god has
One eye

the mystics of
the world's religions

a sermon cycle
by john r. mabry

the apocryphile press
BERKELEY, CA
www.apocryphile.org

apocryphile press
BERKELEY, CA

Apocryphile Press
1700 Shattuck Ave #81
Berkeley, CA 94709
www.apocryphile.org

Portions of chapter six reprinted from *God As Nature Sees God* by
John R. Mabry (Element Books, 1994/Apocryphile Press, 2004). All
rights are held by the author and used by permission.

This book is dedicated to the
people of Grace North Church,
for whom these sermons were written,
and especially to

RICHARD MAPPLEBECKPALMER

my friend, mentor, and partner
in the ministry for lo these many years.

Other books by John R. Mabry

The Way of Thomas
Nine Insights for Enlightened Living
from the Secret Sayings of Jesus

The Monster God
Horrific Images of Divinity in the Religions of the World

Noticing the Divine
An Introduction to Interfaith Spiritual Guidance

Faith Styles
Ways People Believe

God is a Great Underground River
Articles, Essays, and Homilies on Interfaith Spirituality

I Believe in a God Who is Growing
Process Perspectives on the Creed,
the Sacraments and the Christian Life

Who Are the Independent Catholics?
An Introduction to the Independent and Old Catholic Churches
(with John P. Plummer)

Crisis and Communion
The Re-Mythologization of the Eucharist

Heretics, Mystics & Misfits

God As Nature Sees God
A Christian Reading of the Tao Te Ching

The Tao Te Ching
A New Translation

The Little Book of the Tao Te Ching

contents

introduction

I n the *Upanishads*, the most sublime of the all the Hindu scriptures, there is the story of a father who tried to teach his son
something about the nature of God and the world. He told his
son to put a handful of salt into a bucket of water. The boy did
so, and soon after went to bed. After breakfast the next day, the
father told the little boy, "Bring me the salt I gave you last night."

The little boy looked and looked, but he could not find the salt
anywhere in the bucket of water. The salt had dissolved. "I can't
find it, father," he said, distressed.

"How does the water at the top of the bucket taste?" his father
asked him.

"It's salty!" the boys eyes lit up.

"Pour a little off, and tell me how the water in the middle of the
bucket tastes."

The boy did so, and tasted it. "It's salty, too!" he reported.

"How does it taste at the very bottom of the bucket?" asked his
father.

The boy poured off some more water and tasted it again. "Even saltier!" he said, making a face. The father told the boy to toss the rest of the water out and to come and sit on his lap. When the boy wriggled up, he told his father, "I think the salt will always be in that water, now."

His father nodded, and said, "Remember how you were asking about God, and why could you not see him?" The boy nodded. "The world is a bucket of water, and God is the salt. You cannot see it, but it flavors everything. This is the truth, my son. You are salty, too."

When some people approach the topic of mysticism, they do so with great trepidation, as if it is a hard to understand secret, or an academic exercise, but as this marvelous story illustrates, mysticism is simple, perhaps it is too simple, because often children understand it better than adults do. Sometimes adults have to unlearn the ways of the world in order to see things as they really are. This is why Jesus said that we must become like little children if we are to enter the kingdom of heaven. If we are too clever, we will convince ourselves all kinds of crazy schemes are true. But if, like a child, we can behold things simply as they are, our world is transformed.

The mystics throughout the ages have used various techniques to shut off the mind and behold reality unmediated. When they have been successful, what they experienced has been completely beyond the power of words to describe. Fortunately for us, this has not dissuaded them from trying. For their feeble attempts point a way for us to follow, and give us some clue of what they have found.

"Just what is a mystic, anyway?" You might ask, and this is a good question. But I think it will be easier to answer if we first ask, "What is mysticism?" Very simply, mysticism is the pursuit of, or the enjoyment of, union with transcendent reality. In the West, we usually call this transcendent reality, "God." So, for the moment, let us suppose that the mystic is one who experiences no distinction between himself and the Divine. It is as if God and she were one being, and the mystic does not know where she ends and God begins, or vice versa. Likewise, since God is in all things, just as the salt is found in every bit of water in the boy's bucket, the mystic feels similarly at one with the universe, and finds it hard to tell where she ends and her neighbor, or that tree, or even her enemies, begin.

This unitive knowledge may come in a flash, and then subside, leaving only the memory of mystical union, or it may be an awareness that rises like a tide, suffusing all that one beholds, and then gradually subsiding once again. But anyone who has ever had such an experience—and you may very well be one of them, for such experiences are not rare—are never the same again. It is one thing to think, "we are all one." But it is quite another thing to experience that oneness directly. That is the ineffable reality that the mystics find so hard to express, yet it is an experience that transcends culture, or religious tradition, or age, or even piety. Jesus said, "The kingdom of the father is spread out upon the earth, but people do not see it" (Thomas 113). But when you do see it, even for a moment, you realize that you were not at all who you thought you were.

Such visions are scary for some people. They are especially scary to those who hold tightly to a religious orthodoxy. The Southern Baptists among whom I was reared are deeply suspicious of such experiences, and are fond of saying that "Mysticism begins in 'mist' and ends in 'schism.'" But what really scares them is that in the unitive gaze of the mystic, dogmatic boundaries fall away as so much meaningless chaff, cherished doctrines become prisons for the mind, and coloring inside the lines becomes an impossible task. Mysticism is the fundamentalists' worst nightmare, because all the boundaries between "us" and "them" dissolve, sacred and profane become meaningless, and creature and Creator become indistinguishable. This is, of course, heresy, and those who have had mystical experiences have often found themselves at odds with the religious orthodoxy of their day and time.

The Sufi poet Rumi tells the story of a dervish named Bestami. One night, so deep in mystical contemplation that he was drunk with ecstasy, he declared to his disciples, "I am Allah! There is no God but me! Fall on your faces and worship me!"

In the morning, when the ecstatic fever had passed, his disciples told him what he had said. "Oh, dear," he said with great concern. "Listen, if I ever say anything like that again, take your knives and stab me to death. Kill me if I ever say that again." So his students sharpened their knives, just in case.

It was not long, however, before the light of Bestami's reason was snuffed out like a candle. Rumi says that "pure spirit spoke through him." Bestami was not there. The "he" of his personality dissolved; the light of God poured into the empty Bestami and became words.

"Inside my robe," Bestami declared, "there is nothing but God. How long will you keep looking elsewhere?!"

So his disciples drew their knives and slashed at him. But a curious thing happened: though they stabbed at him, they only cut themselves. There was no mark on Bestami, but his disciples lay bleeding and dying.

Sometimes the mystic scares even himself by what he sees. The mystic experience so explodes the containers of religious orthodoxy that there is no choice but to declare him or her a heretic. And yet, what is truth? Is truth the box we construct to contain the Divine, or is it the ineffable presence that cannot be contained by any boxes, dogmas, or orthodoxies? Orthodoxy attempts to mediate between the seeker and the Divine, but the mystic beholds the Divine directly, and any such mediation seems not only unnecessary, but utterly irrelevant, or even harmful.

Naturally, then, mystics are not popular amongst the orthodox of any religion. In fact, almost every one of the religious leaders who founded world religions began their careers as mystics who spoke about what they had seen, and were promptly declared heretics. Just think of the Buddha, of Jesus, or of Muhammad. All of them were heretics, all of them were mystics, and all of them changed the way we view reality.

And they all had a hard time of it, too. The mystical path is not only unpopular amongst "religious" folk, it is sometimes politically dangerous, and it is often personally arduous as well. If you are looking for the easy way out, the mystical path may not be for you. On the other hand, more often than not it is not a path that people choose, but one that chooses them. Moses did not climb through the hill countries on a quest for burning bushes. The burning bush appeared to him, and he was not pleased that it did. It is not an easy path, mostly because it involves a lot of death. For once the mystical vision hits you, you realize that everything you thought you were is a lie, that the universe you thought you were living in is gone, and that all the rules and structures by which you ordered your life are meaningless. It is disorienting and painful. There is no lazy man's path to enlightenment, because once enlightenment hits, the lazy man no longer exists, and the luminous being which has taken his place is beyond recognition, even to himself.

In our own time, scholars of religion have tried to make sense of the mystical worldview, and how it is one comes in touch with unitive consciousness. James Fowler, a developmental psychologist, through extensive study of test subjects, has outlined a theory of religious development. Fowler's theory is kind of baroque, but Scott Peck has done an excellent job of simplifying it in his book *A Different Drum*. Very briefly, this model asserts that we begin life in a state of chaos—nobody but us exists, and we have no moral center. Most young children feel they are the center of the universe, and are oblivious to the needs of others. Some people spend their lives in this first stage of development, although many who are stuck here end up in prison.

Most of us, however, at an appropriate age, move on to Stage Two, which is institutional faith. This stage has very clear rules and regulations, a black and white system of morality, and a clearly defined system of orthodoxy to keep people on the straight and narrow. For people who have lived much of their lives in the chaos of Stage One, Stage Two is a very real salvation—the structure of such a faith rescues them from their own headlong plunge toward self-destruction. Stage Two faith is appropriate for older children and most adults. The great majority of religious people the world over live and die in Stage Two, and it serves them very well indeed.

For some, however, the rigidity and contradictions inherent in orthodoxy become too much to bear, and they begin to question the party line. What if the priests or the gurus or the imams are wrong? What if they are lying to us? What if they are simply ignorant and are stumbling around in the dark like the rest of us? The person who asks such questions has moved into Stage Three, the stage of questioning and doubt. This is a very valuable stage, where idols are smashed, worldviews discarded, and one's true seeking begins. Even though this is a very uncomfortable stage, many people spend their lives here, and find meaning in their lives as activists, or philosophers, or humanists. For them life is a question that has no answer, and yet the question itself contains sufficient substance to sustain them.

But beyond questioning lies another stage, where all the questions dissolve into silence. For the final stage of faith is that of the mystic, where one has fallen in love with Mystery, that Mystery at the heart of all things. In this place one does not need questions, nor does one need answers. The religious traditions of the world are revealed to be arbitrary symbol sets, which are but fingers pointing at a reality which cannot be described, let alone comprehended, but can be experienced and participated in. In this stage, all divisions are illusory, and the distinctions between the universal and the particular disappear. The mystic beholds, as William Blake did, "a world in a grain of sand, and heaven in a wild flower. Hold infinity in the palm of your hand, and eternity in an hour."

The mystic cannot be bound by religious orthodoxy, and yet finds profound value in religious tradition. One who has passed from the questioning of Stage Three into the Mystery of Stage Four may find herself back at the very same church she left years ago, and yet find that though she is praying the same words, their meaning has changed utterly. Like Auden, she may find herself back home where she began, and recognize it for the first time.

Peck notes that we may find people at Stage Two and Stage Four coming to the same church for completely opposite reasons. Stage Four mystics may come to church to become lost in the Mystery, while Stage Two Believers come to church to escape mystery. Well, that is the mystery, isn't it? One comes to this table to be fed exactly what one needs, even though everyone needs something different.

For the past three years, we have spent our summer sermon series looking at the heretics, mystics, and misfits in the Christian tradition, and it has been a lot of fun. But the fun is not limited to the Christian tradition. Heretics, mystics, and misfits abound in every religion. Lizzy Hull suggested last year that I broaden the scope of the series to include those madmen and women of other traditions, and I thrilled to the challenge. So for the next several summers we will be exploring the mystics of the world's religions. We'll be taking them in more or less chronological order, beginning with the foundations of the religious tradition itself, and then examining the particulars as expressed by those mystics who both defined and defied that religion. In this way, we will accomplish two things: we will explore the history of the world's religions, and we will meet those heretics and mystics who challenged their native faiths to embrace more than simply a set of rules and dogmas.

And because we are Christians, and the Christian faith and history is what we know best, we will often examine the teachings of these other mystics in terms of how their teaching supports or challenges the tradition with which we are most familiar. In so doing we will discover as many similarities as we will differences, for even though the cultural clothes of each tradition differs a great deal, the Great Source of Being to which we are all drawn is the same.

Many of these mystics thought they were looking for God, like the boy from the *Upanishads*, who could not find the salt anywhere. Instead, they found themselves, that not only were they salty, but that all the world is salty. I pray we will do the same.

Holy One, in you all things find their beginning and their end.
We seek to describe you, and only succeed
in building boxes in which we hope to contain you.
But you burst through all barriers.
We grasp at you and you pour through our fingers like sand.
We describe you and our words fall from our mouths without meaning.
We look for you, but we cannot see what is before our own faces.
Help us, as we explore the mystics of every age and culture,
to peel away the illusion which separates Jew and Muslim,
Christian and Hindu, man and woman,
rich and poor, creature and Creator.
Give us a moment of clear vision, let us see,
if for only a flash, things as they really are.
And then, O God, give us the strength to bear it.
For we ask this in the name of him
who is the Alpha and the Omega,
in whom we live and move and have our being,
even Jesus Christ. Amen.

⊕ *Preached at Grace North Church on June 22, 2003.*

1 | native traditions

One of my best friends in my years at California Baptist College was a guy named Shawn. When we met I was going through my confirmation class in the Episcopal Church. In my New Testament Greek class one day this very tall guy looked at me in stunned disbelief, and pointed to the book on the top of my stack. It was my confirmation textbook, which this odd fellow no doubt recognized. "Where did you get that book?" he asked me after class. It turns out that he had read that book, and in fact, had even been an Episcopalian for a while.

He had been a lot of things. Shawn had gone from being a Roman Catholic to an Episcopalian, and was, at the time I met him, studying to be a fundamentalist Baptist preacher. Not for long, though. Soon after we started hanging out, Shawn returned to the Episcopal Church, and our conversations ranged far and wide in the field of religious studies. He introduced me to the *Tao Te Ching*, a gift for which I will be forever grateful. He also helped me function on my dinosaur computer, which was so clunky it almost put me off the electronic medium altogether.

After school, Shawn and I stayed in touch regularly. We have always lived a great distance from one another, but we have succeeded in talking on the phone about once a month for the past fifteen years, which isn't bad for staying in touch with one's friends from college, is it?

One of the things that kept our friendship so vital was our common dedication to the weirdness of the spiritual journey. One never knows where the Spirit will blow one next, and that uncertainty, that constant internal wrestling kept us talking. After I finished college, Shawn continued to bounce from church to church, denomination to denomination, even considering becoming an Old Catholic priest at one point.

Then one day, something very strange happened. Shawn called and said that the Goddess had appeared to him in a dream, and had claimed him as her own. He had been reading about neo-paganism, and had certainly been attracted to its nature-based ideology, but the idea of actually *becoming* a neo-pagan had scarcely crossed his mind. That is, until the Goddess granted him a private audience, and shook his spiritual world to its core.

Now, I wasn't alarmed at this news. I was more amused. I saw Shawn as kind of a spiritual pinball machine, a metal ball of a soul shooting from one tradition to another in quick succession. I expected his dalliance with neo-paganism to be just another quick dip in the spiritual pool, but amazingly, this was not to be. It stuck, and stuck well.

So just what is this strange tradition that my friend had gotten himself involved in? Was it some new cult that hadn't yet hit the cutural radar screen?

Far from it. In fact, my friend was practicing the oldest form of religion known to humankind, one common to native peoples the world over. Like every tradition, this one did not emerge fully-formed, but evolved as humans evolved, over millions and millions of years. Lets take a look at how it devolped, and how it has come to experience a revival today.

In our own time we have lost a sense of the hardness of primal life. TV shows such as "Survivor" remind us just how far removed from our native habitat we have become, but for our ancestors, survival was indeed everything. They were powerless over so much in their lives: starvation, disease, and death seemed to lurk around every corner, and like us, they sought to control their fate by whatever means were at their disposal.

This, then, is the very beginning of religion: the attempt made by primitive humans to put a face on the gaping maw of time, to exercise some control over their environment. It took a long time for any concept of deity to emerge, however. Initially, our ancestors intuited a latent force in nature, which was the source of both good and bad luck. The Melanesian islanders call this force *mana*, and historians of religion have followed suit. *Mana* is not "supernatural," it is instead, part of the world. It is both perceptible and to some degree controllable. There is good *mana*, which causes grain to grow and people to be friendly to each other, and there is also bad *mana*, that causes disease and bickering amongst neighbors. Our ancestors sought to increase good *mana* and decrease bad *mana* through the use of charms, incantations, and purification rituals. These were the very first religious observances.

As our imaginations developed, however, our ancestors began to discern personality in this *mana*. They began to speak of "powers" as being entities much like themselves with feelings and motivations. Before long, *mana* had evolved into the "spirits." Spirits became the personified life-force found in all things: trees, rocks, rivers, etc. In Greek mythology these nature spirits survived as dryads and naiads; you might also recall the river nymphs from Norse mythology or Wagner, which is the same idea. Now unlike *mana*, which had no will of its own, the spirits were very much the masters of their own fates. The spirits had minds of their own, and did not necessarily have the good of humans as their top priority. Sometimes the spirits could be helpful, but sometimes they were mischievous or even harmful.

Nonetheless, they were not going away, and the spirits became a normal part of everyday life. They were powerful, but they did not rule over humans. They were just part of the furniture, like the rivers, the meadows, and the forests themselves. In some cultures, the spirits became associated with one's forefathers and foremothers, who could bring good fortune or ill upon the family members who were living. Hoping to enlist the aid of the spirits, or at least to entreat them not to do any harm, humans developed a complicated ritual life that used magic to both appease and enlist the aid of the myriad spirits all around them.

We cohabitated with the spirits in an uneasy alliance for many hundreds of thousands of years. But when we began to set down roots, and became farmers, the scene shifted dramatically. Humans realized that if they planted a portion of grain instead of just eating it, more grain would result! This amazing discovery may be the first known instance of delayed gratification and the great good that can come of such discipline. Knowing how to plant grain gave humans much greater control over their destiny, more security and safety for the tribe. We were able to settle down in one place, and built sturdier dwellings. It didn't take long for us to get attached to the place where we settled down, and humans felt connected to the land in a way that we had never known before. Land became the most important commodity, for fertile land brought this newfound security, and was in great demand. A warrior class emerged both to conquer neighboring lands for one's own tribe, and to defend one's land from one's neighbors!

Almost overnight, the peaceful, matriarchal, hunter-gatherer society transformed into an agrarian culture ruled by warriors. And once one people overpowered another people, chiefs emerged to rule more than one village. Before long, chiefs became kings, and small groups of villages became large groups of villages. Suddenly, there were kingdoms.

And because we humans have a tendency to project our own

political realities onto the spiritual world, the spirits went through a similar transformation: the spirits, like the chieftains, became more and more powerful, until they became gods, ruling like kings with jurisdiction over vast territories. The "spirit of the grove" became the "god of the high mountain." Where there had once been a spirit inhabiting an individual tree, suddenly it was discerned that there was a ruling spirit that had jurisdiction over *all* trees. The river spirit became the river god, with influence over all brooks, streams, and rushing rapids.

Humans began speaking of the sun god, the god of fire, the god of wind, and so on, and as humans conquered larger tracks of land, the influence of their gods grew larger as well. In fact, they grew until we became their subjects. The gods needed to be appeased and propitiated in the same way that human kings needed to be humored if the safety of one's people was to be safegaurded.

As the gods got bigger, the rituals needed to satisfy them became more complicated and specialized, until a class of professional clergy emerged. One can still journey to Greece and see the amazing temples built to Zues, Hera, Apollo, and the other gods of the Greek pantheon. The Celtic peoples still honor the sacred groves where their gods communed with them, and one can scarcely encounter a people who do not have some memory of their native temples and the myths associated with them.

But even with these maginificent liturgies and houses of worship in place, one cannot expect the gods to *behave* themselves. For the gods of most native traditions are every bit as capricious and fickle as human beings. The myths of every people reveal their gods to be at turns loving and jealous, peace-loving and war-mongering, beneficent and unpredictable.

And perhaps that is why we love them so. The gods may not be the paragons of virtue that we in the Abrahamic religions have come to expect, but they were at least comprehensible. We may not agree with their actions, but we understand them.

But the real genius of native religion is this: it does not set up a false dichotomy between human beings and everything else in the universe. I'm not sure exactly when we were bitten by the arrogance bug that made us believe that we were somehow distinct from, or superior to nature, but native religions contain no such hubris. Native traditions see human beings as simply a part of nature, and experience the trees, rocks, rivers and animals as kindred rather than subjects or, god forbid, natural resources.

Houston Smith, in his amazing book, *The World's Religions*, tells of a Native American Onondagan prayer he witnessed that lasted nearly a full hour. During that time, nobody closed their eyes, and everyone listened to the prayer in their native tongue. Smith understood nothing, but when he asked what had been said, was told the entire prayer was devoted to naming everything in sight, animate and inanimate, including spirits of the place, inviting all to join in the proceedings and to bless them.

The Onondagans were not conducting their service as dominators of nature, but as part of it, respectfully inviting all aspects to participate. The Navajos bring the entire world into their homes, as each dwelling is seen as participating in and representing the whole of the cosmos. For native peoples, all things in nature, including humans, have their rightful place which must be honored; all things are kindred, brothers and sisters, and worthy of respect. They invite us to think not of humans embedded in nature, but of nature seeking to extend itself, to grow into new forms and more complex patterns, to behold itself, developing humans as organs of self-awareness.

Later traditions, such as our own, saw nature as something that needed to be beaten back with a stick, and viewed salvation as a way to escape it. This has resulted in attitudes that have had disastrous effects on our environment, because we do not honor the earth as a sacred presence, but as a thing to be plundered and used at will.

But native traditions know better. They know that we humans are inseparable from the natural world, and in these traditions salvation is seen as the encouragement of natural cycles. Since the disruption of natural cycles threatens the tribe, these cycles of fertility, of growth and harvest, must be participated in and encouraged for the survival of all things.

But, you may be asking, is this mysticism? It is indeed, and a very powerful one. In nature-mysticism there is no distinction between natural and super-natural, no divorce of human society from the ecosystem which supports it. There is only the body of the earth, often portrayed as the great Goddess, of whom we are a part, from whose womb we are born, and to whom we will return, to live again in some other form, as the cycle of life on this planet succeeds from one season to another, one generation to another, one era to another.

To know oneself to be part of this larger self—this is to *truly* know oneself. One can participate in the mystery of salvation by encouraging and cooperating with the cycles of nature, by bearing children and making art, by giving due attention to the cycles and seasons of the earth, and by acknowledging and honoring the personified forces of nature, the gods.

As Christianity and Islam spread throughout the known world, the gods of the common people were subdued even as their people were conquered. The word "pagan" comes from the Latin *paganus*, which means, very simply, country-folk, common people. And indeed, as we know from the history of Europe, the church had quite a time ferreting out those who held to the "old ways" and continued to worship the old gods.

Indeed, it was never completely successful in this. Although they tried. Christian society carried on an amazingly successful "smear" campaign against pagan believers. They called them witches, and by some counts, the church burned nearly nine million women in the Middle Ages for the terrible crime of honoring one's family traditions, for the knowledge of what herb can cure a specific ailment, or for believing that certain amulets or incantations might attract love or repel the evil eye. In fact, most of those burned were not witches at all, yet it is a terrible crime nonetheless, even if they all had been believers in the old gods. It is religious genocide, a holocaust largely ignored today, one of the most profoundly shameful events in the history of the Christian church.

Indeed, many people today are fed up with the ideological tyranny of the Abrahamic religions, the violence against other peoples propogated in the name of the One God, and with the environmental violence that has resulted from our specious distinction between ourselves and the natural world that the religions of the One God have inspired. Many are returning to the native religion of their own ethnic peoples. Those from the British islands are beginning to practice once again the old ways of the Celts, many Africans are rediscovering Yoruba and other native African religions.

And though many of those who practice the old ways refer to themselves as witches, more often people will refer to themselves as "Wiccans," from which the word "witch" derives. "Wicca" actually comes from the Old English word "Wicce," which means to shape or bend. Wiccans call on the power latent in the natural world, and through their prayers and rituals, seek to "bend" that power for healing or for the common good.

Many in Western society still buy the medieval propoganda that Witches are in league with the devil, but in fact, nothing is further from the truth. Satan is a deity that belongs to Christian theology, and has no place in any pagan pantheon. Witches do not worship Satan, because they do not believe in Satan. Satan is a Christian belief. It is difficult to accuse someone of worshipping a being that they do not believe even exists.

Modern-day neopagans are not out casting spells trying to cause trouble for people, either. There is a strong belief in the pagan community that any energy that you put out there by means of a spell will come back to you three-fold. That is certainly a powerful reason to put out good energy and not bad.

Wicca has had a very important impact on our culture in recent years. It is one of the fastest growing religions in the United States and Europe, and it is not hard to see why. It has been extremely healing and empowering for women, who, for the first time, are being given permission to take reponsibility for their own spiritual lives instead of handing their spiritual power over to an all-male Christian priesthood. Even more healing, the Goddess allows women to see themselves reflected in divinity, something that the all-male single-parent family of the Trinity never did.

But it has been empowering for men also. Everyone in Wicca is a priest or priestess. There is no heirarchy to which one must bend, and everyone is empowered to take their spirituality into their own hands and to fashion a thing of beauty out of it. I have studied personally with Starhawk, the foremost Wiccan theologian alive today, and though I admit I was scared stiff when I went into my first class, I emerged from that class with a great deal of respect for this tradition, an appreciation for its lively liturgical life, and its complex and multivalent theology. And although I do not see Wicca as *my* spiritual path, I certainly appreciate its importance in the lives of many people whom I love.

My friend Shawn has blossomed and flourished in his own practice of neo-paganism. He has founded and mentored many covens, and, as an ordained interfaith minister, now serves as the only Wiccan hospital chaplain in his area. He continues to call pretty much every month, and I am always eager to hear about his most recent spiritual exploits. After all, if the Goddess deigned to appear to him personally, and to call him to her service, who am I to question it?

We pray today not to any one particular god,
but to the One being who is the universe, the One who answers to many
names, and in whose service every religion strives.

Help us to recognize the hubris of our fathers,
and our own arrogance,
in thinking ourselves better than those who came before,
better than the creatures with whom we share this good earth.
Restore to us a sense of the sacredness
of all creatures and all places,
allow us to recognize the divine face in the wind,
in the fire, in the water, and in the earth herself.
And most of all, open our eyes to the violence
which our arrogance has wrought upon the environment,
upon native peoples, and upon our own psyches.
Heal us and teach us, Great Spirit,
and grant us deliverance from ourselves. Amen.

⊕ *Preached at Grace North Church on July 6, 2003.*

2 | the eleusian mysteries

In the mythology of the Greeks, there is a story of Persephone, who was the daughter of the goddess of grain, Demeter. One day, Persephone was out gathering flowers in the fields, when the earth opened up, and Hades, the lord of death and the underworld, erupted from the fissure riding in a golden chariot. He snatched up Persephone and seating her beside him in the chariot, rode back into the earth to the underworld. There Hades kept Persephone captive, and forced her to marry him and become his queen. Just to make everything kosher, Hades had requested her hand in marriage from her father, Zeus, who granted the request.

Unfortunately, no one had bothered to inform Demeter of the whereabouts of her daughter, nor asked her permission for the marriage. For nine days and nights, Demeter wandered the earth with a torch in hand, searching for her kidnapped daughter. The sun finally let her in on what had happened, and furious at Zeus, she left Olympia and roamed the earth as a bitter crone. In her journeys, she was entertained kindly at Eleusis, where she decided to settle down. She revealed herself as the grain goddess, and the Eleusians began constructing a temple in her honor.

But this did not please her, as the light of her life had still been stolen from her. In her wrath, she refused to allow any crops to grow for an entire year. Oxen and men ploughed in vain; prayers were said, but to no effect. Humans quailed as they saw their extinction looming, and the gods were likewise terrified, because they needed the sacrifices of humans for their own sustenance. Finally, Zeus realized that he had to do something, or the whole world would end. He summoned Hades and made him return his new bride to the world of the living.

Hades reluctantly agreed, but before Persephone left, Hades gave her four pomegranate seeds to sustain her on her journey. Persephone found her way to the surface, and found her mother at Eleusis. When they saw each other, the two embraced and wept for joy. Then Demeter asked her a very strange question: "Did you eat anything while you were down there?"

"Yes, mum," Persephone told her, "four pomegranate seeds. Why?"

Her mother was horrified, because if anyone eats of the food of the underworld they may never return. Indeed, Hades made just that kind of claim over her. "Four months out of every year," he announced to the horrified Demeter, "she will be mine. One month in exchange for every seed she ate."

Demeter had to agree to this arrangement, but she wasn't going to do it without exacting her own sneaky price. "Very well," she said, "and for those four months, nothing will grow upon the earth."

This, for the early Greeks, explained why the earth grew cold and hard in winter, and yielded no fruit at that time; and why in spring the green and the grain returned.

Now, no parent can listen to this tale without horror. There is nothing as terrifying as the kidnapping of a child, and there is no parent anywhere who has not been struck with panic when his or her child is out of sight in a public place. As a corollary, there is no relief greater than finding them to be safe again, either. What parent cannot relate to Demeter's agony, who does not understand her nine-day vigil? Most of us, I dare say, would search far longer if need be. There is an archetypal aspect to this story that makes it truly universal.

The current Disney/Pixar film, *Finding Nemo*, seems to be a retelling of this myth. The little fish Nemo is being reared by his father, a widowed clownfish, when he is captured by a dentist from Sydney, Austrailia, and finds himself trapped in a dental office's aquarium. Nemo's father searches for him doggedly, and after many harrowing adventures, Nemo gains his freedom and the two are reunited.

Finding Nemo seems to be the Persephone myth inverted, as in a mirror. Nemo is a fish, not a human, and it is the story of a father searching for his son, rather than a mother searching for her daughter. And while Persephone is plucked from the surface and dragged to the depths, Nemo is plucked from the depths and brought to the surface. Both are held captive, and while Demeter is wed to the Lord of the Dead, Nemo is promised to the dentist's niece, a little girl who kills fish. Finally, both Persephone and Nemo are rescued through the persistance of their grieving parents.

All the elements of the story are there, and if the box office receipts are any indication, the story resonates as strongly today as it did three thousand years ago in ancient Greece. There is even an initiation ceremony in the Nemo film, which bears resemblence to the Masonic rites which derive in part from those at Eleusis, which makes me wonder just how conscious the Pixar people were of the many parrallels between their story and the myth.

In any case, the Eleusian rites were among the most popular in Greek history. At first they were held every three years, but before long the celebration became an annual festival. It was not a casual spiritual path, however, but required great dedication. To be admitted to the rites, one had to be deemed a moral person. Legend has it that Hercules at one point presented himself as an initiate, but was rejected because of the bloodshed on his hands. He was given penance to do to cleanse himself of his iniquity and make him worthy. These austerities he performed dutifully, and he was eventually admitted to the rites.

Initiates experienced their initiation in three stages. First, were the things that were *done*; second, were the things which were *said*; and finally, there were sacred objects which were *shown*. And afterwards, there was much wine merrymaking, and indiscriminate nookie.

In the first part, in which things were *done*, the initiates lived through the horror of Persephone's ordeal. They were blindfolded and taken into a dark cave—their abduction to the underworld. Following the torches of other initiates—probably representing Demeter's searching for her daughter, they finally found their way to the bright sunlight of the Elysian Fields.

Later, there were things which were *said*: these were liturgies which retold the drama which the initiates had just lived through, commenting on and explicating their experience. This was a kind of theological instruction to help the initiates integrate their experience and make connections between the ritual and their everyday lives.

Finally, the initiates were *shown* sacred objects which no one may behold except those who have gone through the mysteries. Unfortunately, no one was allowed to reveal what these objects were, and they have not survived. This part of the mysteries will indeed forever remain a mystery. At the end of this portion of the ritual, however, the hierophant was revealed. This was a great high priest or priestess selected from the people for his or her piety. The real name of a hierophant was never spoken aloud in connection to the rites, although monuments of prominent Greek citizens often revealed that this or that person had been a hierophant at some point.

I believe these three initiatory experiences, *doing, saying,* and *showing* are instructive, as they reveal three varieties of mysticism embodied by the rites: a physical mysticism, a psychological mysticism, and a spiritual mysticism. These understandings are not exclusive to one another, but complementary and necessary to one another, as one mystery builds upon another.

First, there is the physical mysticism, those things which are *done*. This form is the most primitive, and it is this aspect out of which the myth arises. Why is there winter? Why does the grain refuse to grow? How do we alleviate the anxiety of this time of famine, and encourage the life to come again in the spring? This is pure nature mysticism, in which the rites are performed as a way to participate in the natural cycles of the planet, to encourage the cycles to continue. Humans, the gods and the earth are all part of one piece, the gods need humans, humans need the earth, and the earth needs the gods. Each has their place and is dependent on the other. Survival depended on keeping all in balance, and in motion. This is an important and sufficient understanding of the mysteries, and for thousands of years, was the core of the religion.

But humans are clever folks, and are forever making creative connections that inspire us and invite us into greater depth and meaning. This instinct led the Greeks to personalize the myth: we are all Persephone, we are all dragged into Hell periodically. This is a psychological mysticism which proclaims the universality of the human experience. Like the earth herself, we all go through fallow times. Like Persephone, we are taken against our will into Hell. In the underworld we encounter those aspects of ourselves that we seek to divorce ourselves from, our own personal Hades, if you will, who has power over us only so long as we are ignorant of him, as Demeter was.

In this myth we are also given the hope that we will return from Hell. Like the seasons, this experience is cyclic. We enter Hell and return several times in our lives. In this way we are at one with the gods and the world. As above, so below. The gods live in us, and we replay the myths in our own lives again and again.

Each time we are invited to enter the process with greater awareness and maturity. Each time, the experience adds to our character, and our lives are given greater depth and meaning. The way through this is by talking about it, historically with our friends, loved ones, or the clergy. In more recent times, one's therapist or spiritual director can help one navigate the journey through the underworld. This corresponds to the second experience of the initiate, that of *saying*. We speak our way through the underworld, and we speak ourselves out of it again as well.

But there was a still deeper mystery revealed to the initiates at Eleusis. Like many Greek and Gnostic notions making the rounds at the time, later Eleusian mystics held that unless one dies *before* one dies, one cannot gain eternal life. Socrates said, "The unexamined life is not worth living" and the Eleusians took this further, believing that the unexamined life will not be rewarded after death, either. The Gnostics, likewise, taught that one was not born with a soul, one must grow it during one's life if there is to be anything to carry on after one's death. We can see echoes of this in the Eleusians' rituals. According to them, one must become one with death and resurrection, one must ritually experience the journey to the underworld, one must identify oneself with Persephone to guarantee one's return to the Elysian Fields after death.

Those who have not gone through the initiation are lost—they will not know the way back. But those who have gone through the ritual, who have died, and been led back to the surface are assured that this knowledge will keep them safe in the hereafter. This is an experiential mysticism, where one is *shown* the reality of the mysteries. One lives through them, and afterwards one *lives* through them. In this mysticism a person becomes one with the gods, with death, and with resurrection. We are ourselves the kernel of wheat that falls to the earth in death, and sprouts green in the spring.

Much of this mysticism has been carried over into the Christian faith as well. St. Paul says that unless we die with Christ Jesus we cannot know eternal life through him either. We must lose our life to find it. Unless a seed fall to the earth and die, it cannot live again. Very familiar ideas, no? They were not original to St. Paul or the evangelists of course, but were living and vibrant ideas very popular at the time they were writing. The Pauline authors simply gave these ideas a spin, and replaced the Eleusian ritual with Christian analogues. The correspondences are many and very worthy of study in themselves.

Today, many pagan groups have resurrected the Eleusian rituals, but one need not become an initiate to benefit from the wisdom of this ancient mystery religion. Its mysticism is not exclusive to it, no matter what its adherents once had to say about the matter. For all three types of mysticism celebrated in its history are available to us today.

We know there are things to be *done*: we can acknowledge and celebrate ourselves as part of this planet and its natural cycles. By giving caring attention to the environment we encourage these natural cycles and thus ensure the survival of life. Secondly, there are stories to be *told*: in reciting our own journeys to the underworld and back again, we create meaning in our own lives and give hope to those around us who have also found themselves in difficult places. And finally, there are things to be *shown*: we are invited to pursue the enlightenment that comes about when we die to our ego, and identify with something larger than ourselves. For when that happens, death has no more hold over us. Though we may seem to die, we hold fast to the promise that we will return to the place of the sun. For we know the way *out* of the darkness.

Loving Creator, we know that there is nothing
in heaven or earth that is not likewise in us.
Just as Jesus descended into Hell,

and returned in a glorious resurrection,
give us strength for our own journeys
to the underworld and back again.
Give us proper reverence for the earth,
and kindle in us a fire of responsibility and care for her.
Give us the will to narrate our journeys,
so that those who go after us will not have to go alone.
And give us the grace to die to ourselves now,
that we may live forever as new creatures.
For we ask this in hope that every grain which falls to earth
will sprout again, and will bear new fruit, even Jesus, even us. Amen.

⊕ *Preached at Grace North Church on July 13, 2003.*

3 | the druids

The last time I ever set foot in the fundamentalist Baptist church I attended in high school was on a Sunday evening during my junior year. I had, for a couple of years, hosted a radio show on my high school's FM station, called "Power Music!" featuring rock-and-roll with uplifting, faith-inspiring Christian lyrics. Every Sunday afternoon, I spun records for two hours, and then preached for a half hour, inviting people to call up the station and "get saved" right over the telephone.

Somewhere along the line, our youth pastor got it into his head that rock-n-roll was demonic. He started preaching about its evil influence, how it inflamed the passions and drove youth to unspeakable acts of sexual indiscretion. The prevalent 4/4 beat in rock-n-roll, with its ever-present emphasis on the third beat, was a rhythm derived from the Druids, he told us, and was still charged with their evil influence.

Like the rest of the youth group, I was eager to please both my youth pastor *and* God, so I came home and announced to my father that I was quitting my radio show. His response was swift and sure: "The heck you are. Think again." He then proceeded to

33

give me a fierce lecture on the error of following anyone blindly, and on the importance of thinking for myself, especially in spiritual matters.

Well, this was *not* what they taught us in Sunday school, so I was pretty surprised by this bit of fatherly wisdom. I obeyed, though, because truly, I *loved* Christian rock music *and* being on the radio, and didn't want to part with either one. So I kept doing the show, in defiance of the youth pastor.

Well, the youth pastor, rising to the fight, scheduled a special series of Bible studies for Sunday afternoon—precisely at the time of my radio show, at which, I found out later, he used the Bible to turn the only friends I had in the world against me. Remember, I was quite a religious freak, and didn't really have any friends outside of the church.

On that fateful Sunday night I showed up for choir practice, and to my surprise and dismay, none of my friends would speak to me. Not a word. Finally, at break, my friend Ron turned on me and announced his judgement: "You're a Druid, John. Druid, Druid, Druid, Druid."

"Hmm..." I thought, "I don't think I *am* a Druid." But I knew exactly where he had gotten this. I wouldn't give up religious rock music, so I was a Druid, being as I was so influenced by...well, Druidical influences.

Of course, nothing could more ridiculous. Rock music is no more derived from the Druids than cardboard is from cheese, but it didn't really matter. My youth pastor, and by extension, the youth group, knew nothing at all about Druids, but it was certainly a convenient curse to lay upon someone.

And my youth pastor is hardly unique in his ignorance. *Nobody* really knows much about the Druids; you can say anything about them! Most of our ancient sources on them are Greek and Roman historians, the chronicles of those who attempted to conquer the Celtic peoples. Hacetaius of Miletus first wrote of them in the fifth century BCE, while both Strabo and Julius Caesar weighed in with extensive passages on their faith and customs in the first century BCE.

But the memories of the Celtic peoples are long, and even though there are few written sources from antiquity, many of their myths and legends survive, from which much useful information may be gleaned.

The Celtic peoples, according to most historians, came from Iran and India, and moved into Brittany and the British islands around the tenth century BCE. The Celts believed themselves to be descended from the god of death, which could be an ancient memory of Rudra, or Shiva, the Hindu god of destruction. This "dark" orientation may account for the fact that the Celts count time not in days, but in nights.

They certainly seemed to have a healthy relationship with death. They had no fear of it, which made them fearless in battle, and formidable opponents, as Julius Caesar attests. The reason for this was an absolute confidence in reincarnation—probably another import from their Hindu past. Celtic reincarnation is not the same as Hindu reincarnation, however. The soul migrates from one body to another, sometimes going to a human body, sometimes taking the form of an animal. This was seen not so much as reincarnation as shape-shifting. One "shifted" one's shape after death to another one, and some people, those mystically inclined—some notable Druids amongst them—were able to shape-shift *before* death. Legends say that those who were most adept at shape-shifting in this life had much smoother transitions to other shapes after their deaths. We can see in this belief the beginnings of the legends of werewolves and other were-beasties.

There is one myth about Liban, who was the only survivor in her family after a flood drowned their home. Trapped underwater, she asked the gods to turn her into a fish so that she may live easier in her home. She was turned into a were-fish, or in more common parlance, a mermaid, and her dog turned into an otter. She lived this way for three hundred years until she met up with

St. Comgall. The saint asked her whether she wished to be a mermaid for another hundred years, or whether she would like to be baptized and die straight away. She agreed to be baptized, and was reborn on the other side as a deer with splendid antlers.

"The other side" was also a matter of much concern to the Celts, who believed that there is a mystical world which is inseparably intertwined with our own. The pattern of the Celtic knot is a representation of two worlds which intersect one another at every point. They called the otherworld Faerie, and experienced a constant exchange between that land and their own. Now, Faerie is not at all like the Christian Heaven. It is a place of mystery, of magic, and often, of danger. It is most often accessed by boat, or through holes in the ground. The story of Alice following the White Rabbit through the rabbit-hole and into Wonderland is definitely an echo of these myths.

Caitlin Matthews writes that, "Once within the otherworld, the landscape radically changes...trees in simultaneous leaf and flame, rivers of fire, herds of giant beasts and other wonders abound. A frequent feature of...[the] otherworld is the checkerboard filled with black sheep on white squares and white sheep on black squares." This, again, is echoed in Lewis Carroll's adventures of Alice, when she encounters not checkers, but an animated game of chess underway.

Faerie was not a safe place for mortals, yet again and again in Celtic legends, mortals made a quest into the wilds of Faerie in order to set right something which has gone awry in our own world.

Needless to say, your average citizen did not relish the notion of having to make the journey to such dangerous places, however mystical they might be, and largely left these shamanic responsibilities to professionals: the Druids, of course.

The word "Druid" derives from the Sanskrit word "veda," believe it or not, though I would be hard-pressed to explain how such a transformation took place. Chalk it up to the mystery of etymology. "Veda" means "to see" or "to know," and Druids were definitely the seers in Celtic cultures. The word Druid is also related to the word for "oak," and the oak tree was certainly sacred to the Druids.

The Druids underwent intensive training, often lasting 20 years or more, in which they had to memorize more than 150 songs and legends in which was carried the collective wisdom of their craft. They refused to write anything down, and so all knowledge had to be passed orally.

Druids were both male and female, and they acted as counselors, professors, philosophers, and magicians. A captured Druid could easily fetch the same ransom as a king, which showed in what kind of esteem they were held by the people. They also served as lawyers and judges, settling all disputes in both public and private matters. They led all public rituals, most of which were held in sacred groves, and it was to them that the responsibility fell to cross over into Faerie, to commune with the magical folk, and to bring back that knowledge for the good of the people.

The Druids taught that there was one supreme force in the universe, which was personified by the mother Goddess and the father God. The Goddess began her life by rising from her tomb at Beltane, the spring equinox, while the God rises from his tomb on Samhain, the fall equinox, which we now celebrate as Halloween. Apparently, the Goddess and the God work different shifts, and rarely see each other. Like all native traditions, these festivals were linked to natural cycles, and were times for joy and merrymaking, and—as with the Greeks—more indiscriminate nookie.

The Druids were at the top of the ladder when it came to Celtic clergy, but there were lesser orders. The Ovates were described by Strabo as "interpreters of nature." They were skilled in divination and the healing arts. Many wise women of later times served in a similar capacity as the Ovates, as healers and fortune-tellers.

More esteemed were the Bards, whose job it was to sing the history and wisdom of the Celtic peoples. Bards were professional musicians and storytellers. In the ancient Celtic world, the Bards were libraries on two legs, human bookmobiles traveling unhindered and unmolested from one village to another with news of the world, and tales of the otherworld. Because Bards were the only source of news, they were always granted safe passage, regardless of the political realities in play in any given place, for without the Bards, how would anyone know what was going on?

The highest order, of course, were the Druids, who were proficient in all the arts of both Ovates and Bards, but added to them the shamanic capacity and responsibility of journeying to the otherworld and back again.

One of the most sensationalistic aspects of Celtic religion is the practice of human sacrifice. According to ancient testimony, some of it from Julius Caesar directly, when murder or some other great crime was committed, it was incumbent upon the ruler to sacrifice the offender to the gods to appease their wrath. Often this was performed by placing the victim in an enormous human form made entirely out of wicker, which was then set ablaze.

Now before you get too cocky about the barbarity of this practice and the superiority of more "civilized" religions, allow me to remind you that our own faith is based upon an incident of human sacrifice, and that while Celts sacrificed criminals to appease the gods, we do it today to appease the masses, especially in Texas.

Julius Caesar found the Druids to be especially difficult to deal with, but not because he objected to their religion. It was, in many ways, identical to his own, for the Celtic gods were easily recognizable as analogues to the Indian deities from which the Greek, Roman, and Celtic pantheons all derived. The problem was that these odd clerics held both religious *and* secular authority, and as the Matthews' point out, "The Romans rightly recognized that to overcome the Celts they must first disable their intellectuals" (*Encyclopaedia of Celtic Wisdom*, 185). For though Caesar might capture kings and seize lands, his hold on the people would slip into the woods with the Druids only to pop up elsewhere. This "roving authority" did not fit into the mold of Roman polity, and it had to be squashed. Caesar succeeded in driving most of the Druids from England, but they continued to flourish for centuries more in Scotland, Ireland, Wales, and Brittany.

As Christianity began to take root in the British islands, conflict between the two faiths was inevitable. There are many tales of St. Patrick and his encounters with Druids, most of which end with the Saint besting them at their own game, much like the story of Elijah and the prophets of Baal.

Eventually, though, a very strange thing happened. The Christianity that took root in Celtic lands was so influenced by the Faerie faith, that when it became politically expedient to convert, most people did so easily, Druids included. Ireland may well be the only country on earth that was converted without the shedding of blood. The three-fold ministry of Ovates, Bards, and Druids was roughly analogous to the three-fold Christian ministry of Deacons, Priests, and Bishops, with many of the same responsibilities. The reality of Faerie and the influence of the gods and goddesses were not too dissimilar to Heaven and the ministry of the communion of saints. And it is quite true that Heaven is much closer to the Celts than it is to other peoples—it is the otherworld, and is still intertwined with life on earth, as can be seen plainly in the twentieth century novels of Anglican mystic Charles Williams.

The legacy of the Druids still influences the religious life of the British islands. The Church of England, after breaking from the Church of Rome, quickly returned to the married clergy common to the Druids and the early Celtic church; and the mixing of secular and religious authority held by the monarch is also part of their legacy.

What can we learn from the mysticism of the Druids? For one thing, they teach us that Heaven is not far removed from us, but that the spiritual world is intimately intertwined with our own, and people must frequently make the journey from one world to the other. The spiritual impinges upon us at every moment, and is an ever-present reality. The world to the Celts is a single organism, of which all beings are integral parts. And as life passes into life, as souls journey from one body to another, nothing is ever lost.

It really hurt to be called a Druid back when I was in high school, but I believe that now, I would consider it a bit of an honor. I could think of worse things than being a shaman who moves between the worlds to heal my people. And when I think of how the Druids used to make use of songs to transmit their faith, I remember myself in that radio studio spinning spiritual rock-n-roll. Maybe they were right. It was, after all, a very Druidical thing to do.

God of life and death, master of this world and the otherworld,
help us to see that our life is more than
car payments and stock portfolios.
Grant us sensitivity to behold the spiritual world
which is always tapping us on the shoulder,
always whispering its wisdom in our ear, if only we will hear it.
Help us to see ourselves, not as strangers to the universe
stranded on this island in space, but as part of a
community of souls that transcends the physical world
and affirms the communion of many dimensions with our own.
For we know that life is far too weird to be explained by numbers,
far too rich to be exhausted by accounts outstanding,
and far too marvelous for reason to comprehend.
Grant us, oh God, to believe in magic.
For we ask this in the name of the magician of Nazareth,
even Jesus Christ. Amen.

⊕ *Preached at Grace North Church on July 20, 2003.*

4 | the yoruba peoples

In the beginning, according to the Yoruba peoples, the world was only water and swamp. The great god Olorun ruled the sky and Olokun was the goddess of the waters. There were not any animals then, because there was no land for them to live on. Not everyone was content with this, though. Olorun's son Obatala, looking down from the heavens, said to himself, "It would be so much nicer if there were something interesting down there! There's just water, water, water, and it's boring, boring, boring. If only there were an animal or two, it would be much more entertaining to watch."

So he went to his father and said, "What we need is some solid land down there. Then we could have mountains and forests and giraffes and stuff." And Olorun agreed with him, "Yeah, that would be a lot better than just a bunch of water. But what can we do about it?"

"If you really think it's the right thing to do, father, I will make the dry land," Obatala said.

"It's hard for me to ever say no to you, Obatala, knock yourself out. Make some land."

41

So Obatala went to Orunmila, the seer, and said, "Olorun has given me permission to make some land, but I don't know how to do it."

Orunmila consulted the oracles and told him, "First you must make a chain of gold long enough to reach from the sky to the water. Then you must take a snail's shell filled with sand, a white hen, a black cat, and a palm nut, put them in a bag and carry them when you climb down the chain. That's all you need to do."

Obatala thanked him, and went to find the blacksmith. The blacksmith said, "I can make the chain for you, but it's going to take a lot of gold—I don't think there is enough gold in the sky to make it."

So Obatala went around to all the gods and asked them to contribute. Finally he had collected enough gold necklaces, rings, and nuggets and brought them to the blacksmith, who fashioned the chain. Obatala hooked one end of the chain to the sky, slung the bag full of stuff over his shoulder, and climbed down the chain.

Lower and lower he climbed until he reached the end of the chain, still swinging far above the waters. Then he heard his friend Orunmila shout down from the sky, "Hey! Dump out the sand from the snail shell!"

Obatala reached into the bag with one hand and, taking the shell, he scattered it. Then Orunmila shouted, "Okay, now drop the chicken!"

Obatala took the hen from the bag and dropped it straight down. It flapped its wings, and landed on the sand safely. The chicken then began scratching at the sand, tossing it to and fro, creating hills and valleys in all directions.

Finally, Obatala saw that there was enough ground to support him, so he jumped the rest of the way and tried it out. It felt good! He walked around the land, feeling very proud of himself. Then he celebrated by planting the palm tree.

The palm nut sprouted and grew into a huge tree, dropped its nuts and more trees sprouted up. Obatala made a house out of them and lived there in peace with his cat.

Then one day he said to himself, "I love my cat, but I need people more like myself to relate to." So he began to dig in the ground. Some of the sand had turned to clay, so he began fashioning little people out of the clay. After awhile, though, he grew tired and thirsty. "I know what I need, a little wine!" he said, so he made some palm wine, drank it, and continued his labors. But as he got drunker and drunker, the people he was fashioning started coming out misshapen. Some had arms or legs that were longer than the others, or they were hunchbacked or had withered limbs. But Obatala was too intoxicated to notice that.

After he had a nice little stack of figures, he called out to his father, "Olorun, listen to me! I have created people out of clay, but only you can breathe life into them and make them live. Please do this for me so that I can have companions!" Olorun heard his prayer and did what he asked. He breathed life into the figures and they became human beings.

When the wine wore off, Obatala walked around cradling his aching head and looking around at what he had made, and it was only then that he realized that some of the people he had made were far from perfect. He felt terrible about this and vowed that he would not only swear off wine, but would also devote his life to protecting these people who were suffering because of his carelessness.[1]

The city Obatala founded was Ife, which is the greatest and most holy of all the Yoruba cities. The Yoruba are a number of loosely-related peoples who live in the south-western part of Nigeria. The Yoruba city-states were traditionally subdivided into twenty-five different kingdoms, of which Ife is the most important. Most scholars believe that Ife was founded about 850 CE, while the second oldest city, Oyo, was founded in 1350 CE.

When Christian missionaries first came among these people they decided that they were non-religious, even atheistic, because they did not set aside a certain day for worship, and only seemed to visit the priests when they were sick. In fact nothing could be further from the truth: the Yoruba people do not say that they "believe" in God, because the reality of God is self-evident, and the power of the gods is always present to them. The Yoruba, far from being a godless people, are a people literally swimming in the Divine. All activities are religious activities, all relationships are holy, and all places are sacred. The Christian missionaries' compulsive need to separate "sacred" from "profane" made little sense in a place where *everything* was sacred.

For to the Yoruba, the gods are literally in everything. How they got there is a very entertaining story as well. Originally, there was only one divine spirit living on the earth. His name was Orisha, and he lived in a house at the foot of a cliff. He had a slave named Eshu, who was himself a god, though not a very lucky one up until that point. Eshu hated Orisha and was tired of cooking all his meals and cleaning up after him. So one day Eshu climbed up to the top of the cliff above Orisha's house and, using some leverage, caused an enormous boulder that was teetering on the edge of the cliff to topple. It fell straight down and utterly smashed Orisha's house—and Orisha. In fact, the splinters of the house and little bits of Orisha himself flew in all directions.

The many splinters of Orisha became the 601 Orishas, the divine spirits that live in all things. Every tree, every river, every mountain has an Orisha, and human beings also can be indwelt by the Orishas and become their mouthpieces. In fact, the high point of ecstatic worship among the Yoruba people is the possession of one of the worshippers by one of the Orisha, who often has encouraging words, or sometimes warnings to give the worshippers.

What is amazing among the Yoruba people is that there is very little jealousy amongst the gods. It is unthinkable to the Yoruba that one would only worship one of them to the exclusion of others, although everyone has their "special" deity. When a Yoruban child is born, the seer is consulted. The seer consults the oracle and declares which Orisha claims the child. The child grows up under the special protection of his or her Orisha, and has a special relationship with that particular god. But when it is time for that child to marry, he or she cannot marry someone who is dedicated to the same god that they are. Instead he or she must marry someone dedicated to a different Orisha, so that there will be a balance of worship in the home. Likewise every village contains numerous shrines to many Orishas, so that they will all feel cared for and loved. And good old Eshu will even punish those who do not honor all of the Orishas, but maybe that's just because he feels a little responsible.

Now this is in marked contrast to the Jewish deity we have inherited, who declares that he is "a jealous god." Indeed, the deity of the Abrahamic religions does not know how to share and does not play well with others, if the Old Testament stories of the wholesale slaughter of people who worship any other god but him is any indication.

It seems a shame, because this has left us with a very impoverished sense of who God is. Like most native religions, the Yoruba do not insist that their deities be perfect, and by extension, they don't beat themselves up for not being perfect themselves. After all, Obatala was drunk, and *made* us imperfect. It's not our fault! This is very liberating.

It is also a shame that the Christian missionaries to Africa could not break out of their cultural prisons and see how very much their faith and the Yoruba religion have in common. Just as it was the son of God who created the world in the Yoruba myth, Christians believe that through Jesus "all things were made, and without him nothing was made that has been made" (John 1). They also believe that the Orishas are parts of god, and the children of God in much the same way as Jesus is part of God and God's Son. Furthermore, the Orishas serve as intermediaries between humans and the high God, much as the saints do in

Roman Catholicism. In fact, when the Yoruba peoples were brought as slaves to the new world and forced to convert, the Orishas fit neatly into the pantheon of saints, and the religion was able to survive under a thin veil of Catholicism.

When I was in Salvador, Brazil, I was amazed by the amazing number of churches in the city—over 150! And a hundred years ago, there were over 300 Catholic churches in the little town. Why? Because every Orisha has to have its own shrine!

One very interesting thing about Yoruba religion, however, is that while the high God, Olorun, is honored, he is never prayed to directly, and there are no shrines or churches built in his honor. Apparently, he is too scary, too powerful, and people would rather not attract his attention. Instead, they worship the Orishas, who are much more intimately concerned with human life, and less likely to visit destruction upon them if they are angry. A very powerful God can be useful, but dangerous. Better to simply lay low.

Although this does not have a parallel in Catholic teaching, it certainly does have a strong connection to Catholic practice. Many people feel that God the father is too judgmental, too demanding, too scary, and instead make their devotions to Jesus, or Mary, or to the saints. This is a pretty primal instinct in human beings, isn't it? If Daddy is being mean to you, you need to run to Mommy!

So what can we learn from this? It's pretty clear that the Yoruba people have developed a very complex and subtle theology. It is a kind of qualified monotheism that acknowledges one God, but sees this divinity as diffused throughout the earth. They are intimately connected to the divine spirits that inhabit the natural world, and see the world as an interconnected community that cares for them, and for which they care in return. This is a very well-developed nature mysticism, with a large body of mythology and a vivid and dramatic ritual life in which the gods literally speak to the community. It is a symbiotic culture, where humans and gods need each other, love each other, and together care for the earth. It is a religion that does not dwell on perfection, but instead finds a little waywardness to be a healthy trait in humans and gods alike. It is balance, not perfection, that they strive for, including balance between the gods.

The faith of the Yoruba people appeals to many, and is a very fast-growing religion indeed. There are over 30 million adherents in the world, 800,000 of them right here in the United States, though we call it Santeria here, where it is usually mixed with elements of Roman Catholicism.

Our theme sentence, "The effort one makes of forcing another to be like oneself, makes one an unpleasant person" speaks to the great tolerance and respect for the "other" in Yoruba culture. Sad to say that we Christians have certainly been very unpleasant people in the past. This need we have for everyone to act like us, look like us, and believe like we do is a very destructive impulse that we are just now beginning to shake off. We can learn from Yoruba that all peoples, all faiths, all deities should be shown respect, even if it is not ours to reverence each one of them.

High God, we are used to addressing you directly,
but the Yoruba people are right:
you can be a pretty scary guy.
Especially in our Old Testament,
you did and said things that just don't behoove a loving deity.
Yet it is we who decided that for some reason you had to be perfect.
You never said that yourself,
and we're sorry to have projected onto you
something that no human or deity can ever live up to.
Likewise, we are far from perfect people.
I'll tell you what: you forgive us, and we'll forgive you.
This will probably be easier for you than it will be for us,
but if you will grant us an ounce

of the good common sense of the Yoruba people,
we'll try not to be so hard on you in the future.
Sound good? Okie-dokie, then. Amen.

⊕ *Preached at Grace North Church on August 3, 2003.*

NOTE

1 Adapted from *World Mythology* by Donna Rosenberg (Chicago: National Textbook Company, 1986).

5 | black elk

In the late seventies a trilogy of books was published that completely captured my imagination. *The Chronicles of Thomas Covenant the Unbeliever* gave Tolkien fans the world over what they had been slavering for: a trilogy that could hold a candle to *The Lord of the Rings*. Oh, sure, it was derivative. But unlike *The Sword of Shannara*, it wasn't a hack job—it at least approached serious literature. And unlike Tolkien's own *Silmarillion*, published around the same time, it was actually readable.

It was more than readable, in fact. I have returned to the Covenant trilogy several times in my adult life, with almost the same frequency and excitement with which I return to Tolkien. In the Covenant books, our hero is more of an anti-hero. Thomas Covenant is a best-selling author in our own world. But not long after his name becomes a household word, disaster strikes. He contracts leprosy, his wife leaves him, and his neighbors pay his utility bills so that he has no reason to come into town.

Determined to pay his own phone bill, thank you very much, he walks into town and, wouldn't you know it, gets run over by a police car. When he wakes up he is not in our world at all. He finds himself instead in a place called the Land, a place that, not surprisingly, bears more than passing resemblance to Middle Earth. He is apparently sent there by the Land's creator, chosen to be the savior who will rescue the Land from the evil clutches of Lord Foul. His wedding ring, he learns, is made of white gold—an alloy that does not exist in the Land, and with which he can wield unlimited power—if only he can figure out how to use it.

This is a marvelous setup except for one thing. Thomas Covenant is a putz. The phrase "unwilling messiah" does not begin to describe this infuriating misanthrope. Never before in all of my reading days have I actually thrown a book across a room in frustration and disgust, but that's exactly the kind of reaction Thomas Covenant elicits, not only from readers, but from the inhabitants of the Land as well, who don't understand why, if a man *can* help a people in danger, why *won't* he help?

This is precisely the question that plagues us when we consider today's mystic, Black Elk. Born in July, 1864, in what is now Wyoming, Black Elk belonged to a tribe of Oglala Lakota, a branch of the Sioux people. His father was both a warrior and a medicine man, and his tipi was a crowded one, with five daughters and two sons. Black Elk's second cousin was a man of some fame; perhaps you've heard of Crazy Horse? It is said that the resemblance between the two was uncanny.

When Black Elk was five, he had his fist vision. His grandfather had made him a bow and some arrows. He was riding in the woods and saw a kingbird sitting on a limb. Black Elk went to shoot the bird, but was rattled when the bird spoke to him. "The clouds all over are one-sided," the bird said. The boy didn't know what this meant, but then the bird said, "Listen! A voice is calling you!" Then he looked up at the clouds and two men were hurtling down from the sky like arrows, straight for him. As they came, they sang a song, "Behold a sacred voice is calling you. All over the sky a sacred voice is calling." But just before they reached him, they wheeled about and dissolved into a constellation of flying geese. Thunder crashed, and then rain soaked the boy. He was so freaked out by this occurrence that he told no one about it, and wondered long and hard as to its meaning.

It wasn't until he was nine, however, that his *big* vision struck. It was a long, complicated vision that is like nothing quite so much as the psychedelic shewings of St. John in the *Book of Revelation*. Black Elk was in a fever for twelve days, but in that time he saw things that he could scarcely describe in words, including four groups of horses that remind me of the four horsemen of the apocalypse. The high point was meeting the six grandfathers of the six sacred directions who told him that he was to be the savior of his people. They gave him a cup of water "to make the day live," and a bow with the power to destroy. They gave him a sacred pipe with the power to make peace, and they gave him the good red day. They gave him a sacred staff and hoop, and told him to plant the staff within the hoop, and to watch it bloom.

Black Elk was just as frightened and freaked out by all of this as you or I would be, and he was afraid to tell anyone about it, because he was only a nine-year-old boy, and he didn't think anyone would believe him.

Hard times were to come upon his tribe very soon, however, and Black Elk regretted his silence for the rest of his days. His people were decimated and displaced, and at the age of twelve, Black Elk fought beside his cousin Crazy Horse at the Battle of Little Big Horn.

One thing that amazed white people about the Lakota was that they did not withdraw when it was time to eat, but just sat down in the midst of the battle. During the battle, in fact, Black Elk and his friend Red Crow did just this. They had a seat, and watching the battle rage all around them, placed a little pile of jerky between them and began their meal. A bullet struck the dirt between them and kicked dust all over their jerky. They simply dusted it off, and calmly continued eating. "If I had been killed there that that moment," Black Elk would later say, "at least I would have died with food in my mouth."[1]

Little Big Horn was a disaster for the Lakota people. Crazy Horse was killed and the remaining warriors fled to Canada. Three years later, at the age of fifteen, Black Elk returned to join his people on the reservation to which they had been restricted. Slowly he began to reveal his vision to his people, but his confusion about what it meant and what was required of him grew. He studied the ancient ways of his people and was fast becoming a respected medicine man, and yet his studies brought him no peace and few answers. Troubled in his soul and unclear as to his path, he felt that the fate of his people rested on his shoulders alone and he could not muster the courage or the clarity to carry such a burden. Finally, he snapped and did what most of us would do in similar circumstances: he ran away and joined the circus.

Buffalo Bill's Wild West Show, to be exact. Black Elk did medicine dances and discovered he was a bit of a performer. He traveled with Buffalo Bill to New York, and then on to London to perform for Queen Victoria, whom he called "Grandmother England." They toured the better part of western Europe before he finally bought passage for himself back home. He arrived back on the reservation in 1889, but it was a sad homecoming indeed. "Before I went," he later told his daughter, Lucy, "some of my people were looking well, but when I got back they all looked pitiful."[2]

In 1890 he discovered the Ghost Dance, and saw in it great power, and he hoped, some sense of what his purpose might be. The dance united the native peoples, and their spirits began to be lifted. They found healing in the dance, and fame of the dance spread far and wide, with newspapers around the country running stories on the odd religious spectacle taking place on the plains. The soldiers were not happy about this, of course. They saw anything that gave power to the Indians to be a threat to their own fragile dominance, and they swiftly sought to destroy this new religious threat. The Ghost Dance precipitated the Battle of Wounded Knee, where Sitting Bull and three hundred Lakota warriors lost their lives.

Black Elk lived through this battle as well, but he was an extremely conflicted man. He possessed the "soldier weed" given to him by the thunderbeings in his vision, and believed that one touch of this rare herb would cause instant death. But he was a tender-hearted soul, too, and even though he had seen the soldiers do terrible things to his own people, he could not use the awesome power he held against them. Maybe he was afraid to, maybe he was afraid the soldier weed wouldn't work, and it would just make things harder for his people. Or perhaps he knew he actually held the power of life and death in his hands and he could not bring himself to wield it. He had seen death, and he did not want to be the cause of it.

And yet his vision was clear: kill and show no mercy. But he could not bring himself to do it. He finally knew what he was supposed to do, and chose not to. That decision would haunt Black Elk for the rest of his life, as he saw his people suffer more and more. He was the chosen one, with the power to save them. And yet he did not do it.

In 1892 he married Katie War Bonnet, who not long after, converted to Catholicism. All of their children were baptized Catholic, and yet Black Elk continued to practice the traditional medicine of his people. He was forty years old, and he lived with a heavy heart and a great sense of dis-ease. His father, brother, and one of his own sons had died, and in 1903, his wife Katie died as well. Black Elk was bereft.

Many of the Lakota people were becoming Catholics at this time. The Jesuits brought western medicine, science, and education to the reservation, and though the Army tried to stop them, the "black robes" as they were called, just kept coming. Black Elk's friend, Sam Kills Brave, was the leader of a nearby community, and he encouraged Black Elk to convert. Black Elk refused, but it was clear that Christianity was just one more conflict this troubled man had to carry.

Not long after Katie's death, Black Elk was summoned to the tipi of a family whose little boy was gravely ill. He was just bending to enter the tent, when a black robe thundered up in a horse and buggy. "Get out!" the priest ordered him. "The boy is baptized!"

Black Elk was a powerful medicine man. He had power and knew he had power, but for some reason he felt dwarfed by the spiritual power of the Jesuit. He sat down in the dust and felt all his power and all of his hope drain out of him. He felt useless. When the black robe was finished ministering to the boy he snapped at Black Elk, "You, come with me."

He took Black Elk to the mission, where he stayed with the priests and became an avid student of Catholicism. Finally, on the feast day of St. Nicholas, December 6, 1904, Black Elk was baptized a Roman Catholic. He took the name of the saint of his baptismal day, and was thenceforth known as Nicholas Black Elk.

Catholicism brought Nick Black Elk new hope. Finally, he felt he was relieved of some of his burden as he relinquished his sense of duty to the authority of the church. He found an amazing congruence between Catholic teachings and his own native religion. And though many people accused him of converting just to survive financially, and others accused him of turning his back on his own tradition, the truth is probably closer to the middle. Nick saw Christianity as the fulfillment of his vision, the missing piece that made it all make sense. He honored the ways of the Lakota and would continue to do certain rituals, but other rituals he would not do.

He understood the sacred staff in his vision to be the cross, and that it was his job to plant it in the sacred hoop of his people, where it would bloom and bring life to them. He threw himself into this new teaching with a vengeance. He became a catechist and a liturgist, traveling far and wide on the reservations preaching, teaching Catholic doctrine, and, when no priest was available, leading prayer services and baptizing people. He was apparently a very charismatic preacher, and people often remarked on his skill as an orator.

He was also skilled as an apologist, and one time when a Protestant minister asked him how he could honor the Virgin Mary, Nick asked him, "Are the angels good people?"

"Yes," the minister replied.

"And the Holy Ghost, is he good?"

"Yes, of course," the minister agreed.

"Well," Nick told him, "if all these honored her, why shouldn't I?"

Nick Black Elk was a dedicated Catholic teacher for the rest of his days, but he also kept alive the rituals and theology of the Lakota. When the poet John Neihardt interviewed him in 1932, a book resulted titled *Black Elk Speaks*, which has become one of the most famous accounts of Native American mysticism that we have. Further books were compiled, as anthropologists mined his memory for knowledge of the Lakota tradition that was fast disappearing. Nick felt that the teachings of his people were important, and cooperated. He also performed ceremonies for tourists. Perhaps he felt like he was selling out, performing the sacred dances for pay, but perhaps he had developed into a bit of a ham while traveling with Buffalo Bill, and a part of him enjoyed performing. Or perhaps he just desperately needed the money. In any case, Nick Black Elk continued in this bivocational vein, praying with both the pipe and the rosary, dancing the sacred dances and teaching Catholic doctrine until he fell ill in 1948 and could no longer dance.

Just before his death he asked his son to take him to the top of Harney Peak in the Black Hills to pray. While they were journeying up the mountain he told his son, "I feel like something is going to happen today. I am going to pray, and if I have any power left, the thunderbeings should hear me. There might even be a little rain." This seemed unlikely as they were in the middle of a terrible drought. Nick Black Elk reached the top of the mountain and prayed. He broke into tears and confessed that he had never been able to bring the sacred staff to bloom. He prayed that if there was any life left in the sacred tree, it might one day bloom after his death, and that his people may someday be saved, and return to the ways of peace and plenty that they had known before the white men had come. While he was praying thunderheads gathered, and rain fell on Black Elk as he wept.

Was Black Elk a failure or not? That's hard to say. He refused to cooperate with his vision, the power he was given went unused, and his people were subjected to a horrific fate. Yet, he refused because he chose the way of peace, even at the cost of great personal suffering for him and his people, and he found in Catholicism a rich and powerful mythology in which he might be able to justify, or some would say, rationalize, his decisions.

And yet there is much that we can learn from him. Although the Black Robes would have preferred that he repudiate and denounce his native teachings, Black Elk steadfastly maintained that "the good red road" was a gift of the Creator, and even if its fulfillment was to be found in Christ, the road was a blessing nonetheless. Black Elk did not see the different religions as being in conflict, but as being complementary. Just as the circle of a tipi is set into a larger circle of many tipis, Black Elk saw the religion of his people as one tipi, the religion of the Catholics as another tipi, and other religions as other tipis; and yet each of these tipis were set into a larger circle of faith. The Lakota call God *Wankan Tanka*, "the Great Mystery." Black Elk did not denounce the faith of his people, nor did he simply pay lip service to the Jesuits. Instead, he saw many religions as paying faithful witness to the Great Mystery, anticipating by nearly fifty years the proclamations on the validity of non-Christian religions issued at the Second Vatican Council.

In the Thomas Covenant books of Stephen Donaldson, Covenant had two main difficulties to overcome. First, he didn't believe he was in the Land at all, but dreaming. And second, though he pitied the people who looked to him for help, he didn't know *how* to help them. Black Elk certainly believed in his vision, but like Covenant, it was the *how* of it all that stumped him. In Black Elk I see a template for the post-modern mystic. We know the fate of the world is hanging in the balance, we know that the Great Mystery is counting on us to bring about the vision of peace and true fulfillment given us by our many religious traditions, but we are a little fuzzy on the details, and we feel small and impotent in the face of such great need.

Black Elk, it turned out, was not the savior of his people as the thunderbeings had hoped. He was not faithful to his vision, and he did not destroy the white man. But he was a man of great vision; he saw what others were afraid to see, and he spoke his visions even in the midst of his own uncertainty. And so we honor him today, not as savior, but as a very human soul, a conflicted man and a genuine mystic, who was able to walk in two worlds and recognized the Great Mystery as being active in each.

Great Mystery, we stand before you in much the same condition
as your servant, Nicholas Black Elk.
We see that the Land is in great need,
that the people have no vision and little hope.
We quail at the horrors that may be visited upon us,
or more likely, that we will visit upon ourselves.
And yet, we do not know what to do about it.
We are small, and weak, and often our best efforts
do more harm than good.
We ask you for a vision of healing for our land,
for the knowledge of how to bring it about,
and for the courage to act in the face of doubt, distress, and danger.

Help us to find our place in the sacred hoop,
and bring to flower the sacred tree you have planted in our midst.
For we ask this in the name of the one who hung upon the tree,
and thereby brought us life, even Jesus Christ. Amen.

⊕ *Preached at Grace North Church on August 17, 2003.*

NOTES

1 Raymond J. DeMallie. *The Sixth Grandfather* (Lincoln: University of Nebraska Press, 1984).

2 *Ibid.*

6 | lao tzu

At a used book store several years ago, I purchased a copy of Raymond M. Smullyan's book *The Tao is Silent* on a whim. I had heard of the Tao, and was intrigued by the little information I had. I had not heard of the *Tao Te Ching*, but I soon gained respect for Taoism's philosophy as Smullyan interpreted it. Halfway through the book a friend came for a visit and saw it. His jaw dropped open and he looked at me in an odd way. "Are you...into the Tao?" he said tentatively.

"Well," I replied, "I like what I''ve read."

"Have you read the *Tao Te Ching*?"

"No, but I wa..." Before I could finish he dashed out of the house and slammed the door. I contemplated this peculiar behavior and wondered if perhaps I had overlooked a manic tendency in my friend. I certainly hoped he wouldn't hurt himself. Before I could finish my musings, the door had swung wide open once again. My friend hovered in the frame with a crazed look, clutching an enormous dog-eared trade paperback.

"This," he said, panting, pressing the book to my chest, "is the holy word of God."

"You don't say," I returned, flipping through the treasured tome. It was Gia-Fu Feng and Jane English's translation, beautifully illustrated with Chinese calligraphy and Ms. English's stunning nature photography. "Can I borrow it?" I asked.

He chewed his lip a moment and I had my first glimpse of how terribly important this book really was to him. "I would really love to read through it. It's not long. I'll get it back to you soon. Promise." I lied. From the first few chapters I was entranced with the book's simplicity and awesome profundity, and living with it has seriously affected my life, both spiritually and socially.

The *Tao Te Ching* is a book of Chinese philosophical poetry, written sometime between the seventh and the fourth centuries BCE. According to tradition it was written by a quiet librarian named Lao Tzu, which in Chinese can mean, curiously enough, either Old Man or Old Child. Lao Tzu was said to be a contemporary of Confucius, although many years his senior, and the legend of their ideological rivalry is very popular. It is said that both their reputations traveled before them, so when they met face-to-face Lao Tzu was anything but impressed. He sternly rebuked Confucius for his arrogance, greed, and ambition. When the audience was over, Confucius is recorded as saying:

"I understand how birds can fly, how fishes can swim, and how four-footed beasts can run. Those that run can be snared, those that swim may be caught with hook and line, those that fly may be shot with arrows. But when it comes to the dragon, I am unable to conceive how he can soar into the sky riding upon the wind and clouds. Today I have seen Lao Tzu and can only liken him to a dragon."

Scholars nowadays doubt the historicity of the person Lao Tzu and many believe the *Tao Te Ching*, the book attributed to him, to be a composite work collected by an early Taoist school, much the same way that Jews and Christians today doubt the historicity of the Mosaic authorship of the Torah. Whether Lao Tzu actually wrote every word of the *Tao Te Ching* is unimportant—most probably he is the founder of a school, the teachings of which are best represented by this book. He is, nonetheless, its traditional author, and for the purposes of this sermon, we will give him the credit.

In the *Tao Te Ching* we once again encounter a form of nature mysticism, but it is a unique and amazing form. As in other nature religions, in Taoism humans are not separate from nor dominant over nature. We are a part of nature. The Taoist sees him or herself as equal to all other things in Creation, and in fact, it is from observing nature that wisdom is gleaned. There is no revelation in Taoism. Nature reveals everything we need to know, if only we have the eyes—and the patience—to see it. Nature, in Taoism, is always correct and has the answers to every problem. Humans think too much and that gets us into trouble.

So what is the Tao? This is a difficult question, and Lao Tzu tells us right off in his first poem in the *Tao Te Ching* that "The Tao that can be described in words is not the true Tao." Like most mystics, however, he does not let the impossibility of his task deter him, and spends the next eighty poems trying to do just that. We are used to thinking of deity in terms of God or the gods, but Taoism demands a very different orientation. The Tao is not a god, ruling over subjects, or wielding power over nature—the Tao is a part of nature, or more accurately, nature is a part of the Tao, and therefore the Tao is not a separate personality, like the Christian God. The Tao is impersonal. This sounds like a negative thing, and irreconcilable to the Christian conception of God, but it is in fact neither. *The Tao is God as nature sees God.* The sparrow, who cannot fall without God's knowledge (Matt. 10:29), does not have a "personal relationship" with God. The sparrow does not perceive God as a personality but as the very web of being in which it moves and of which it consists. The Taoist follows the example of the animals and the Earth herself, and perceives of God in the same way.

The Tao is simply that which is. By observing nature we can discern certain characteristics about it, and also discern healthier ways of being human as well. There is no one to pray to in Taoism, there are no rites to be performed, no liturgy to be recited. There is simply the world as-it-is, and we will either find our proper place within it or we will suffer.

According to Lao Tzu, all things in nature are in balance. The Tao consists of both Yin and Yang, opposing forces that define and sustain each other: good and bad, light and dark, matter and spirit. The *Tao Te Ching* speaks of matter and spirit as if they were partners, one incapable of functioning without the other. Taoists speak of spirit as "non-being," implying something that exists in objective reality, but which possesses no physical manifestation, or "being." Synonyms for spirit/non-being are emptiness and non-existence. Meister Eckhart, in our own Christian tradition, spoke in similar terms when he said that "God is a being beyond being and a nothingness beyond being."[1] This unitive vision of spirituality is difficult for Westerners reared with pervasive dualism. Lao Tzu asks, as if speaking directly to us, "Being both body and spirit, can you embrace unity and not be fragmented?" (poem 10).[2]

To illustrate his vision, Lao Tzu presents non-being as absolutely necessary for physical realities to "function," and vice versa, saying, "Thirty spokes join together at one hub, but it is the hole in the center that makes it operable. Clay is molded into a pot, but it is the emptiness inside that makes it useful. Doors and windows are cut to make a room, but it is the empty spaces that we use" (poem 11).

The first time I read these verses, chills ran down my spine. I felt that I had been told a great secret that was the most obvious thing in the world: the relationship between matter and spirit. One is not dominant. "Existence and non-existence produce one another," Lao Tzu explains. "Existence is what we have, but non-existence is what we *use*."

In addition to non-being, which is thing, or noun-oriented, Lao Tzu also offers a matching concept which is action, or verb-oriented: non-action. The Chinese word for non-action is *wu-wei*. *Wu-wei* literally means "not doing," but it has many applications.

With this concept, Lao Tzu speaks directly to twenty-first century Westerners and our fast-paced culture. He tells us, "If you spend your life filling your senses and rushing around 'doing' things, you will be beyond hope." It is difficult for some of us to slow down and not feel guilty.

Instead, Lao Tzu asks a difficult question: "When Heaven gives and takes away, can you be content to just let things come or go? And even when you understand all things, can you simply allow yourself to be?" (poem 10).

Slowing down enough to hear the voice of the Spirit, or to observe the way of the Tao, is in my experience one of the most important spiritual disciplines of all. An old joke reminds us that Westerners say, "Don't just sit there, do something!" while Eastern wisdom says, "Don't just do something, sit there!" The value of not-doing is every bit as great as the value of non-being, or spirit, and the health of our non-being/spirit is utterly dependent upon our ability to not-do.

In the *Tao Te Ching* Lao Tzu also concerns himself greatly with leadership, both political and spiritual. There is a tradition that the *Tao Te Ching* was originally written as a guide for a young ruler on how to rule well. Lao Tzu's advice is about as counter-intuitive as we in the west can imagine.

"Loving all people and leading them well," he asks, "can you do this without imposing your will?" This is a great and important question for us who are surrounded by traditions notorious for spiritual coercion. Unfortunately, we often unwittingly perpetuate the cycle of coercion. But Taoism suggests that, like water, all things simply flow out and return, void of any notions of "right" or "wrong."

The key to being successful in spiritual leadership, according to Lao Tzu, is to *not try*. "Therefore the sage, not trying, cannot fail," says Lao Tzu. "Not clutching, she cannot lose." Likewise in our own spiritual lives, "The truly good person does not try to be good." Goodness needs to come naturally, effortlessly, like breathing or hearing. The sage is not concerned with being good, or even with being a good spiritual leader. He or she does not give it a thought. It is not a goal. The goal is to respond humanely—as a human would—to whatever situation life gives.

I have told you before the story of Agnes, the Chinese grandmother I worked with in San Francisco many years ago. I was agonizing over some minor indiscretion—something I said that might have offended somebody. I was *kvetching* about this aloud when Agnes snapped. She threw down the papers she was carrying and pointed her stubby finger in my face, "You too goody-two shoes!" she said. "If you Chinese, we take you to doctor!" I was shocked, but after reading the *Tao Te Ching*, I finally understood her. When things are in balance, they are healthy, when they are out of balance, they get ill. All of Chinese medicine is based on this principle, and it is certainly healtheir than our constantly berating ourselves for not being "good" enough. According to the Tao, if you are too good, you are just not healthy.

Taoism, then, not surprisingly, has a very different conception of sin than we are used to in the West. "Sin" in Taoism is not about doing evil or disobeying authority. Instead it is simply going against the grain, and one's punishment is immediate and in this world: a life of stress and struggle. "Salvation" on the other hand, is simply going with the flow, finding a life of freedom and security, because one knows how the universe works and can cooperate with it. There is no "guilt" language in the *Tao Te Ching*. The Tao's love is universal and unconditional. It is not for the enlightened only, or the holy or even the moral. The Tao is there for all. "It is the good person's treasure," Lao Tzu writes, "and the bad person's refuge... Why did the sages of old value the Tao so much? Because when you seek, you find. And when you sin, you are forgiven." How healthy is that?

In Lao Tzu's philosophy, success comes not from achievement or from the accumulation of spiritual merit or power. Instead, success is measured by one's ability to simply be, free of stress, free of striving, free of conceptions of what one "should be" that is in any way at odds with how one simply is.

Legend tells us that Lao Tzu, in his old age, finally despaired of teaching humanity anything, and gave up on us as a lost cause. He packed his yak, and headed for the wilderness where things were sane. At the top of a mountain pass, the last outpost of civilization, the gatekeeper persuaded Lao Tzu to commit his philosophy to paper before he left humankind forever.

The human race will be forever indebted to the foresight of this gatekeeper, as Lao Tzu's book, consisting of just 5,000 characters, is one of the most sublime, meaningful, and downright practical works of mysticism in the human canon. If you have not read it, please pick up a copy on your way home, or print it out from my website. I guarantee that if you read it with prayerful attention, it will change your life as well.

Holy Creator and sustainer,
who knows and cares about each sparrow that falls to earth,
help us to see the world as you see it, as nature sees it.
Help us to see ourselves as part of the whole,
and that the proper balance of all things depends
in part upon us and our awareness.
Help us to lead by following, to achieve by not-doing,
to be good by not trying to be good.
Help us to be at peace with ourselves as we are,
to recognize the holiness of the world as-it-is,
and to rest in the lowest place, as water does.
For we ask this in the name of the one who sought out the lowest place,
who nourished it and gave it life, even Jesus Christ. Amen.

⊕ *Preached at Grace North Church on September 7, 2003.*

NOTES

1 Matthew Fox, OP. *Meditations with Meister Eckhardt* (Santa Fe: Bear & Co., 1983).

2 Quotations from the *Tao Te Ching* from *God As Nature Sees God* by John R. Mabry (Rockport, MA: Element Books, 1994).

7 | chuang tzu

several years ago, my wife Kate and I were up in Alaska visiting my parents. It was just before we were married, and
she was meeting them for the first time. As usual, my stomach was tied in knots, and I was a bumbling idiot, as I so often
am when visiting my parents. I never understood why I was such
a nervous wreck the moment I stepped through their door, and
my transformation from general competency to blathering klutz
was mystifying to Kate.

After a day or so, Kate became more withdrawn and grim. I
thought the trip was going fine so far—or as fine as a trip to my
parents *can* go, when, in a moment alone, Kate dropped the
bomb. She said, "John, do you realize that your Mom hasn't gone
five minutes without criticizing you?"

My first impulse was to say, "What nonesense!" But the sensa-
tions in my body distracted me. My stomach churned and my
throat thickened up. "Do you think that's really true?" I asked,
trying not to cry.

"Don't you?"

But I could longer see Kate. It wasn't that my own tears were obscuring her but a vertigo had overtaken me. The wheels of the universe had shifted and locked into place, and for one mystical and fleeting moment, much in my life made sense that had been a mystery to me before. And then I started to notice. I began to count on my fingers the critiques as they rattled off. "Why do you walk that way? Won't studying that stuff confuse you? Don't slouch. How can you stand to eat curry?"

Now, to be fair to my mother, I am aware that she says these things not to be mean, but in that weird, twisted way that many mothers share, out of a sincere desire to make me a better person. I know in my heart of hearts that she is motivated to say these horribly wounding things by love, as bizarre as that might seem.

And mothers aren't the only purveyors of this kind of senseless, non-stop criticism, either. The religion we practiced also heaped on the negativity. "You are a craven, corrupt soul who deserves to burn in the fires of Hell for all eternity," I was told from the pulpit every week. I was convinced of my own depravity, as every authority in my life drilled the same message into me: "You worthless turd. God sees you and wants to puke." I was surrounded on every side by well-meaning moralists telling me in great detail how to live without pissing off God. I learned the rules, and for the most part kept all of them, though I never did learn to walk to my mother's satisfaction.

Our mystic of the day, Chuang Tzu, would have understood well my delimma. He, too, was surrounded on every side by zealous moralists dictating the proper way to do just about every aspect of a person's life. In his case, the moralists were the Confucianists, who followed the philosophy of Confucius, naturally. Confucius began with an egalitarian message: noble birth does not convey nobility. A person is as noble as he or she behaves, and everyone can strive to be a superior person. But being a superior person was a lot of work: there was a proper way to do just about everything. Confucius piled on the rules until even a person who had all the money and leisure in the world could not be properly observant. It was into this world, a world obsessed with Confucian rules and regulations into which Chuang Tzu was born.

He lived in the third century BCE, in a district of China known as Meng, which most scholars locate as being near modern-day Honan, south of the Yellow River. His first name was Chou, and he worked for a while in the state lacquer garden. But due to his disregard for propriety and rules, it is not likely that he held the job for long. Which was probably just fine with Chuang Tzu, who was deeply influenced by the Taoist philosophy of Lao Tzu, and took his master's teachings about "not-doing" to heart.

Much like Plato writing about Socrates, Chuang-Tzu's writings recount many tales of Lao Tzu, and expand upon his philosophy. Just as Socrates wrote nothing and Lao Tzu wrote little, both Plato and Chuang-Tzu wrote voluminously about the teachings of their mentors, complete with their own unique spin, of course.

In Chuang-Tzu's philosophy, one did not need to memorize the Confucian rules for being a superior person, nor did one need to keep them. The endless harangue of how one *should* be, or what one *should not* do irritated him, and seemed to him not only pointless, but destructive. And this is why: according to Chuang Tzu, everything is okay exactly as it is. The universe is One, Chuang Tzu taught. The moment you say something is not-okay, you make a distinction and do violence to the whole. Once you start making distinctions, once you say something is good, it implies that something else is bad—and suddenly you have up and down, hot and cold, pleasant and unpleasant, right and wrong, good and evil, useful and useless, light and dark, big and little, *ad infinitum, ad nauseum.* All of these things are illusions created by the human mind. Then ten thousand things rise from the One and fall back into it again. Seeing the One instead of the ten thousand things is not hard to do, and is the only way, in Chuang Tzu's system, to stay sane.

"Life, death, preservations, loss, failure, success, poverty, riches, worthiness, unworthiness, slander, fame, hunger, thirst, cold, heat," he writes, "these are the alternations of the world.... Day and night they change place before us and wisdom cannot spy out their source. Therefore, they should not be enough to destroy your harmony."

The efforts of Confucius and the other moralists were pointless, he said. Human nature is human nature, it is what it is, it is part of the Tao. Trying to change it is crazy, and doomed to failure. "The Way has never known any boundaries..." Chuang Tzu tells us. "So, those who divide fail to divide; those who discriminate fail to discriminate. What does this mean, you ask? The sage embraces things. Ordinary men discriminate among them and parade their discriminations before others. So I say, those who discriminate fail to see."

Not suprisingly, Chuang Tzu is an iconoclast. Skewering sacred cows is one of his favorite pastimes; he delights in bursting the bubbles of every self-inflated ideologue who crosses his path. One of his best friends, Hui Tzu, was also his constant foil. One time Hui Tzu said to him, "I have a big tree in my yard—it has a trunk that is so gnarled and bumpy that it is absolutely useless to any carpenter. Your teaching is just like that tree—big and useless!"

"And yet" Chuang Tzu said, "it had the wisdom to grow so gnarled and bumpy so that no axe will ever touch it. Nothing will harm it. If there's no use for it, how can it come to grief or pain? And is it really useless? Why don't you relax by its side and do nothing? Or lie down underneath it for a free and easy nap?"

Unlike Confucius, who spent most of his adult life chasing after political appointment, Chuang Tzu eschewed all political power. One story relates that Chuang Tzu was fishing in the P'u River when the king of Ch'u sent two officials to him to offer him the job of governor. Chuang Tzu just continued fishing and without even turning his head, said, "I have heard that there is a sacred tortoise in Ch'u that has been dead for three thousand years. The king keeps it wrapped in cloth and boxed, and stores it in the ancestral temple. Now, would this tortoise rather be dead and have its bones left behind and venerated? Or would it rather be alive and dragging its tail in the mud?"

"It would rather be alive and dragging its tail in the mud," said the two officials.

Chuang Tzu waved his fishing pole at them and shouted, "So go away, and leave me to drag my tail in the mud!"

Chuang Tzu knew that the moment he accepted such a post, he would cease to be a free man. Sudenly there would descend upon him responsibilities and stress, and expectations and propriety, and all the things that steal a person's freedom. And that is the secret to understanding Chuang Tzu. His philosophy can be reduced to one word: freedom. Freedom from all the things society tells us we *should* do or *should not* do, freedom from stress and striving, freedom from arbitrary rules that senselessly shackle us.

And it isn't just freedom from the expectations of society. Chuang Tzu finds the lives of those who eschew the world and go off to live in caves to be just as imprisoning. There's nothing free about the ascetic ideal with its fasting and silences and self-conscious denial of every earthly pleasure. Instead, Chuang Tzu's philosophy advocates freedom from the ideologies, prejudices, rules, structures, proprieties, and all the anxiety that comes in the wake of all such man-made nonesense.

Chuang Tzu teaches that all loyalties are suspect, including one's loyalty to the state, to one's ruler, to one's family, to an ideology or a religious doctrine. The only loyalty that has any value is the loyalty to one's true nature, to the Tao itself. Instead of chasing after cock-eyed notions of "right" and "wrong," Chuang Tzu invites us to see beyond such arbitrary distinctions and to rediscover an authentic way of being in the world. He wants us to respond with authenticity, rather than through the filters of propriety. To react humanely—as a human would—to any given situation, just as a fish reacts as a fish would, or a bird reacts the way a bird would.

Just before leaving my house to go down to the coffee shop to write this sermon, I remembered that I had a full trash bag sitting by the kitchen door. Now, there is about a fifty-fifty chance that if I left that bag where it was, my dog Clare would have ripped it open and scattered its contents across the entire kitchen. Clare does not rip open a trash bag because she is a bad dog, nor does she refrain from ripping it open because she is a good dog. She is just a dog, and responds as a dog responds, depending on just how enticing an aroma might be coming from that bag.

Just as a dog does not fill his days with worry over how to respond to a given situation, Chuang Tzu wants us to just be and respond from our true and inner nature. When a dog is tired, it sleeps; when it is hungry, it eats; when it itches, it scratches; and when it smells a delicious bit of trash, it helps itself. So, instead of putting labels on Clare, like "good dog" or "bad dog," labels which mean nothing to her anyway, I simply took out the trash, since where there is no temptation, there can be no transgression.

Not bound by artificial rules or rituals or scripts, Chuang Tzu says that human beings can discover who they were truly meant to be. And "*be*" is the operative word. Not what they are to *do*, what they are to accomplish, what they can achieve. But who they are to be, in their most unaffected, unmediated, and authentic selves. Only by discovering this true self can one hope to, in Chuang Tzu's words, "stay in one piece, keep oneself alive, look after one's parents, and live out one's years."

Chuang Tzu tells us, "You never find happiness until you stop looking for it." Happiness can be found, but not by striving. "The pursuit of happiness" enshrined in the *Declaration of Independence* would have seemed backwards to Chuang Tzu. One is happy only when one ceases pursuing and striving and *trying*, and allows oneself simply to be.

When Chuang Tzu was about to die, his disciples started planning a sumptuous funeral for him. Not surprisingly, he protested, saying, "Why do you need to do anything? I will have heaven and earth for my coffin and coffin lid, the sun and moon for the pennies on my eyes, the stars and constellations for my jewelry, and the ten thousand things for my parting gifts. The furnishings for my funeral are already prepared—what more is there to do?"

"But if we don't bury you," his disciples protested, "the crows and kites will have at you!"

Chuang Tzu calmly replied, "Above ground, I will feed the crows and kites; below the ground I'll feed the crickets and ants. Tell me, what do you have against the birds?"

We don't know how long Chuang Tzu lived, but he has left a record that is unparalleled in the history of philosophy. He is one of the only figures in philosophical history to have used humor as one of his main teaching tools, and his challenge to us remains as amazing and earth-shattering to us today as it did twenty-five hundred years ago. His invitation to throw off the bonds of propriety and social conformity is both refreshing and frustrating as it is often difficult to discern exactly where society ends and our authentic selves begin. But that is the journey. I have to say that while it is easier to visit my parents today than it was in the past, revisiting the burdens of distinctions that I walked away from so long ago is still painful and tedious. I try not to let my mother's haranguing get to me, but I have, at least, made peace with the way I walk. Let us pray, in whatever way is authentically yours....

Eternal Tao, nameless and formless,
you have blessed us with life and brought us forth from the garden.
We suffer only because we struggle against nature
and do not recognize our oneness with you.
Help us to relax, to let go of the fetters of "should" and "should not"
and to discover the subtle essence of our true selves.

Help us to find our home in the world, our help in you,
and our identity in the unity of all things. Amen.

⊕ *Preached at Grace North Church on September 21, 2003.*

8 | hinduism

One of my favorite films of the past several years is *The Truman Show*, which features what is probably Jim Carrey's finest dramatic performance to date. Instead of the ludicrous, madcap characters he normally plays, in *The Truman Show* he is an unsuspecting everyman, and he plays the role with great depth and poignancy.

For those of you who have not seen the film, Truman is more or less an average Joe. He works at an insurance company at a job he doesn't really like all that much. He has a pleasant wife, but his marriage lacks passion. The island on which he lives is idyllic, but a little boring. Truman realizes he wants more, but it is then that he starts noticing some very odd coincidences. There are no elevators where there should be elevators. His friends and his wife are behaving strangely.

What we know, and his wife and friends know, but what Truman *doesn't* know, is that he is not a no-name, hapless schmuck after all, but a world-famous TV star. From birth, Truman has been raised in an artificial world, constructed entirely for the television cameras, as every second of his life has been captured on film and watched by millions. His life is the ultimate reality-TV show, and he is completely unaware of it.

He does begin to suspect, however, and the great pleasure of the film is watching him put the pieces together, confront the people he thought were closest to him, who are revealed to be only actors, and come to grips with the existential crisis that overwhelms him.

Finally, he puts it all together. He is angry that he has been a dupe his entire life, that he has been manipulated and used for the entertainment of others, without his knowledge or consent. And it is ultimately the knowledge of his fate that liberates him, for once his eyes are opened to the artificiality of his world, he knows precisely how to leave it and be free of it forever.

But it is what happens *after* Truman walks away that interests me, and this the movie doesn't show us. Once Truman leaves the world of illusion and is lost in the sea of anonymity, what then? A sequel would probably not be nearly as much fun as the original film, but the questions haunt me nonetheless.

I feel a little bit like Truman whenever I contemplate Hinduism, our next stop on our tour of the mystics of the world's religions. For Hinduism teaches us that the entire world is merely an illusion. None of it is real, none of it has any ultimate value, other than simply this: the entertainment of the deity. According to the Hindu faith, the universe is *lila*, a Sanskrit word that means, "play." The world is God's playground, a vast illusion spun solely for the amusement of the supreme Being. Just as in *The Truman Show*, all that we see is fabricated, a show, and all of our struggles, our suffering, our joy, our drama, and our happiness exists solely for the enjoyment of the observer.

And also like *The Truman Show*, the people who populate this artificial reality are just characters in this show. In Hinduism, we, too, are just illusions. We seem to have personalities, we appear to ourselves to have independent consciousness, but this, too, is an illusion. In Hinduism there is only one thing in the universe: God. And all the myriad beings that populate this world are merely bits of God at differing stages of awareness of their true identity. The world, then, is an enormous game of peek-a-boo that God is playing with himself.

One significant difference from *The Truman Show* is that in the film everyone is trying to keep Truman from discovering the secret that the world is a sham. In Hinduism, however, that message is proclaimed from the rooftops. It is no secret that the world is an illusion, and Hinduism is filled with myths and rituals that try to bring this truth home to us. And just as this knowledge allowed Truman to escape from his prison, so true knowledge of the world in Hinduism permits us to escape the endless cycle of death and rebirth.

But this mystical teaching did not fall from heaven, fully-formed, of course. It took a long time for Hinduism to develop into the subtle and complex mystical system that it is today. When it began, it was simply a nature religion like any other we've been studying. The gods were personifications of natural forces: Indra, the god of thunder and king of the gods, Agni the god of fire, Vayu the god of wind, and literally thousands of other local nature deities are attested to in early Hindu literature.

The most famous collection of early Hindu mythology is a collection of hymns called the *Rig Veda*. No one knows when it was written, but it is a good guess that it goes back a good 5,000 years or more. The *Rig Veda* is largely composed of hymns to Indra and the other early Hindu deities, and revisions of it were compiled to arrange the hymns for liturgical use. There was no talk of play among the gods in these early myths—in fact, the business of the gods was deadly serious. In one myth we are told that the gods did not start off as the gods at all, but as demons opposed to the gods. The gods and demons worked together to churn the ocean into soma, the magical elixir that granted unlimited life and power to any who drank it. Then, when the gods weren't looking, the demons stole the soma and drank it. They, then, became the new gods, and the old gods became the demons.

Unlike in our Western religions, the terms "gods" and "demons" don't necessarily refer to the morality of the beings involved, but to their power. Those with the power are the gods, those without the power become, by default, the demons, the enemies of the gods. Religious practice at this time was concerned with the generation of *tapas*, the Sanskrit word for "heat" which also means "spiritual power." Demons could become holy men or women, and by means of sacrifice, gain enough *tapas* to be a threat to the gods. Likewise, the gods need the sacrifices of human beings, but they don't want humans to be *too* holy, or their *tapas* would rival their own, and also pose a threat to their supremacy. The gods in Vedic Hinduism, then, are concerned with maintaining a balance of power: keeping the gods fed with sacrifices, but also keeping humans and demons in their place.

Sacrifice is the primary means of worship in Vedic Hinduism, especially the fire sacrifice. As the priestly caste grew in influence and wealth, the sacrifices gradually became more and more elaborate and difficult to perform, not to mention expensive. At the height of the Vedic period, the horse sacrifice often took weeks to perform, involved the killing of hundreds of horses, and nearly a score of priests working around the clock to do it correctly. One slip, and it would have to be started all over! The last known horse sacrifice was performed in 1986, and filmed for posterity. And just to relieve your squeamishness, gourds were sacrificed in place of actual horses. I have seen this film, and it is a kaleido-scope of obsessive-compulsive priestcraft, fit only for the hard-core fan of Hindu history.

About this time a major shift occurred in Hinduism. Nobody knows how it happened, but someone discovered that the sacri-fice could be performed internally rather than externally. By the use of vivid imaginal practice, a person could perform an entire sacrificial ritual in his head. Not only was this far cheaper than killing hundreds of horses, but it seemed to be just as efficacious as the physical ritual.

So now you have all of these priests sitting still, going through this long, fourteen-day ritual in their heads. What do you think is going to happen? One of them veers off into the bliss of meditation, and *boom*! Enlightenment. One of them, and then another of them, has the experience of unitive consciousness as a result of their imaginal experiments, and suddenly meditation is born.

Well, these holy men realized they were onto something here, but it was not a popular discovery amongst the priestly caste, for a number of reasons. First of all, anyone could meditate and know this sublime mystery, which threatened their monopoly on spiritual power in their culture. Anyone could become a yogi. Second of all, the experience of unitive consciousness had grave implications for their theology, in effect, invalidating it. The mystery they glimpsed in meditation went far beyond the placation of nature spirits upon which the entire edifice of Vedic Hinduism was built.

Though the Brahmins tried, they could not stem the tide of this new religious awareness. People of other castes began meditating and they, too had the same experience of unitive consciousness, and Hinduism quickly transformed into a very different animal altogether. It went through what scholars today call the "Upanishadic Shift," named for the new scriptures that were appearing to explain and document this new awareness, the *Upanishads*.

According to the *Upanishads*, there is only one being in the universe, which these writers call Brahman. Brahman is the ultimate ground of all being, yet inside each and every being is a corresponding spirit, the Atman. The Atman is that bit of Brahman that lives in each of us. Brahman and Atman are one being. You and God are one being.

In Christianity, the Atman is analogous to the Holy Spirit. Just as Christians believe that the Holy Spirit is that part of God that dwells in us, the Hindus teach a very similar doctrine, and call that Spirit, Atman. Thus all of the Vedic gods were merely parts of Brahman, the One Being who fills the universe.

Brahman apparently did not have much of a personality, though, because Hindus quickly supplanted him with gods they liked better, especially Shiva and Vishnu. Ultimately, in Hinduism, it doesn't matter what you call this One Being: Brahma, Shiva, Vishnu, Kali, Durga, any name will do. For though there is only one being, that being can wear any face. One has merely to discover the mask of God to which one feels the most attraction, and pray to that face. I have read that there are more Hindu gods than there are living Hindus! In Hinduism, it doesn't matter which god you appeal to: they are all the same god, in the end.

There is a wonderful myth that illustrates this Upanishadic Shift. Indra, the king of the gods was building a gigantic palace that would be a fit reflection of his glory. But every time he visited the royal carpenter to see how the work was progressing, he got another idea of how to make it larger, grander, more worthy of his greatness. Finally, the carpenter was stressed out, and realized that if Indra keeps making more and more demands, he'd never be done with the project. So he goes to Brahma, the creator, and explains his problem. Brahma is sitting on a lotus which grows out of the navel of the sleeping Vishnu. Brahma tells the carpenter to go home, something will be done to help him.

The next day a beautiful blue boy, surrounded by other children, appeared at the gates of Indra's palace. Indra summoned the boy to him, and said, "So why have you come to see me?"

"I have heard that you are building a marvelous palace, more grand than any Indra before you has ever built before."

"What do you mean, 'Indras before me'? I am the only Indra there is!"

But the boy laughed at him and said, "That's what you think. I have watched Indras come and go, come and go. Vishnu sleeps in the ocean of the cosmos, and the lotus that grows from his navel is the universe. Brahma sits on the lotus, and when he opens his eyes, a world comes into being, and that world is ruled over by an Indra. And when he closes his eyes, the world disappears, and its Indra disappears with it. Each Brahma lives nearly 500,000 years. Then the lotus dries up, and anther grows in its place. How many Indras have there been? How many drops of water do you think there are in the ocean?"

Just then, Indra noticed an army of ants marching across his palace floor. The boy pointed at the ants and said, "See those—those aren't ants at all, they're all the Indras that have ever been."

Needless to say, Indra, who thought he was the highest god in heaven and earth, was brought down a notch or two, as were the Brahmins, the professional clergy. This story certainly illustrates the shift that happened in the popular religious imagination, as Hinduism morphed from a polytheistic nature mysticism to a qualified monotheism, becoming one of the most complex and satisfying mystical systems the human race has ever known.

Hinduism reveres every god in its past, but reserves the pride of place for Brahma, the creator, Vishnu, the sustainer, and Shiva, the destroyer. Brahma isn't really worshipped all that much, but he does get a lot of lip service. Most Hindus today honor either Vishnu or Shiva as the most supreme expression of divinity, and just as Catholics and Protestants have fought wars over which system is right, so Vishnites and Shivites have fought each other over which god best represents The One.

Shiva is a scary fellow, and full of contradictions. He lives in a graveyard, and dances on the bones of the dead. He is an ascetic, and master of the practices advocated by the yogis, especially meditation. But he is also a husband and father, and together with his consort, Shakti, he is the master of the Tantric schools of mysticism as well. In Tantra, the man assumes the identity of Shiva, the woman assumes the identity of Shakti, and in their sexual union the illusion of separateness in the universe is dissolved, creating a fast-track to enlightenment that is not only expedient, but a heck of a lot more fun than sitting your butt down in the ashes of the dead muttering mantras all day.

Vishnu, on the other hand, is not nearly as scary or weird. Vishnu is the preserver of life, and constantly intercedes on earth to make sure that the balance of power is not upset. "Whenever evil seeks to destroy the sacred order," Vishnu says, "I take myself a body and put things to rights." Vishnu has had many incarnations, being born into a human body to be the savior of humankind, over and over again. Krishna is probably the most famous incarnation of Vishnu, and Rama is a close second. Vishnu incarnates in much the same way as Jesus is understood to be the incarnation of Yahweh, the Jewish God. In fact, since Hinduism can honor any god as a face of the One God, ever since its contact with Christianity, Jesus has been seen by Hindus as an incarnation of Vishnu. And why not? It sounds as plausible to me as any other theory of the incarnation.

Vishnu does not ask his followers for heroic ascetic practices, as Shiva does, but instead, offers a much more devotional path. One can reach liberation from the cycle of death and rebirth by the grace of Vishnu, merely by worshipping him. We might call it the lazy man's path to enlightenment, but that would be inaccurate, especially if you have ever been to one of the marathon mantra sessions the Vishnites love so much, where they can go on for *days* chanting the names of Vishnu. It may be the path of love, but it's still a heck of a lot of work.

But this is part of the genius of Hinduism: there is no *one* right way to reach liberation. The path that is right for me may not be the path that is right for you. Hinduism recognizes four broad paths: the way of knowledge, the way of devotion, the way of compassionate action, and the way of psychospiritual exercises. Any of these paths can bring you to unitive consciousness. And it makes sense: if there is only one thing in the universe, God, then any path you take is going to lead you back to God in the end.

You just have to find out which path is *your* path, and walk it, just as you have to decide which face of God is *your* face to worship.

All of this is mystically very satisfying, but less satisfying is when we get to the problem of evil. Hinduism says that evil and suffering are simply part of the illusion, that they have as little ultimate reality as anything else in this gigantic game of peek-a-boo, and are therefore unimportant. But I believe that is small comfort to someone who is really hurting. It may help put things into perspective after the fact, but I really have a hard time believing that telling someone in the throws of unbearable suffering that their pain is ultimately unimportant is very compassionate or really even all that helpful. Still, that is the answer that Hinduism gives us. Evil is just part of the game.

This is illustrated poignantly in the great Hindu epic *The Mahabharata*, where prince Arjuna is surveying the battlefield just before a great war. Circumstance has put Arjuna and his brothers in one army, and his cousins, teachers, friends, and other loved ones in the enemy camp. Arjuna knows he is about to go out into battle against people he loves, and he simply can't do it. He despairs and his bow falls to the dirt. Krishna is Arjuna's chariot driver, conveniently, and just before the big battle commences, he opens Arjuna's eyes to behold the world as-it-is. Arjuna has a profound mystical vision that is related in the *Bhagavad Gita*, one of the most beloved scriptures in all of the Hindu canon.

In this vision Arjuna beholds the entire universe as Krishna himself, and since Krishna never dies, death is itself an illusion. Krishna tells him to buck up and go and do his duty.

The problems inherent in this text were brought home to me profoundly a few months ago while I was in the recording studio. My band Metaphor has been working on a twenty-minute adaptation of this great battle scene, which will appear on our next CD, *Entertaining Thanatos: Seven Cheery Songs About Death*. At the end of the song, Krishna is singing to Arjuna, "So yeah, go out and kill, but do it with a twinkle in your eye. Yeah, go do what you will, 'cause everything is me and I don't die." I recorded these words the very same day we dropped our first bomb on Baghdad.

This, then, is Hinduism: one of the most enduring and amazing mystical systems known to humankind. As such, it is a mass of contradictions and competing impulses. It is both compassionate and dispassionate. It has room for both the pacifist and the warrior. It is moral and amoral. It is simple and complex. In fact, just as it is almost impossible to say what Hinduism *is*, it is equally difficult to say what it is *not*. It has subsumed into itself every religious tradition that has come into contact with it, and all without any system of centralized authority. It's magic is derived from one very simple mystical insight: *tat tvam asi*, which is Sanskrit for "Thou art that." No matter what you look at in the universe, your mother, your dog, the sky, a hamburger, a fence-post, or a pile of dog-doo on the sidewalk, the same mantra applies: *you are that.* Because there is only one thing in the universe, one being—and you are that being. And just like Truman, we are all trapped in an illusory existence until we really, truly, at the core of our being, understand that truth.

God of day and night, of life and death,
of heaven, earth, and all the myriad hells,
we bow before you even as we recognize
that the Being before which we bow is our very Self.
Alpha and Omega, beginning and end,
all worlds find their origin and their dissolution in you.
Help us to become aware of the Atman,
that flame in the heart that burns in the heart of the sun as well.
Help us to realize that our true selves are not the names
on our drivers' licenses, or the faces we see in the mirror,
but that, in fact, our true identity is in you.
God of all worlds, bring us the peace of knowing
our true Self in you, and liberate us from all illusion. Amen.

⊕ *Preached at Grace North Church on October 19, 2003.*

9 | the vedantists

I am about to confess to you something I have never told anyone else in my life. It is not something I am proud of. Indeed, it has caused me much personal suffering, especially as a boy. When I was in fourth grade, there was a bully who taunted me mercilessly. My fourth grade teacher was a waify woman who had not a single clue how to control a classroom, and as a result we "softer" children were ever at the mercy of those who would take advantage of us.

Now, I was a good boy. I mean, I was a *perfect* little boy. I agonized over the smallest infraction, and obeyed my parents in all matters, large and small. I was, as my mother is fond of saying, the very "sort of child the psychologists warn you about"—because eventually boys and girls who are "too good" snap and overcompensate in the other direction. This did indeed occur some ten years later, but in fourth grade, I was still the image of obedient perfection.

I was at a complete loss as to what to do about being picked on. I complained to my teacher, I wrote a letter to the principal.

My father did not hide his shame that he had raised such a pansy who could not even stand up for himself. I felt that shame and was paralyzed by it.

And then one day, the worst bully in our class arrived with a new toy in his pocket. It was a magnet about two inches square. It was the largest, most powerful magnet I had ever seen in my life, and I was mesmerized by it. I coveted it. Nay, I craved it. It seemed so unfair that someone so evil should be afforded such a great prize. I didn't quite know how to cope with the feelings of envy and betrayal that were surging through me, and I did something that was entirely unmeditated, and utterly unlike me.

At lunch I went back to the class to grab my sweater, and realized that I was alone. Without thinking, I walked to the bully's desk and raised the hinged top. There was the magnet, unprotected, grinning up at me, daring me to take it. I slipped it into my pocket, and rushed outside, my heart pounding in my throat.

When the class returned after lunch, the bully discovered his missing prize, of course, and holy hell was raised. I put on my best, "Who, me?" face and trembled inside. Fortunately, no suspicions were cast in my direction, and I boarded the bus for home sweating from the stress, but safe, and with the magnet safely in my pocket.

When I got home, I told everyone I had *found* the magnet—I *had* found it in a desk, after all—and started playing with it. I got into the neighbor's car to go to the store, and in a moment of clumsiness, the magnet fell down between the back seats of the Cadillac, and it was gone. I was unable to retrieve it, and I felt bereft.

The next day I also felt horribly, inconsolably guilty. The incident had shaken my self-image to the core. I was not strong, was miserable at any sports, did not get particularly good grades, and hung out with kids more brilliant, and amazingly, even geekier than I. The only thing propping up my fragile self-esteem was my belief that I was *good*, that God was pleased with me. And now I had done a very bad thing. I was a thief, and one with nothing to show for it either. I realized suddenly that I was *evil*, and the word rolled over and over on my tongue like icky cough syrup.

This threw me into my very first existential crisis of any real magnitude. Who was I? What was I worth now? Was I a good person who had done a bad thing? Or was I a bad person who was pretending to be virtuous? I was confused and scared. I wasn't yet adept at tolerating paradox, and it terrified me.

The fundamentalist religious tradition I grew up in taught me the standard Calvinistic doctrine of the utterly corrupt nature of the human soul. And yet, these same horribly corrupt people included William Wilberforce, who with his fellow fundies had mandated an end to English slavery. Conservative religious people the world over have done much to alleviate suffering. We all know people like this: people so doctrinally rigid a brisk wind might crack them in two, and yet possessed of a caring and compassionate soul. My own family is like this. Again, we are faced with a paradox that is difficult to resolve.

Paradox is religion's stock in trade, I'm afraid, and we humans have always struggled with how it is we can be silmutaneously angel and beast, good and evil, loving and vengeful, individual and corporate. How is it that we are children of God and at the same time capable of causing so much suffering? Are we divine or not divine, or both—and if so, how?

In the East, the form this great paradox has taken is not "how it is possible to be both good and evil," but "how is it possible to be both a person with individual consciousness, and a part of God at the same time?" Of course, many people have answered this question in many different ways. This morning we will look at how three broad schools of Hindu philosophy deal with such paradox, the Vedantists.

Born in the late eight century of the Common Era, Sankara was born in a little village in India called Kaladi. His parents had been praying for a child, and legend has it that Shiva appeared to them and gave them a choice: they could have a short-lived but brilliant son, or a long-lived dullard. They chose brilliance.

Sankara's father died soon after the boy was born, and his mother did her best to support them by performing religious ceremonies. Sankara did what he could to help by begging door to door. One day, when he was a teenager, he was bathing in the river when a crocodile took hold of his leg. Sankara was sure he was about to die, and he instantly surrendered to the moment, sinking into deep meditation, ready to meet his fate. The crocodile was so freaked out by such unusual behavior by its prey that it let go. Perhaps he thought Sankara dead and was only interested in fresh meat, or perhaps the blissful vibes radiating from Sankara spooked him. In any case, Sankara lived, and from that moment on knew that he was supposed to be a *sanyassi*, a Holy Man.

Soon he had found a guru, who was so impressed by Sankara's intellect that he sent him off to roam the lands and write commentaries on the Hindu scriptures. Many of Sankara's classic writings were composed while he was still a teenager, which is some feat, considering one almost needs a PhD in philosophy to understand them even today.

Sankara developed a school of philosophy called Advaita, or "non-dualism." He taught that there was only one thing in existence, Brahman. But Brahman is not just God, Brahman is God without attributes. If God is one, then all else you might say about God is partial and ultimately erroneous. You cannot call God loving or all-knowing or eternal, as all of these things are attributes and so incomplete as to be simply wrong. It would be like me describing Fr. Richard as "Mr. Swollen pinky, with a hangnail," and proceeding to refer to him only in reference to his little finger. There is, of course, so much more to Richard than his little finger that any such descriptions are simply laughable. And yet, says Sankara, that is what we do to God all the time.

For Sankara, liberation from the bondage of illusion means realizing one's identicality with Brahman, knowing that the me I think of as me is simply an illusion crafted by karma, which is ephemeral and ultimately unreal. The means of gaining liberation from such illusion was deep meditation and the acquisition of true wisdom. This is salvation through *jnana, gnosis,* or as we say in English, knowledge.

Once we have gained this knowledge, and know ourselves to be only Brahman, then, at death, we leave all our illusions behind and are absorbed utterly into Brahman. All our notions of independent existence or experience are dissolved into the One and we no more remember nor are remembered. From the One comes many, and the many become One.

One of Sankara's favorite things to do was to travel from place to place and stage debates with other philosophers. He was a wicked opponent, and as legend has it, had a perfect record, leaving a massive string of converts in his wake. One day Sankara set out to debate the greatest Buddhist philosopher of his day, but as his opponent was on his deathbed, the Buddhist teacher directed Sankara to his chief disciple, Visvarupa.

Sankara and Visvarupa made a wager. If Visvarupa won the debate, Sankara would take off his *sanyassi* robes and get married. If Sankara won, Visvarupa would become a Hindu *sanyassi,* and Visvarupa's wife would likewise convert. The debate lasted for weeks, and Visvarupa was just about to concede defeat, when his wife, who, oddly, was judging the event, asked Sankara about the art of lovemaking. Sankara, having been a *sanyassi* since his early teens, knew absolutely nothing about lovemaking, and so in a state of meditation, he psychically entered the mind of the king, and experienced all the King's memories of his many amorous conquests. Sankara's eyes snapped open and he answered all of the woman's questions perfectly. Visvarupa conceded and became Sankara's most devoted disciple. Unfortunatley, we don't know what happened to his wife.

Finally, at the age of thirty-two, Sankara had had enough of the world, and retreated to a cave where he entered into meditation, and achieved *samhadi*, ultimate liberation, and there he died, leaving behind an enormous body of philosophical work and many converts and communities.

But his arguments did not convince everyone. In the year 1017, Ramanuja was born in the village of Perumbudur, not far from Madras. Like Sankara, Ramanuja also lost his father at a very early age, and surrendered to the life of a *sanyassi* when still a boy. He was ordained into Sankara's system, and yet it left him unsatisfied. He began to question his teacher, Yadavaprakasha, and so forcefully challenged him that Yadavaprakasha decided to take the life of this young upstart. But Ramanuja was warned of the plot against his life, and he fled into the forest.

Ramanuja found other teachers who were not as threatened by his brilliance, and became a convert to the Visishtadvaita school of Hinduism. This school, of which Ramanuja was to become the premiere spokesperson, holds that though everything is God, you cannot speak about God except through metaphor and attributes. Not only that, but attributes have a limited existence of their own, though not distinct from Brahman. In other words, everything is Brahman, but Brahman takes many forms, some of which are eternally enduring.

Visishtadvaita literally means, "qualified non-dualism," and this is a very good distinction. For Ramanuja, a person may reach liberation from the cycle of death and rebirth, and enter into the bliss of complete union with Brahman, but one is able to actually enjoy this bliss as one retains a vestige of individual consciousness. In other words, for Ramanuja, one can be fully united with God and *know* that one is fully united with God. This is a *conscious* union, unlike the unconscious union of Sankara.

As you can imagine, this school of thought has much appeal. People generally *like* to think that a part of them endures beyond the grave. It's much more appealing than imagining that you simply drop into a pool of forgetting, however sublime you're told to believe it is.

Unlike Sankara's God, who is largely impersonal, Ramanuja's deity was intensely personal, and one's liberation came through heartfelt love for Vishnu in one of his many forms. This is the path of *bhakti*, of devotion, and salvation is granted not so much because of one's great effort, but also by the grace of God.

When Ramanuja was initiated, his guru Nambi told him the world's most powerful mantra and swore him to secrecy, for anyone who chanted this mantra would attain certain salvation, and it must be reserved only for those who are worthy of it. But Ramanuja was filled with compassion for humanity, and he could not keep such treasure a secret. So he went up on top of the roof of the temple and began to shout the mantra to anyone—of any caste—who would listen. Nambi almost had a heart attack. He was livid and when he went to confront Ramanuja, the young disciple said, "Please punish me appropriately, but I would much rather suffer in Hell if it meant that multitudes of others might be saved by hearing this powerful mantra." Nambi's heart melted and instead of punishing Ramanuja, he blessed him.

Ramanuja, like Sankara before him, wandered the land, founded communities, and wrote commentaries on the *Upanishads*. At the ripe old age of 120 years, he finally entered into full union with Brahman, and hopefully, knew that he did so.

But as you might guess, the pendulum had further to swing. Sankara's non-dualism was challenged in the 13th century CE by the dualistic school of a man named Madhva. Now, Madhva was quite an athletic youth, born in Velali in southern India. He was so swift of foot that people considered him to be an incarnation of Vayu, the wind god. His nickname was Bhima, after the Hercules of Hindu mythology. He loved pushing his body to the limit, but eventually his love of learning won out, and he became a holy man at the age of twenty-five.

The rumors of his divine origin spread, and people told many tales about the miracles he was able to perform. Not surprisingly, given his pedigree, these miracles were overwhelmingly of the meteorological variety. Like Jesus of Christian mythology, Madhva was able to still the waves and calm the storm on the sea. Though, in Madhva's case, it wasn't because anyone was in any danger, he just wanted to take a bath.

Madhva's system is called Dvaita, the dualistic school, and affirms the five real and eternal distinctions: the distinction between the Supreme Being and the individual soul, between spirit and matter, between one soul and other souls, between souls and matter, and between one bit of matter and another bit of matter. Matter, in other words, mattered a great deal to Madhva.

For Madhva, one achieved liberation by marking the symbols of Vishnu upon one's body, naming one's children after incarnations of Vishnu, and singing hymns. He also advocated the practice of the presence of God, in much the same way Brother Lawrence did in the Christian tradition.

But Madhva's liberation would have seemed unthinkable to Sankara. For Madhva, one never fully unites with Brahman. One is always eternally separate from Brahman, yet can still enjoy the bliss of liberation from the wheel of *samsara*, the cycle of death and rebirth.

Perhaps the most famous group to follow Madhva's school known to us in California is the Hare Krishnas, who say, "I want to taste sugar, I don't want to *be* sugar." For followers of Madhva, we are meant to enjoy God, but we shall ever be distinct from God.

So which is it? Is reality truly and indivisibly One? Are all particularities only illusion? Or are we eternally distinct? Or, as Ramanuja declares, is the truth somewhere in the middle? People have fought wars over such questions, and I doubt that we are going to solve anything definitively, here. But we do have a source of knowledge that the three great Vedantists did not have. We have post-modernity, and the crazy wisdom imparted to us by quantum physics, which has taught us that reality looks different depending upon what you expect to see.

One mirror in a room will do its job without fail—it will reflect. Yet *what* it reflects, what it reveals will be different for every person in the room simultaneously. A person over here will see this corner reflected, while a person over there will see that corner reflected. Which is the truth? Of course, they all are.

Just so, reality always reflects back to us what we expect to see. If we insist that the world is a hard and cruel place, it will without a doubt be a heartless place to live. If we are convinced that the universe holds us in love, then we are swaddled and held. We may never know what awaited Sankara, Ramanuja, or Madhva upon their liberations, but I am convinced of one thing: it was a very different experience for each of them, as it will be for us.

Likewise, people who have near death experiences generally experience what they expect to experience. Those who trust Buddha for their liberation find themselves in the Pure Land. Those who trust in Jesus are generally met by him. And those who believe themselves to be unworthy of Heaven generally have the most atrocious near-death experiences.

So what was I, as a little boy: good or bad? I was precisely what I believed myself to be. I still am.

To whom should we pray? To the God of Sankara?
If so, then only silence is appropriate.
To the Gods of Ramanuja or Madhva?
If so, then let us sing praises.
Instead, I ask you to enter the cave of your heart,
and pay attention to the God you find there.
For that, truly is the Holy One. And thou art that. Amen.

⊕ *Preached at Grace North Church on June 27, 2004.*

10 | mirabai

Krishna has a thing for cowgirls. It's true! In the literature of the epic period of Hindu history we find numerous stories about the Lord Krishna and his exploits with, well, cowgirls. The Sanskrit word for cowgirl is "gopi," and the gopis quite clearly had a thing for Krishna, too. I'd like to tell you one of these stories:

One night Krishna decided to go dancing with the gopis, so after midnight, he took his flute and went out into the woods and began to play. You've heard of the pied piper? Can't hold a candle to Krishna! The cowgirls went bonkers. They flew out of bed, made hasty excuses to their parents or their husbands and took off for the forest.

Now, when the gopis found Krishna, like the playful lover he is, he teased them, saying, "My goodness! How nice of you all to drop in on me like this! But really, it's a little late, and you should be in bed." This only made them laugh, because Krishna has never been one for following the rules or being discreet.

So then Krishna said, "The forest is a dangerous place with animals like tigers, bears, jackals, and wolves. Your families must be worried about you. You should hurry back home at once." This of course also made them laugh because they were in the presence of the supreme identity of the Godhead and they weren't the least bit worried about tigers.

Krishna kept teasing them and trying to get them to go home, and they finally got a little miffed at him and told him not to be so mean. They said, "Krishna, we love you so much and you promised us we would have you as our husband." So then Krishna kissed them all and they started to romp through the forest, singing and dancing.

And then suddenly, Krishna was gone! He just disappeared.

Well the Gopis were dismayed and started to look everywhere for him. They broke out the flashlights and organized a search. But you know, when Krishna wants to hide, really, what can you do?

Finally they gave up and just started to play. Then they started to play like they were Krishna! One of them pretended to be the demon Putana, and another became Krishna taking her milk. One gopi became a handcart and another kicked her legs as Krishna did in another myth to break the cart. One gopi played on a flute. They had a wonderful, wonderful time.

Then they got tired and they sat down and started chanting that "Hare Krishna" chant. (It's very old!) And then suddenly ...there he was, standing before them! Lord Krishna suddenly came out of hiding. The gopis made a seat for him in the sand and put nice cloth over it. Sitting on the seat with the gopis, Krishna became even more beautiful. He said, "Sometimes I hide from you, but do not think I was away from you. I was very near and watching you. Please don't be disturbed. Just be happy." And so Krishna began to dance hand in hand with the gopis. He put his hands on the shoulders of each gopi on both sides of him. He danced with every one of them, though each one thought only *she* was dancing with Krishna.

Now a lot of people think that the Rasa Dance, as this story is called, doesn't have anything to do with dancing, but with love-making, which really isn't all that different, really. And since each of the cowgirls felt like they had married Krishna that night, there might be something to that.

After the Rasa Dance finished, just an hour or two before sunrise, Krishna said, "It is time to leave." They did not want to go, but they did. And they were all ecstatic, because for one unbelievable night, they had each been Krishna's lover.

This is one of the most famous and beloved of all the Krishna stories, often to the chagrin of the Hindu Brahmins and gurus, because, as we said, Krishna doesn't play by the rules, and if it were anyone other than Krishna cavorting with all these women out of wedlock, they'd all be stoned to death or suffer some other horrible fate. After all, this tale supports cheating on one's husband, and is vaguely orgiastic, and if everyone behaved this way, the priests feared, society would crumble. Holy men, in general, are fairly puritanical, and the Rasa Dance pushed their buttons big time.

But the common people loved the story, which is why it has survived. One woman, Mirabai, who was herself a princess, took it so much to heart that she lived it out, much to the horror of her family.

Mira was born in Samvat, India sometime in the sixteenth century of the Common Era. When she was a little girl, she was watching a marriage procession pass in front of her house with her mother. The bridegroom passed by, and in his finest clothes, he was impressive. Mira was transfixed and asked her mother, "Mama, who is my bridegroom?" Her mother, wanting to tease her a little, pointed to the image of Krishna being carried in the procession and told her, "There is your bridegroom, Lord Krishna." This is a cautionary tale: parents be careful what you tell your children.

For Mira took this jest to heart, and grew to love the statue of

Krishna with all her soul. She bathed and dressed the image, she worshipped it, she even slept with it. She danced before it and sang for it and talked to it constantly. Her favorite story, even from childhood, was of Krishna the mountain-lifter.

In this story Krishna had been telling the villagers not to worship Indra, the sky god any more, but to worship the mountain instead, which was a part of himself. Indra was so furious that he sent down rain and thunderbolts upon the village. But Krishna, unperturbed, lifted the mountain high over his head and used it as an umbrella to shield the village from Indra's wrath until the sky god's fit of fury was spent.

Eventually it came time for Mira to marry, and her parents had arranged for her to wed the prince of Chitore, Rana Kumbha. She did wed him, and by all accounts was a dutiful wife. Yet everyday, after her household duties were fulfilled, she rushed off to the temple of Lord Krishna to dance before his image and converse with him. According to legend, the idol of Krishna would come to life when she visited him, play the flute for her, and talk with her for hours.

This odd behavior did not sit well with her husband's mother and sisters. This is kind of the Indian Cinderella story. They demanded that she worship Durga, the goddess, but she refused. Her sister-in-law decided to frame her. She told Rana, Mira's husband, that Mira had secret lovers, and that they rendezvoused in the temple of Krishna. Rana grabbed his sword and went straightaway to kill her. But an older relative caught him by the sleeve and said, "Be slow to judge this. She may be being setup. Make sure you have your facts straight before you do anything rash." Rana agreed.

Then one night Rana's sister took him to the temple. Rana broke down the door and rushed in, expecting to find Mira in the arms of her lovers. Instead he found her talking to the idol of Krishna. "Who are you talking to?" he demanded. "Where is your lover?"

"Why there he is, my husband, the one who has stolen my heart," and she pointed at Krishna. Then she fainted.

Rana was deeply perplexed by these bizarre devotionals, and he was also embarrassed, because people were beginning to whisper. So he decided to do away with Mira and take a proper wife. So he sent a basket containing a poisonous snake to her. But when she opened it, all she found was a little statue of Krishna. Then he sent a cup full of poison to her, saying it was nectar. Mira offered it to Krishna as an offering, and after her worship, drank what was left, much as we priests do with the extra wine at the end of our Eucharist. But instead of poison, it had become real nectar. Finally, Rana commanded her to sleep on a bed of nails, but when she lay down upon it, it was miraculously changed into a bed of roses.

Mira was unharmed, but nonetheless disturbed by all of these attacks on her life. So she wrote a letter to a nearby saint and asked him what she should do. The saint sent back a reply, saying, "Oy, relatives, what can you do? Listen, abandon those who are the enemies of Vishnu, even if they are your relatives. All the great saints have had to do this, so you are in good company. Your relationship with God is the most important relationship, all others are secondary." Mira pondered these words and wondered what to do.

Once, the most famous musician in the land came to visit Mira, as he had heard about the marvelous songs she made up in front of the idol of Krishna. So he hid in the temple and was so moved by Mira's poetry, that when she passed near his hiding place, he touched her feet. Somehow news of this reached Rana, who flew into another of his famous rages. He confronted Mira and commanded her to drown herself in the river for bringing such disgrace upon his family.

Mira obeyed. She went down to the river to drown herself, singing a hymn to Krishna as she went. She went gladly, dancing the whole way. When she was almost at the river, she leaped into the air in her dancing, but someone caught her from behind. She looked over her shoulder and saw the Lord Krishna. Then, once again, she fainted. When she came to, Krishna smiled at her and said, "My dear, dear Mira. Your married life to this man is over. You are free. Be happy, for you are mine alone. Go now to the Bowers of Vraja and look for me. But be quick, for you are in danger." Then he vanished before her eyes.

Mira went immediately as Krishna told her. Along the way people greeted her joyously as if they knew she was coming. When she reached the bowers, she found there the image of Krishna, and she knew she had arrived. The community there embraced her and she quickly became famous for her love songs to Krishna.

There was a well-known saint who lived nearby named Jiva Gosain. Mira wished to attend a devotional service performed by Jiva, but because she was a woman, the saint refused to see her. Some saint! So she sent him a letter saying, "Before God, we are all women. Only Krishna is the true man. Only today have I learned that there is another man his equal in our fair city."

Jiva was so chagrined by this response that he sent for her immediately and apologized. Another time, a wandering mendicant was so taken by her beauty that he lusted after her and demanded that she sleep with him, saying that Krishna had ordered it. In her quiet and wily way, Mira did not protest, instead, she prepared herself for a night of love, and prepared a bed for them—in the middle of the temple compound where the entire community could gaze on. The whole congregation gathered and watched to see what would happen. "Well, what are you waiting for?" Mira asked. "I thought you wanted to have a good time." The man was so ashamed he rushed from the compound never to return.

Mira's devotion to Krishna, and her novel and out-there sexuality horrified many people around her, but Mira didn't care what anyone thought but her Lord alone. She didn't follow any of the religious rules of the time—she didn't fast at the proper times, nor did she perform the duties or rituals required of her by her religion. Instead, she sang and danced before Krishna and simply loved him with all her heart.

Her devotion was not mediated by priests or rituals or scriptures—her communion with God was direct, intense, and very personal. Most religions begin with a story such as hers. Someone has a direct mystical experience of the Divine, and it changes their life and the lives of all those they come into contact with. But in trying to preserve and pass on this intense experience, religions are born, scriptures are written, rituals are invented, and the direct experience of the divine becomes a fading memory, leaving people attached to the rituals and scriptures rather than the Divine itself.

Just look at our own tradition: Jesus was a man who had an intense experience of communion—and union—with God, and it changed the lives of everyone he met. But after he was gone, his followers scrambled to find ways to preserve and pass on the quality of experience they had from him. In doing so, they invented the church with its scriptures, rituals, and traditions, none of which hold a candle to simply being in Jesus' presence.

The mystics of our tradition know this, and have sought this unmediated communion with God ever since, which is precisely why they have often been declared heretics, because like Mira, they have little need for rules and regulations, dogmas or doctrines, rites or rituals. If you *have* God, why would you possibly settle for a *picture* of God, after all?

In our parish, we worship according to the Anglo-Catholic tradition, but we do not worship these traditions. Our scriptures, creeds, and rituals are not God, but merely windows through which, if we are lucky or persistent, we might glimpse God, draw near to God, and commune with God. And if any of these things do not move you towards God, who cares? They are not important. As the Buddhists say, all this is merely the finger pointing at the moon, not the moon itself.

Unfortunately, it is the way of religions to take themselves too seriously, to elevate scriptures and rituals to the status of the Divine, and to obfuscate the direct experience of ecstatic communion with divinity. With Mira, let us say "nuts to that" and go dancing. The gopis had the right idea after all.

Mira did not die of old age. Legend has it that eventually her old husband Rana realized how badly he missed her, and he sent some men to beg her to return to him. She refused to listen to them, so they appealed to her compassion by going on a hunger strike. Finally she relented, and agreed to return to Rana. But as she was walking to her home to gather her things, the idol of Krishna reached out and, grabbing her arm, drew her into the idol itself to be forever united with him; an image, in legend, of the very absorption into God that she had enjoyed her whole life. She was never seen again. Though Rana, her old husband, missed her, it was Krishna, her true husband, who could not bear to lose her. And that, my friends, is truly the love of God.

Holy God, lover of our souls, in holy scripture
you speak to us as your beloved,
and tell us that you long to wed yourself to us forever.
Help us to be faithful partners, to enjoy you with a whole heart,
and not to settle for a pseudo-religion that is a poor substitute
for the true communion which you desire so much to have with us.
Help us to hold out for the real thing, and be faithful to us.
Do not make us wait, but come amongst us and dance with us,
even as we celebrate in this Holy Communion
a foretaste of that great feast where we will be united to you forever.
For we ask this in the name of our bridegroom,
even Jesus Christ. Amen.

⊕ *Preached at Grace North Church on July 18, 2004.*

11 | the buddha

Not long ago I put an ad in the Episcopal Diocesan magazine, *The Pacific Church News,* for my Gospel of Thomas lecture. I'd given it at a couple of Episcopal churches, and it had been very well received. So I thought I'd cast my net a little broader and get the message out in as many churches as I could.

Last week I got a call from one woman interested in scheduling me to come and speak at her parish, and she soon began grilling me on exactly how I was going to structure my talk, very intent that, regardless of how I roamed in it, I would come back at the end and affirm her particular brand of orthodoxy.

Since I have absolutely no interest whatsoever in affirming anybody's orthodoxy, the phone call turned into a bit of a push-pull match. After a couple of tense exchanges, I realized this talk might not actually come together at her parish, and she began to grill me about my own beliefs. "You *are* a Christian, aren't you?"

"Well, I am a priest," I said.

"Huh," she snorted, "*that* doesn't mean anything."

Fair enough, I thought. So I put on my seminary professor hat and did a little razzle-dazzle dance about high and low Christologies, a dash of soteriology, and an "eschatological" thrown in for good measure. But she was not phased by such tactics, and kept pressing me about my personal relationship with Jesus Christ.

So I pulled out the big guns and gave her my best shot. "Let me be clear with you," I said. "I follow Jesus, and I trust in him for my salvation. Now, exactly what that *means*, I'm not entirely sure."

"Oh," she said simply. "That's all I wanted to know. When can you come?"

Now, I don't know what this woman *thought* I meant by that, but it was the most that I could affirm for her in the moment. For you see, at heart, I am an agnostic. Was Jesus God? Did he come down from Heaven? How are we saved? How will we be judged? What is Heaven like? I don't know the answers to any of these questions. I can tell you the history of each question, and outline half a dozen theories along with the biographies of their chief proponents throughout the long march of Christian history, but answers? I haven't got a one.

Now some of you who don't know me very well may think that this is a very strange position for a clergyperson to take. But I say, on the contrary, it is the only way that has any integrity, at least for me. Plus, I'm in excellent company, as one of the greatest spiritual leaders of all time was a dedicated agnostic. I am, of course, talking about the Buddha.

He was born Siddhartha Gautama of the Sakyas, the prince of a small kingdom in India approximately 2500 years ago. According to legend, before he was born, his father consulted an oracle, who warned, "If he remains in the world, he will unify India, and become its greatest king. But if he forsakes the world, he will become the greatest saint, and redeem the world."

His father was not very excited about this sainthood business, but the greatest king thing he liked. So he set out to protect his son from any influence that might cause him to take up the path of religion. The king built high walls for the palace, so the young prince could not see outside. He surrounded Siddhartha with only beauty and luxury.

Despite his strenuous efforts to protect Siddhartha from the painful realities of the world, he was not successful. One day the young prince was traveling from one palace to another, and saw three things he was not supposed to see. First he saw an old man leaning on a cane. The king had never allowed the prince to see anyone older than the king himself. The prince stopped in his tracks at the sight of the old man. Old age...the idea had never occurred to him before, and he shuddered.

Next, however, he saw a woman wracked with disease. The young prince had never seen anyone who had anything worse than a cold. Siddhartha's attendants had to restrain him from running to embrace the sick woman—who knew what she had, after all? Siddhartha felt sick himself, and wanted to understand the mystery he was encountering—how widespread was sickness and disease? What was its cause and its cure? His head swam as his journey continued.

Not long after this, the caravan ground to a halt, for there in the middle of the road was a corpse. Siddhartha had never seen a dead body before, and the sight of it horrified him. "Is this my end, and the end of all people?" he asked. He jumped from his carriage and, oblivious to his attendants' desperate protests, he cradled the dead man's head and wept.

Finally he was roused from his grief, and was able to continue his journey. But before he reached his destination he saw something else he had never seen before, something that gave him some hope. He saw a monk begging for alms. The man wore simple, rough clothes. He was unconcerned with wealth. He was lord over no one, and it looked as if he had no home. Most striking of all, he looked happy.

Siddhartha realized that, by comparison, his world, luxurious as it was, seemed superficial and empty. Having learned about the realities of old age, sickness, and death, he desperately wanted to find an answer—an escape from these conditions. He wanted to help people and alleviate suffering. He could no longer lounge in his palace eating figs and Ben & Jerry's, for all pleasure in these things had left him. The monk had shown him that there was another, a better way to live, and he desired that life more than anything else.

So it was that one evening, under cover of night, the prince said goodbye to his wife, his son, his father, and indeed, left behind his entire kingdom. He would not rest until he had found the key to stop the suffering of all creatures.

For years Siddhartha worked hard at being a Hindu holy man. He studied under a couple of gurus, and lived and practiced with a group of forest-dwelling monks. The teachings he heard emphasized asceticism, so he starved himself until, as he said, he could "see his spine through his stomach." He lived exposed to the elements, and practiced many extreme techniques such as holding his breath until passing out.

After several years of this, Siddhartha realized, "Look, this is crazy. If I don't cut it out, I'm going to kill myself. And then what good will I have done? There has to be a better way." With that he renounced asceticism, realizing that his body was the only vehicle for enlightenment that he had and that he had to care for it properly if it was going to be of any service to him. His fellow forest-dwellers did not take kindly to this "heresy" and banished him from their company.

Unswayed by their derision, he found a place in the forest by himself and continued his practice. One day, after intense study, he sat down beneath the Bodhi Tree, and he vowed that he would not get up again until he had achieved enlightenment. The legends say that Mara, the Evil One, tempted him with Desire, a beautiful seductress, but Siddhartha was unmoved. Mara then attacked him with terrible forces of nature—hurricanes and flaming rocks—but all turned to a rain of flower petals before touching him.

Mara then challenged his right to do what he was doing. Who did he think he was, after all? He was a prince, not a holy man. He did not belong here. Siddhartha did not answer with words. Instead, he simply touched the earth, and earth responded, "I bear witness." All of nature roared. Mara fled, and the Buddha sank into deep meditation. He removed himself from the center of his universe, and allowed his consciousness to expand until it was at one with everything.

And then suddenly he was no longer Siddhartha. He was Buddha, the One who is Awake. In a flash of unitive awareness he saw through the veil of seeming reality to the deeper reality of which we are a minute part. He saw all of existence in one glimpse. He saw everything *as it is*. In this flash of insight, called *satori*, he transcended his separate self, and realized that all of the universe was one, and that he, too, was that one. He saw—and knew—that his most authentic self was not Siddhartha at all, but Existence itself. His identity transferred from Siddhartha's ego to the cosmos in all its multidimensional glory.

He saw in that moment the impermanence of all things, that all things rise, and then fall, only to rise again in new forms. He saw that the past is a shadow and the future is a dream, and that to live in either is to live in a fantasy world, for there is only the *now*. He saw that it is this very grasping after the illusory that caused so much of our suffering, and that we would continue to suffer so long as we resist what *is*.

In that moment, he not only transcended his ego, but also the cultural paradigms that ordered Indian society. He realized that every creature suffers and is worthy of compassion, from highest to lowest. The caste system which dictates who should serve and who should be served, an idea central to Hinduism, became meaningless to him, and he saw all people as equal. (Unfortunately, there were some exceptions to the Buddha's clear sight—he still regarded men as superior to women, though he would soften on this as his ministry progressed.)

He likewise saw all of the Hindu teachers' talk of gods and religion to be utterly unecessary. "There may be gods," he taught, "and there may not be. It is not important and has no bearing on reaching enlightenment." This was the beginning of the Buddha's agnosticism—the first religious agnostic! He wasn't simply agnostic about the matter of whether or not there are gods, he assumed an agnostic view on most metaphysical matters.

This did not please people, of course. One of his students complained, "Whether the world is eternal or not eternal, whether the world is finite or not, whether the soul is the same as the body, or whether the soul is one thing and the body another, whether a Buddha exists after death or does not exist after death—these things the Lord does not explain to me. And that he does not explain them to me does not please me, it does not suit me." The Buddha would just smile. Sometimes the Buddha could be downright infuriating.

Because he had no need for gods or religious rituals, he did not claim for himself any divine authority. He didn't want people to accept his teaching out of fear or coercion or any religious illusions. "Don't take my word for it," he told his listeners, "instead, try the practice out and see if it works. If it does, use it; if it doesn't, leave it behind."

Thus, what the Buddha founded was not so much a religion as a technology; a method of practice that could help the seeker reach his or her goal. What is the goal? For the Buddha it was the ceasing of suffering. His four Noble Truths, one of the most basic Buddhist creeds, tells us that first and foremost, "life is suffering." This sounds pretty dour, but the next three Truths give us hope: "Suffering has an identifiable cause," "It is possible for suffering to end," and finally, "There is a path that can be followed to end suffering."

So what is that path? The Buddha condensed his teaching into eight principles which, if followed, can lead to liberation:

Right understanding
Right thought
Right speech
Right action
Right livelihood
Right effort
Right mindfulness
Right concentration

What constitutes what is "right" in any of these formed the basis of much of the Buddha's teaching, as he sought to mediate the unfathomable to the clueless. Like Lao Tzu, the Buddha was often frustrated with his students, but he persevered. Some of the members of his old forest community became his first followers, and before long his ministry flourished. People came from far and wide to join his community. People of low caste found that in the Buddha's community they found respect and equality. Eventually even his wife and his mother became nuns, forsaking the palace even as young Siddhartha had done, and walking the path to liberation.

What did it take to follow the Buddha? Not faith, as we have come to understand conversion in Christianity, but a concept that might at first sound strange: refuge. As the young Siddhartha found out, the world could be a scary place. Those who followed him did so by seeking safety in three things: in the Buddha, in the community of followers, and in the teaching he handed down through the ages.

Now, in my lecturing on the Gospel of Thomas, I highlight the similarities between the Buddha's teaching and that of the Jesus of Thomas. They are, in fact, nearly identical, which has led me to the opinion that the Thomas school represents nothing other than a native Jewish school of Buddhism, which might at first seem a shocking notion.

Yet, like the Buddha, the Jesus of Thomas does not appeal to any heavenly authority, nor does he require even belief in God. He is instead concerned with the re-identification of the individual from one's ego to the universe as a whole. I do not consider myself a Christian in any orthodox sense, but I do consider myself a Christain of the Thomas school, and in so doing, I likewise take refuge in three things:

I take refuge in Jesus. He is the way-shower, the one who has reached enlightenment, and like the Buddha, he is the one who shows us how to do the same.

I take refuge in the community of followers. You, here, are my *sangha*, my church, my fellow travelers on the way. As I hold you and support you in your spiritual journeys, you likewise hold and support me. I can do the work I need to do because you are here loving, affirming, and encouraging me.

Finally, I take refuge in the teachings of Jesus as I find them in the Thomas gospel, and elsewhere in the Christian tradition. Granted, I don't take any of these documents uncritically. But considering carefully each one, and weighing their value for my own path, they provide wisdom, encouragement, and, I trust, salvation—whatever that means.

I believe the Buddha would approve. And maybe the Jesus of Thomas, as well. I propose this Buddhist rule for your own consideration, especially in the context of this spiritual community. For we do not require any statement of faith. We do not insist you accept any teaching, nor require any intellectual assent whatsoever.

We only ask these three things: Do the stories of Israel and Jesus inspire and assist you on your spiritual path? Can you find safety and support and friendship in our midst. Can we laugh with you, cry with you, hold you when you are scared or troubled, and rejoice with you when you are glad? And finally, do the words of our prayer, the rituals we enact together, and the teachings of Jesus and the prophets and the mystics of the world's great traditions feed and heal your soul?

If you answer "yes" to these three, then you are probably a member here. And if you are not, be careful or you may become one! As the Buddha shows us, the critical way in religion is not about blind faith, but about seeking refuge, a place of safety, and that includes the safety to inquire freely, to ask the tough questions, and to say, "I don't know." That is real safety.

This kind of safety served the Buddha well for many years. He lived to a ripe old age, traveling around India, and preaching the way of liberation to anyone who would hear him, of whatever caste. Finally, he knew his body was wearing out, and that his students were prepared to carry on without him. So he accepted an invitation to dinner from an old friend. Unbeknownst to his friend, however, the meal contained poison mushrooms. Now, later legends say that the Buddha, in his omniscience, knew that the meal would be fatal, but out of hospitality, could not deny his host. This is probably mythology, but nonetheless, soon after completing the meal, the Buddha laid down and with the peace that passes all understanding, slipped into Nirvana, finding at long last the liberation and release he had worked his whole life to promote.

May all beings have happiness, and the causes of happiness;
may all be free from sorrow, and the causes of sorrow;
may all never be separated
from the sacred happiness which is sorrowless;
and may all live in equanimity, without too much attachment
and too much aversion, and live believing
in the equality of all that lives. Amen.

The Four Boundless Meditations—Buddhism

⊕ *Preached at Grace North Church on August 22, 2004.*

12 | the bhikkhunis

In our Gospel reading for the day (Mattew 9:18-26), Jesus is out mixing it up with the villagers, teaching, preaching, and healing the sick. When all of the sudden, he stops in his tracks and says, "I felt power go out of me—who touched me?"

Now, this seems like a silly question to his disciples, because Jesus is being pressed on every side by a whole crowd of people. Jesus was being touched by lots of people, so what did he mean, "Who touched me?"

As it turns out, there was a woman who was suffering from a flow of blood, a hemmoraging that no doctor in her day could address. In spite of her suffering, filled with hope and desperation, she had heard that Jesus, the famed healer, was passing through, and she sought him out.

But she didn't expect him to pay any attention to *her*. Who was she, after all? Just a poor peasant woman. But she had faith that if she just touched him as he passed by, that would be enough. And so it was that when she reached out and touched the hem of his robe, he felt a surge of healing power pass from himself into her, and he stopped in his tracks.

Now, I'd like you to note that this woman violated a number of taboos in her pursuit of healing. First of all, women and men were not supposed to touch, unless they were wed or family. The disciples got upset at Jesus elsewhere in the Gospels for even speaking to a woman—far too unseemly for a rabbi in good standing.

Second, Jewish law dictates that all women when they bleed are ritually unclean, and touching her would have defiled any man. This isn't because blood makes one dirty, but because Jewish theology says that spiritual power is contained in blood, and coming in contact with it is to appropriate such great spiritual energy as to be dangerous to oneself and others. To defile a rabbi against his will was a big no-no, and it took a great deal of courage.

And yet, this woman's suffering was so great, she was willing to violate the taboos of her society to find some relief at the feet of the Holy One. Her story is not unlike the stories of many women who, five hundred years earlier, sought out another great teacher in the hope of finding some balm for their own suffering, even though their society forbade it.

I am speaking of the bhikkhunis, the women who followed the Buddha, even when he himself did not allow it.

If you recall from our last sermon on the Buddha, young Prince Siddhartha had found a way to end the hopeless cycle of birth, suffering, death, and rebirth that plagues all beings. Having attained enlightenment, seeing the universe as it really was, and being freed from the bondage of karma, he set out traveling throughout India, preaching and teaching the Dharma, and ordaining anyone who chose to take refuge in him, in the community of monks, and in the teachings he offered.

Unfortunately, for the first several years of the Buddha's ministry, he only ordained men, and assumed that only men could reach enlightenment. Yet the Buddha's own female relatives, especially his aunt, Maha Pajapati, had faith in him and petitioned him mercilessly to ordain them.

In an effort to force him to see things their way, Maha Pajapati led a parade of aspiring Buddhist nuns on a pilgramage to demand ordination. They walked hundreds of miles, and the Buddha was so overwhelmed by their determination that he relented and ordained them.

Now, there are still Buddhists who believe that one must be reincarnated as a man to reach enlightenment, yet there are writings that reach far back to nearly the beginning of the Buddha's ministry that refute this, not the least of which is the poetry written by these early female followers.

Now, this is primitive Buddhism, very close in time to the historical Buddha himself. There are no grand mythologies about the Buddha as a savior, no bodhisattvas, no wrathful deities—these things would take centuries to develop. Primitive Buddhism such as the Buddha taught is known as Theravada Buddhism, the Way of the Elders, and it is still practiced in many parts of the world today, most notably Sri Lanka and Thailand.

In Theravada Buddhism the Buddha does not save us, he simply shows us the way to achieve liberation. He points out the roads, we still have to walk it under our own power. The image that is often used in the Buddhist tradition is that of a river. We are on one side, the place of suffering, and we long to reach the far shore, which is nirvana, the place of liberation. The only rafts available are small—there is only room for one person on them. So if you are going to get from this shore to the other, you will have to paddle your own canoe.

This is why Theravada Buddhism is sometimes called "Hinayana," which means, "the little raft." But be careful using this term, as it is a pejorative term used by other varieties of Buddhists. Using this term would be like Protestants talking about those "idol-worshipping Catholics." Not a term to use in mixed-Buddhist company.

It takes great effort to pass from one shore to the other, and tradition tells us that it often takes hundreds of lifetimes of effort to accomplish. But the cycle of rebirth, *samsara*, is hard to break, and for many of the bhikkhunis, it took an experience of profound suffering to push them over the edge into enlightenment.

In the writings of the Bhikkhunis there is preserved the story of Ubbiri, a peasant woman who had lost everything. Due to various unconnected accidents, her parents, her husband, and her two small children all died within a period of just a few weeks, and Ubbiri was inconsolable. Nearly mad from her grief, she confronted the Buddha in the charnel ground where she had just burned the body of her daughter.

The Buddha did not chasten her or shame her. Instead, he revealed to her that this was not the first child she had left behind in this same charnel ground. Indeed, she had left thousands of children in these grounds over innumerable lifetimes, and in each one, her suffering had been incapacitating.

She saw in that moment the wheel of endless torment she was bound to, she saw in a flash the millions of lifetimes of grief and sorrow that had brought her to this moment, she saw the futility of her rage and disappointment, and in finally beholding things as they are, she broke through and became enlightened. She left her grief behind along with the body of her daughter, and found liberation.

For many of the bhikkunis, it is their grief that is the catalyst for enlightenment. In another story a young woman named Kisa Gotami was in such denial over the death of her sick child that she continued to carry her baby's corpse around as if the child were still alive, hoping against hope that she might eventually find a medicine that could cure him. When she found the Buddha, she begged him for such medicine.

The Buddha had compassion on her, and told her that if she would bring back some mustard seed from a house that had not known death, he would give her such medicine. Now, mustard seed was a common spice, and every home had some. But as she went from door to door, every house she visited had had a person who had died in it—a mother or grandfather, a child or a friend. Every house had known death, and as she wandered those streets, she uttered these words:

"No village law is this, no city law,
No law for this clan, or for that alone;
For the whole world—and for the gods, too—
This is the law: All is impermanent."

Kisa returned to the Buddha empty-handed. She had no mustard seed, but the knowledge she had gained eventually led to her enlightenment, and some of the most beautiful verses in the writings of the bhikkhunis.

For both men and women, desire is the great culprit. Now, we could point out that Buddhist tradition seems a little sexist to us today in how it depicts desire. Men are shown craving after wealth and worldly power, while women are shown craving after family or beauty. We should perhaps not be too hard on this tradition, since social roles of the time indeed dictated to a large degree what people lusted after and longed for. C.S. Lewis' admonition against chronological snobbery is certainly appropriate here.

The blessing of living in such a liberated age as ours is that we men are not bound to only identify with the men in these legends, nor women only identifying with women. Women today can find themselves resonating with the young prince who eschews wealth and power, just as we men today can feel our hearts broken by the stories of these mothers grieving for their lost children, and that without shame.

I certainly have found some resonance with the woman suffering from the flow of blood. For the past year I have suffered from a condition that causes intolerable headaches, persistent night sweats, and full-body nausea, which is only temporarily and incompletely alleviated by a constant barrage of antibiotics. I have been to the dermatologist, the gastrointerologist, the endrocrinologist, and the ear, nose, and throat specialist, all in search of the elusive cause of this infection. Each of them have thrown up their hands, and each has admitted that they have no idea what is causing my condition. I have good days and bad days, but my patience with this persistent illness is wearing thin, and I sometimes lapse into despair.

So I feel like I know a little bit about how that poor woman must have felt, who could find no cure for her hemorrhaging. Her doctors gave her no hope, and so she reached out and took hold of Jesus' robe, desperate for an end to her suffering.

And thank God, when she did reach out, Jesus did not turn her away, as his society said he should. Likewise, the Buddha did not turn away the women who came to him to end their own suffering. For suffering is not for men alone—women certainly know their share, as I'm sure you all know very well. Indeed, all beings know suffering, and all beings desire release, healing, and liberation from their pain.

If my illness has taught me anything it is the ubiquity of suffering, for just as I do not know if I will awaken on any given morning feeling merely nauseous or with a full-blown headbanger, so none of us knows what loss, what grief awaits us around the next corner. Life is suffering, as the Buddha said, but suffering is not an end in itself.

If we are lucky, our suffering can function as a wake up call. Our own pain can wake us up from our perpetual slumber to the profound magnitude of suffering that surrounds us on every side, and can move us, if we are sensitive and determined, to do something about it. Our own suffering can inspire compassion for the suffering of others, and can move us, like the Buddha, to leave behind ambition and desire and work to alleviate the suffering of others. It can awaken us, as it did so many of the bhikkhunis, to the knowledge our suffering is not something we can prevent, but is part and parcel of the human condition.

For only when we are willing to acknowledge the futility of human life can we make the leap of faith that will allow us to transcend it. And only this knowledge can inspire us to pick up the paddle and make for the far shore under our own power. For if the Theravadans are right, no one is going to do it for us. Not Buddha, not Jesus, not some magical Daddy figure in the sky. Continue to suffer, or stop suffering. The choice is yours alone. And the power to make it stop is in your hands, alone. The question is: do you want to work that hard? You will, maybe in this lifetime, maybe a hundred lifetimes from now. You'll know when you're ready, and you have plenty of time. And when will you be ready? When you realize, *"I have suffered enough."*

May all beings come to saving knowledge;
may all beings have the courage to break society's rules
and claim for themselves liberation.
May all beings eventually be free from the wheel of death and rebirth
and know the peace of nirvana.
May we all wake up from the nightmare that deludes us,
and relinquish craving, desire,
and the pain that inevitably follows in its wake.
May all beings find refuge;
may all beings find enlightenment;
may all beings find peace. Amen.

⊕ *Preached at Grace North Church on September 12, 2004.*

13 | bodhidharma

Several years ago I regularly attended a support group here in Berkeley. It was the practice of those of us who met there to retire to a nearby pub for socializing after the meeting. Needless to say, it was not an AA group! I recall one member of the group vividly, because of the acute pain he was in. He was a divorced man who was trying to come to grips with the fact that he was gay. Now this can be difficult under the best of circumstances, but these were *not* the best of circumstances for this gentleman—for you see, he was an evangelical Christian, of quite a fundamentalist stripe.

As he wrestled with feelings he could not control, he was filled with a deep and vicious self-loathing, and I was really very scared for him; scared that, in his agony and despair, he would do something drastic. I was faced with a bit of a dilemma. As a spiritual director, it is not my job to try to argue anyone out of their beliefs, and yet as a pastor, it is difficult to watch someone suffer due to caustic theology. So I talked with him, night after night, and spoke from my own experience and understanding.

One night as he was nursing a diet Coke after the meeting, he worried about the future, about how his ex-wife would be in Heaven in the hereafter, and would forever watch him as he writhed in agony in the fires of Hell, as the scriptures promise. Now, Jesus, in a parable does mention that those in Hell can see those in Heaven, but nowhere does scripture suggest the other way around; that would only become popular in the middle ages. Still, this was not the time to split hermeneutical hairs, and I tried to keep my attention on him.

"I have a question for you," I said. "If God is everything he's supposed to be, and Heaven is everything we've ever heard, do you really think that anyone could actually *enjoy* Heaven as long as there was even one person in Hell?"

He looked at me like I had suddenly switched to speaking Swahili. He was not someone who was trying to break free of fundamentalism—he believed it with his whole heart. What he was struggling with was accepting himself in all of his maddening complexity in light of such a simplistic system. He was trapped by his beliefs, and didn't have the theological wiggle room to extricate himself from the paper bag he was thrust in at birth.

"I think you're fooling yourself," I told him directly. "You think you have to face this alone, when in reality Heaven and earth are pulling for you; not to repent, but to accept yourself as you are. Here's what I believe: nobody goes it alone. Either everyone is saved or everyone is lost. It's all or nothing. And you get to choose what it's going to be."

This was heresy, of course, and he didn't understand how a priest could get away with saying such things. I told him, with considerable pride, that I serve a very weird church. He smiled, but it was not a broad one. I paid my tab, drained my beer, and left him alone, still clinging to his self-hatred, and indeed, to his sins. I wasn't sure I'd done him any good at all, and I left that night depressed and a little anxious.

This tension between individual and universal salvation is a common one, and every religious system has dealt with it, sometimes in very creative ways. In our last sermon on Buddhism we discussed how the Buddha had discovered a way to see through the illusion of separateness and escape the endless cycle of suffering, of death and rebirth. It was a way that insisted on giving up everything and devoting oneself to spiritual practice full-time, and even then it may take hundreds of lifetimes of practice to achieve liberation.

The fact is, though, that most people cannot quit their jobs and go and meditate in caves for the rest of their lives, even if they had a mind to do so. The way is simply too hard. So, as Buddhism grew and developed, an easier system evolved. Tradition tells us that though the Buddha's discourses were written down and declared scripture, another tradition, an oral tradition, was also transmitted by the Buddha, which shed a very different light upon things. The oral tradition said that instead of entering into Nirvana upon his death, the Buddha declared that he would not enter into bliss until all beings were liberated. He would himself liberate them through his own efforts.

Now in primitive Buddhism, this world is viewed as one side of a river. The other side of the river is Nirvana, but if you want to get from here to there, you have to paddle your own canoe. The new oral tradition, however, said that instead of a canoe, the Buddha has a gigantic raft, big enough for everyone to climb aboard. The Buddha is the cosmic ferryman, who carries all beings across. One doesn't need to become a monk or a nun, nor does one need to practice full time. All anyone needs to do is simply have faith in the Buddha to enjoy the fruits of his salvation. This form of Buddhism became known as Mahayana, which means "the big raft."

The Buddha became the first bodhisattva known to humankind, but lots of men and women followed in his footsteps and vowed that they likewise would not enter into bliss until all beings were enlightened. Before long there was a vast celestial pantheon of Buddhas and bodhisattvas, past, present, and future, and Buddhism began to look an awful lot like the Hinduism it had tried to correct. Nonetheless, it was this new, esoteric version of Buddhism—Mahayana Buddhism—that really caught on outside of the Buddha's native India.

One monk in this tradition was Bodhidharma. His early life is a lot like the Buddha's, actually. He was a prince in southern India, born sometime around 482 of the Common Era. He studied to succeed his father and rule his people, but then he came in contact with the teachings of the Buddha, and it rocked his world. Like the Buddha himself, Bodhidharma left his family and his kingdom behind, and went to study with a renowned Buddhist teacher. He was an amazing pupil, and when his teacher died, he transitted the Buddha mind into Bodhidharma directly, whereupon Bodhidharma was enlightened and succeeded his teacher.

For unknown reasons, Bodhidharma took the teachings of his master East, traveling from India to China. In the year 527 he received an invitation from the Emperor in Nanjing, who was himself a Mahayana Buddhist, and had heard of Bodhidharma's fame as a teacher. Bodhidharma accepted the invitation, and presented himself before the Emperor. This ruler had done much to advance the cause of Buddhism in China, and was quite proud of this fact. He had financed the building of temples, and the translation of sutras. He supported countless monks and nuns, and was sure he was burning through his karma quickly by doing so, which is also known as "acquiring merit." He thought that Bodhidharma might have a good read on how well he was doing, so when the teacher presented himself, the emperor outlined all of his good works, and asked, "so how much merit have I accrued?"

"None to speak of," said Bodhidharma with a yawn.

"What?" the Emperor wailed. This did not square with what his other teacher had told him, which was that you get as good as you give, so he was stymied and didn't know what to think. In fact, this didn't sound like any Buddhism *he* knew of. "Well, then what is the meaning of Buddhism?" he asked.

Bodhidharma picked his teeth with a splinter and replied without looking up, "Vast emptiness and no meaning whatsoever."

The Emperor's jaw dropped. He simply did not know what to think. "Who *are* you?" He asked the monk.

"I have no idea," Bodhidharma smiled up at him.

The Emperor was so shaken he dismissed the teacher and went to process this meeting with his own regular teacher. "Who was that guy?" he asked.

"Do you not know, your majesty? That was Avalokiteshvara, the transmitter of the Buddha mind." Now, this is not an easy name to pronounce—don't try this at home. But, just for a little background, Avalokiteshvara is the same being known to those in China as Quan Yin, and to those in Tibet as the Dalai Lama, the Bodhisattva of compassion.

In fact, Bodhidharma was part of a school of Mahayana that felt that all the heavenly beings, bodhisattvas, and wild mythologies had gotten, well, *too* wild, and advocated a kind of back to basics form of Buddhism—kind of a middle way between the extremes of both the Theravada and the Mahayana schools. That middle was was called Ch'an in China, better known here in its Japanese form—Zen.

Unshaken by his encounter with the Emperor, Bodhidharma went north and, finding a suitable cave, settled in to meditate for about nine years. Legend has it that he was having trouble meditating, so he cut off his eyelids. As soon as his eyelids touched the earth, tea plants miraculously sprung up. Zen Buddhists to this day meditate with their eyes open, and drink green tea to help them stay awake.

One day a retired general named Hui K'o arrived at his cave. The general was deeply perplexed because he could not find peace of mind. He begged Bodhidharma to instruct him, but the great teacher refused. Once he stood outside Bodhidharma's cave in the middle of a snowstorm to show his sincerity, but the teacher remained resolute. Finally, the general took out a hacksaw, hacked off his own arm, and threw it at the teacher's feet. For a guy who had lopped off his own eyelids, this was apparently a good move, because Bodhidharma recognized him as a kindred soul, and finally agreed to instruct him.

"What do you seek?" Bodhidharma asked him.

"Peace of mind," replied the general.

"Show me this mind of yours and I will pacify it."

The general thought for a minute, and finally said, "But when I seek my mind, I cannot find it."

"*There*!" Bodhidharma announced, "I have pacified your mind!"

"So you have!" Hui K'o agreed, and laughed his head off.

What can I say? Zen is weird.

Anyway, eventually Bodhidharma happened upon the monastery of Shao Lin, where the monks were barely scraping by. He had compassion upon them, and instantly began instructing them. He told them that the Buddha had eschewed asceticism and embraced the middle way, which means that you take care of your body, so it can take care of you until you reach enlightenment. He taught them a less rigorous method of meditation, and he also insisted that the monks practice daily exercises designed to strengthen their bodies, sharpen their perceptions, and afford them some protection from bandits. He called this series of exercises Kung Fu, but contrary to popular opinion, he never called anybody "grasshopper."

Bodhidharma brought the monastery back to life, and the monks under his tutelage renewed Buddhism all over China and the East. He left behind many sermons and teachings, which became foundational documents for the Cha'n, or Zen schools. Fundamental to this teaching is the eradication of all dualities— hey we've heard that one before, haven't we? But he struck a new chord by stating that there are not some beings that are enlightened and some beings that are not enlightened. Instead, he taught that *all* beings are enlightened—they just don't know it yet. He taught that there is no difference between Nirvana and Samsara, the phenomenal world. The only difference is how one perceives it.

While reading Bodhidharma's sermons, I was reminded of my friend from the support group, and I wish that his religion was not so strict that he could not entertain wisdom from other sources, for I believe that Bodhidharma has much to teach him. For, if Bodhidharma is right, Heaven and Hell are the same place, the only difference is how you perceive it. My friend, for whom self-loathing was his constant companion, was most definitely in Hell. It is sad that he chooses to stay there, for Heaven is closer to him than his own heart, if only he had the eyes to see it. Likewise, if every being is enlightened and just doesn't know it, in the West we would say "every being is saved, and just doesn't know it." There is no Heaven or Hell we can be sure of beyond what we create right here, and by our actions we shall surely either all perish or we shall all flourish. Samsara and Nirvana, after all, are not separate realities. None of us have individual fates—the world will survive or it won't.

I can't help but think that the coming election is a time for us to decide that fate one way or the other. Of course, this is hyperbole—yet many small decisions do add up to large ones, and I encourage you to vote your conscience.

Bodhidharma passed from this incarnation in 536, and a stupa was built to honor him. A few years later, a Chinese official swore that while traversing the mountains of central Asia, he ran into Bodhidharma, who was walking west holding a staff with a single sandle dangling at the end of it. The two traveled together for a short distance, and Bodhidharma told the official that he was traveling back to India. After many years, news of this story reached the Shao Lin monks, who after much debate, finally decided to open the master's tomb and peep inside. What do you think they found there? The tomb was empty, except for a single sandal. Bodhidharma had one foot on the earth and one foot in the sky. Indeed, he denied 'til his dying day that there was any difference between the two.

St. Therese of Lisieux once said,

"All the way to Heaven is Heaven."
God of all compassion,
look upon us with the eyes of lovingkindness;
see the places where we have deluded ourselves,
where we torture ourselves unnecessarily.
Touch us and heal us, that like Bodhidharma,
we too can go forth and proclaim the Good News
that the Kingdom of Heaven is not in the sky,
nor is it in the future, but that it is here, now,
if only we have the eyes to see it.
For we ask this in the name of Jesus,
who is Bodhisattva for us,
and whose raft we will ride to the other shore. Amen.

⊕ *Preached at Grace North Church on October 10, 2004.*

14 | padmasambhava

Several years ago, I had just been hired as editor of *Presence*, the international journal for spiritual directors. I was representing the journal at the annual conference for spiritual directors, which was being held close to home that year, in Burlingame. Unfortunately, when hired, I had a prior commitment on my calendar to marry a couple that same weekend as the conference. Trying to honor all my commitments, I upset my boss by leaving my post at the conference Friday night to drive down to Santa Cruz for the wedding rehearsal. But as I left the conference center, a wave of fatigue washed over me that I feared would utterly overwhelm me. I had been working non-stop for days preparing for the conference, and the idea of driving down to Santa Cruz in Friday's rush hour traffic and back again seemed like *way* too much. I was weary and literally staggering. I simply did not know how I was going to do it all.

Then, in a flash of irrational insight, I paused beside a large tree near the parking lot. I embraced the tree as far around as I could and begged it to help me. I told it how exhausted I was, and all that I had yet to do that day. And as I poured my heart out to this tree, I felt a mysterious energy pass from its bark into my skin. It was the oddest thing, and I'll never forget the feeling. But whereas moments before I thought I might just collapse, I was suddenly teeming with strange energy.

Riding on this renewed vigor, I hopped in my car and sped down to Santa Cruz. The wedding rehearsal went quickly, and before I knew it I was standing once again in front of the tree. I was speechless in my gratitude, and I simply said, "Thank you." I hugged the tree again, and I felt the strange energy leave me and enter back into the tree. But it didn't leave me as tired as I was before. I still felt strangely renewed, though no longer buzzing with life as I had been. I wished there was more I could do than simply say, "Thanks." I wished there was a way to return the favor.

Okay, I know some of you are ready to break out the Thorazine, but I swear to you this happened just like this. And such experiences are not, I have discovered, that unusual. Nature gives to us in ways that are inexplicable and mysterious, but rarely do we know how to give back. Sure, we know how to destroy nature, but we do not know how to bless it.

One man who found a way, however, lived over a thousand years ago near the border of Afghanistan and Pakistan. His name was Padmasambhava, the man who brought Buddhism to Tibet.

His story really begins lifetimes ago, when a fallen goddess was born as a woman named Dechogma. She had four sons, but died before the stupa in her honor had been completed. Her four sons vowed that in a future life they would be born as a Dharma king, a learned holy man, a tantric master, and a messenger that would reunite the brothers.

Flash forward several hundred years, after many incarnations had passed. A righteous king named Indrabodhi opened the doors of his treasuries to the poor, and gave away everything he had. When the treasury was exhausted, the poor threatened him, for not all of them felt they had received an equal share. So the king set sail to procure the wish-fulfilling jewel from the crown of a mystical beast. He was successful in his quest, but on the way home he came upon an amazing sight.

There, floating on the water was a lotus, and emerging from the lotus was a little boy. The king questioned the child and asked where he had come from, and to which caste he belonged. Ominously, the child intoned, "My father is the self arisen, my mother is the sphere of reality, my caste is the union of primordial wisdom and the Dharma, and my name is the glorious Padmasambhava."

The king was delighted, and raised the boy as his own child. Padmasambhava grew up to be a righteous king, and was known as "the sovereign with braided hair." But Padmasambhava was not content with being a ruler. He realized that temporal power and spiritual power are oxymoronic, and to resolve the situation, he surprised everyone by murdering the child of an evil minister and exiling himself. A neat, if nonintuitive, resolution to his dilemma.

For several years thereafter, Padma hung around cremation grounds and cemeteries performing mystical rituals, becoming a powerful tantric master. Having accomplished all that he felt he could sitting on burial mounds, he set off for a tour of India, and sat at the feet of every master and guru he could find. He mastered the teachings of every one of them, and became known as "The Supreme Love Endowed with Wisdom," which sounds clumsy in English, but has a ripping ring to it in Tibetan.

He took as his consort a princess named Shastradhara, retired to a lovely cave, and with her help, excelled in tantric attainment. Feeling like he had finally atoned for his crime, he returned in disguise to his old kingdom, but the people recognized him and like the villagers in the old Frankenstien movie, chased after him in a mob to burn him at the stake.

Once the fire was struck, however, it was mystically transformed into a glassy sea covered with lotuses. Padma shook off his bonds, and taking his consort's hand, led her to a giant lotus in the middle of the mystic waters, where they sat in state upon their flowery thrones. The people were overcome with wonder, and they worshipped him.

Meanwhile, Padma's other three brothers from his previous life had come into their own as well. True to their vows, one brother was born as King Trison Deutsen, 38th king of Tibet. Another brother, the king's messenger, then summoned the great Khenpo Shantarakshita and Padmasambhava. Once the reborn brothers were back together, they vowed to work together, and used their pooled resources to fuel a Buddhist missionary drive that transformed Tibet and gave birth to a form of Buddhism that we today call "Vajrayana" or "Tibetan Buddhism."

There are two main branches of Buddhism: Theravada is the closest to the actual teachings of the historical Buddha, and hew closest to the earliest Buddhist scriptures. Mahayana Buddhism claims to continue the oral teachings of the Buddha, revealing a complex mythology in which the historical Buddha is just one of many buddhas on many worlds. Tibetan Buddhism is an offshoot of Mahayana, but adds to it the Hindu Tantric tradition and many elements from the Bonn religion, the native tradition of Tibet.

From the Bonn and Hindu influences, Tibetan Buddhism reveres a variety of deities, some beneficent, some of wrathful demeanor. By meditating upon a succession of such deities, aspirants can effect powerful psychological and spiritual processes that can lead one to liberation.

Unlike other forms of Buddhism, in which the body is cared for as a vehicle, but given little importance otherwise, Tibetan Buddhism embraces the body utterly, and sees an embodied spirituality as a fast track to enlightenment. Forms of prayer in Tibetan Buddhism are filled with rituals: turning prayer wheels, flying prayer flags, making prostrations and perambulations, sometimes for days on end. The body is not just a vehicle to be tolerated, but the very engine of enlightenment, and worthy of veneration in its own right.

Tantra is so important that Tibetan Buddhism is sometimes called "Tantric Buddhism." In Hindu Tantra, a male partner ritually assumes the identity of Shiva, while his female partner assumes the identity of Shakti. In a sacred ceremony, the two enter into sexual union that aspirants believe dissolves the illusion of duality, and speeds the attainment of enlightenment. Tibetan Buddhism substitutes Tibetan deities, but the idea is the same. Of the many orders of Tibetan monks, only one of them is celibate: sex is way too important to Tibetan spirituality for any of this abstinence nonsense.

Ironically, the very moral conflict that drove Padmasambhava to murder, and later, to his destiny (the conflict between spiritual and temporal power), was eventually brought together once again in Tibet. The Dalai Lama, whom Tibetans believe to be the reincarnation of Avalokiteshvara, the Buddha of Compassion, is both king and pope of the Tibetan peoples, and has vowed to continue to reincarnate until his people are liberated.

I have recently heard that the most recent Dalai Lama has vowed that he will not reincarnate again. This is quite a change for Tibetan Buddhism, which has always counted upon the presence of a realized Buddha in their midst, but since the Chinese invasion and destruction of the Tibetan culture in the past century, there is little about the Tibetan way of life that has endured.

After planting his wild form of Buddhism in the hearts of Tibet's people, Padmasambhava headed out to likewise convert the land. Legend says that he wandered the land for over fifty years, and left not even the space of one horse-hoof unaffected. He walked the width and breadth of Tibet, blessing every part of it as he went. Every lake, every mountain, every cave, every valley, every grove, and yes, every tree he blessed. And as he blessed them, he hid within them treasures of wisdom for future generations to discover and incorporate into the tradition. For he knew that people could only handle so much change so quickly—over time they would discover his hidden teachings and come to the fullness of the truth.

It's taken us in the West a long time to uncover the secret wisdom that the body and the natural world are as holy and fruitful sources of spiritual wisdom as any dusty tomes ever were. But Padma knew it and preached it, and today it is a living tradition shared by millions of believers the world over. Our only nod to this in our own Christian tradition is the Feast of Saint Francis, when we deign to bless liturgically, on this one day of the year, the many creatures that give their lives in love for us.

Closer to master Padma's own reverence for the natural world, however, are a group of Buddhists in Thailand. Several years ago, the Thai government approved the destruction of a forest held to be sacred by many. Instead of suffering the trees to be cut down, the local Buddhist officials draped the trees in ochre robes and ordained them. Since, according to Thai law, it is forbidden to kill a monk, the trees, newly ordained as Buddhist monks, were spared. This is more than mere blessing, it is an acknowledgement of the sacred function that nature plays in the spiritual lives of human beings.

As I think back to that incredible experience I had with that tree in Burlingame, I often wonder just what I could have done for it that would in any way repay it for its kindness to me. I'm not sure that ordination to the priesthood would have meant very much to it, even were I a bishop and in a position to bestow such an honor. We have to be careful not to be too anthropomorphic about these things. Still, it seems that my simple "thank you," was not enough. Like St. Francis, Padmasambhava, or the Swedenborgian missionary Johnny Appleseed, I could perhaps roam the land blessing nature as I go. But, as romantic an idea as that is, it is impractical for an unenlightened schlub like me with the physical constitution of the Pillsbury Dough Boy.

But one thing I can do is bring attention to those who have gone before, fess up to my own freaky mystical experiences with trees, and ask you here today: in what way do we honor the natural world and its contribution to our spirituality? How much do we still buy into the Gnostic hatred of the body and world? And how might we, in the future, bless the trees, the groves, the mountains and the valleys? It is no accident that most of us feel closer to the spirit when we are in nature. It is no accident that church groups regularly go into the wilderness on retreat. Yet we rarely say why. The truth is that nature is untouched by our theologies of illness and disease. Nature knows nothing of our ideologies of greed and mindless waste. Nature ignores the irrational self-aggrandizement of our species. It is only itself, unthinking, unspoiled, and unphased by our philosophizing.

Nature *is* blessed. Padmasambhava may have blessed the land, but it was no doubt for the benefit of the people more than for the benefit of the land. It is *we* who need to be reminded of its holiness, not nature. It is *we* who need to be reminded of the holiness of the body—for the body already possesses this wisdom. It is *we* who need to be awakened to the sacredness of sexuality—for certainly our bodies have never forgotten the sacred union for which they were made. Tibetan Buddhism is a huge affirmation of the flesh, the body, the world, and nature, all of those things we have for so long denigrated in the West. Not only are they not barriers to salvation, they are, as Padmasambhava preached so long ago, the very instruments of liberation.

Creator of earth as well as heaven,
we have been sold a bill of goods here in the West.
We have been told that our bodies are bad,
that the world is corrupt, that the material plane is worthless.
Yet you, in thine own infinite wisdom,
married thyself to the material world for once and for all
by being born a babe at Bethlehem.
Help us to throw off the shackles of centuries of bad press,
and embrace corporeality as you meant us to do.
Help us to behold this world and say with thee, "It is good."
And like Padmasambhava, help us, when we leave it behind,

to leave it more blessed than we found it.
For we ask this in the name of the Word become flesh,
even Jesus Christ. Amen.

⊕ *Preached at Grace North Church on May 29, 2005.*

15 | mahavira

ast Sunday, I was feeling like a very bad priest indeed. Everything was going fine up until the giving of blessings, when Flavio came up for his travel blessing. He was going on a business trip this past week, and without thinking, I asked him in front of all of you when he would be returning. The moment I did so, I flinched inside as if I had cut myself. Of course I knew he would be returning Wednesday night, and I had asked him that publicly for the benefit of the congregation. But did he know that? Or did he think I had forgotten? From the look on his face, I was sure I would catch hell about it when we got home, and I felt icky about it throughout the Eucharistic prayer.

Then, while distributing communion, I completely spaced on Lizzy's name. Now, just between you and me, I think the person who thought up saying a person's name while distributing communion either a sadist, or, if a priest himself, a masochist, because the personality type attracted to the priesthood generally has a brain like a sieve, and trying to get through the communion line each week without forgetting a name is like running some kind of excruciating gauntlet. Theologically, I love the idea, for Jesus says he has called us all by name, and being called by name as we receive him is a precious and touching thing. Unless you are the priest, in which case it is a nerve-wracking invitation to failure.

And I didn't just space on the name of a newcomer, someone whom I had yet to truly internalize, I spaced on Lizzy—who has been here almost as long as Charlotte! To make it worse, I could see that Lizzy was having a hard day when it happened. As I finished the line and headed back up to the altar, my inner critic kicked in like Jet Li and started throwing punches. "Great way to kick a girl when she's down," I hissed to myself, and cringed through the rest of the service.

Afterwards, of course, Flavio didn't know what I was talking about, and Lizzy brushed away my apology like it was a cobweb. Later on, as I was reflecting upon all this, I realized that it's not the big things I do wrong that really get to me. If I decide to chance the carpool lane when I'm late and driving solo and I get a ticket, I deserve it, take it, and don't complain about it. No, it's the little screwups, where I don't mean any harm, but do it anyway, that really smart. It's days like last Sunday that make me just want to say, "Forget this—I'm going off to the wilderness to live with dogs—dogs who don't go on business trips and don't care if you forget their names."

I despair sometimes that, despite my best intentions, I don't seem to be able to get through a single day without stepping on someone's toes, putting my foot in my mouth, or inadvertently pissing someone off. To go through a day without doing any damage? That just seems like a very tall order sometimes, and this makes me feel sad. And frustrated. And sometimes, like a very bad priest.

I wonder if any of you can relate? Since it's Father's Day, I'll tell you what my own father might say if he could hear me now. I can just hear him rolling off one of his beloved clichés: "You can't make an omlette without breaking a few eggs," he'd say. To which I would like to reply, "I'll have cereal, thanks."

That is certainly the answer that today's mystic would have advocated, for his dilemma was similar to mine, although he did things in a much more dramatic fashion. I am talking about Mahavira, the founder of Jainism, a man who really, really didn't want to hurt anyone, and who never did anything half way.

Mahavira—whose name means "the great hero"—was a contemporary of the Buddha, and like the Buddha, he started a Hindu reform movement that sought to deflate the power of the Brahmin priests, who had a stranglehold on society from high atop their self-congratulatory caste system. There are many ways in which Mahavira and the Buddha are alike. For one thing, Mahavira's father was named Siddhartha, which was, of course, the Buddha's given name. Mahavira was also a prince, just as the Buddha was, and again like the Buddha, when he was a young man he left the palace and his wife and child behind and went into the forest to seek a different kind of wealth.

However, when Mahavira got to the forest and started practicing austerities, he went into them whole-hog. He went completely naked, and brutalized his body whenever possible. He would bake out in the sun until he got sunstroke, and would refuse to put on a sweater when things turned chilly.

Whereas the Buddha had second thoughts about this kind of abuse, and advocated a "middle way" that cared for the body while still striving to transcend it, Mahavira, as I said, wasn't going to do anything half way. It was attachment to the body, and matter in general, that was the problem, and Mahavira wasn't going to give it any quarter.

Mahavira taught that while there might be gods, they were not very important. The only thing that was important was escaping the wheel of death and rebirth. Once again, this is very close to the Buddha's teaching. But while the Buddha taught that individual consciousness ceased upon entry into Nirvana, Mahavira taught a different doctrine.

He taught that souls, or *jivas*, were eternal beings of pure consciousness that longed to be free from the bonds of matter. What keeps these souls trapped in matter, in bodies? Why, karma, of course. Karma, in Mahavira's system, is like a snakebite—through no fault of our own we have been bit and infected with a substance that poisons us and immobilizes us.

If we want to be free of matter, if we want to shed the world and the body, and reclaim our original heritage of pure and undefiled consciousness blissfully floating in the ether, we must neutralize and eradicate the effects of karma. We must, as it were, pay our karmic debt, and exit this world with a zero balance if we are ever to rise above it.

For many people, this takes lifetimes. But Mahavira believed that anyone could achieve liberation in this lifetime if they just worked hard enough. Unfortunately, "worked hard enough" meant doing a lot more than sitting naked under the Indian sky without sunblock.

Mahavira taught a doctrine called *ahimsa*, non-violence, or not-harming. By practicing non-violence one can slowly deplete one's karmic debt. But how does one get through an entire lifetime without hurting anybody? The same as the rest of us—one day at a time.

But we're not talking about not hurting people's feelings, here, although that is indeed part of it. Mahavira always took things to extremes, and so he taught his disciples to cover their mouths with a kerchief so as not to breathe in any insects accidentally. He told them to sweep the path in front of them and to step slowly and carefully so as not to trod upon anything. He forbade them to eat animals, or even any sprouting grain or other living food.

Just taking your car for a spin around the freeway would have horrified Mahavira—just think of all the creatures who were sacrificed for your little joy ride! The bugs against the windshield, those ground under the tires! A driving vacation to Tahoe could rack up enough karmic debt to keep you on the planet for another hundred lifetimes.

Yes, Mahavira really did take things to these extremes, and those followers who came after him did likewise. The word "Jain" comes from the Sanskrit word *jina* which means, "victor." The Jains hope to be victorious over the power of matter, to eventually escape it through the eradication of their own karma, and this is never so hard as when a person is old. For a Jain to attain liberation, it isn't enough to simply live without harming anything—that just gets you to the threshold. To actually cross the threshold and enter into bliss one must practice the ultimate austerity and starve oneself to death. Not every Jain must starve him or herself to death, just those who are reasonably certain they have paid off their debt. If you have not worked it hard enough to be at that place, then by all means have another bowl of curried lentils, you can always try again in your next life.

There are many interesting features to Jainism, however, that go beyond being naked and famished, and are a fair sight more appealing. The doctrine of *anekantwad* states that things are not always what they seem, and that there is no one right way to view things, because everything changes depending on the perspective of the observer. The Jains say that there are at least seven ways to view any given thing or event.

First, from one perspective, it seems as if a thing *is*.
From another perspective, it seems as if a thing *is not*.
From another perspective,
  it seems as if a thing both *is* and *is not*.
From another perspective,
  it seems as if a thing is simply not describable.
From another perspective, it seems as if a thing *is*
  and is still indescribable.
From another perspective, it seems as if a thing
  is not and is indescribable.
From yet another perspective, it seems as if a thing *is*,
  is not, and is indescribable.

I'm glad we cleared all of *that* up. Now, critics of the Jains complain about this, saying that the Jains are upholding illogical and contradictory statements. The Jains say, "Silly Buddhists, we aren't making declarations about the objective reality of a thing, but only about how it appears to a person from different perspectives." This does not satisfy the Buddhists, and only leads to another argument. Apparently, arguing is not a form of violence for Jains.

Mahavira asked his followers to take five great vows: 1) to harm no living thing; 2) to speak only the truth; 3) never to steal; 4) to be celibate and renounce all worldly pleasures; 5) complete non-attachment to people, places, or things.

Striving to uphold these vows himself, Mahavira traveled throughout India preaching his new doctrines, and often getting beat to a pulp for his efforts. Eventually, however, after thirty years of preaching, he felt he had paid his karmic debt, and like a good Jain should do, starved himself to death, and entered himself into bliss.

After Mahavira's passing, the Jain movement sputtered and almost disappeared. But his followers rallied and became actively evangelistic, taking his teachings to the furthest reaches of the Indian subcontinent. While Buddhism was absorbed back into Hinduism in India and completely disappeared there as a separate religion, the Jains have endured, living side by side in peace with their Hindu neighbors, often holding positions of great prestige and responsibility.

Later Jains, concerned that their religion be seen as more ancient and enduring than it seemed, started teaching that Mahavira was not actually the founder of Jainism, but instead simply the last in a string of twenty-four teachers. And for all of their commitment of non-violence, they simply could not resist fighting each other. Jainism split into two competing factions. The Digambaras hew closest to Mahavira's teaching, and insist on complete renunciation, including the eschewing of clothing. But their rivals, the Shvetambaras, would agree with Mark Twain that "Clothes make the man, and naked people have very little influence in society." So they took to wearing white clothing, and eased up a bit on the austerity thing so that people could still belong to the faith, but could also have families and hold down jobs—little things like that.

The feud continues to this day, with one side shouting "sell-outs" and the other shouting "extremists," because, you know, arguing is *not* violence and apparently does not rack up any karma so long as no actual blood is spilt.

So what meaning does Mahavira offer us, today? Although few of us would agree that any of his ideas should be taken to the extremes he advocated, there are many of his ideas that are valuable, indeed, essential to our lives today. Mahatma Gandhi was powerfully influenced by his doctrine of *ahimsa*, or non-violence, and this teaching became the cornerstone of Gandhi's own philosophy, leading to Indian independence from Britain, and also informing the American civil rights movement of the 1960s.

Secondly, Mahavira's doctrine of seven ways to view things is extremely relevant. Quantum mechanics has verified the truth that the observer changes that which is observed, and that all things are relative depending upon one's perspective. Once again, this is a case of science taking twenty-five hundred years to catch up with the mystical insights of the East. This is a very important teaching for us, today. We have emerged from a great Dark Age in the West where we felt we had all the answers, we could explain everything, that objective reality was quantifiable, packagable, and marketable. In fact, however, nothing is more slippery than reality, and as Mahavira teaches, it is an impossible thing to know divorced from our own lenses, prejudices, and perspectives.

So the next time you feel like chucking it all and running off to the country because you just can't seem to get through a single day without hurting somebody, stop and think for a minute. How many beings are you likely to hurt in your allegedly innocent flight to the country? It may not be impossible to get through a day without causing any suffering or harm, but it is very, very hard indeed. Who can blame someone for trying to live his or her life that way? Mahavira was a man of great conviction, who wore his deep feelings and beliefs on his slee...bicep. He may not be someone we all will want to emulate, but he is a man whose deep feeling and fearless critique of the religious establishment of his day we can admire, whose story we can pass on to future generations. Not everyone will view him the same way, but then, as he himself said, there is no one right way to view anything or anybody.

God, Mahavira didn't say that you don't exist,
but he didn't esteem you very highly, either.
Please don't hold that against him, because,
honest to Pete, the man has suffered enough.
We only ask that you grant to us a measure of his conviction,
that we would go out of our way to avoid hurting others.
But also grant us the wisdom not to hurt ourselves,
for we do not have to be Jains to admire them.
Help us to care for both ourselves and others,
and remove from us the arrogance that insists
that we are right about anything.
For we ask this in the name of the one
who took upon himself our own karmic debt,
even Jesus Christ. Amen.

⊕ *Preached at Grace North Church on June 19, 2005.*

16 | zarathushtra

Once upon a time, a prophet appeared who preached that the world is locked in an eternal battle between good and evil. He predicted that this war would rage until the end of days, fought by endless armies of angels, demons, and human beings. Finally, a savior would appear upon the earth and vanquish utterly the powers of darkness. Then would commence the final judgment, where every woman and man receive their due. Once the judgment is complete, the bodies of all those who died will be resurrected. Time will be no more, and all beings who have embraced the good will be ushered into the Kingdom of God to enjoy eternity.

Sound familiar? No, it's not Isaiah or Jeremiah, or Daniel, or one of the other Jewish prophets, and it's not Jesus, either. It is, in fact, the preaching of a humble Persian clergyman by the name of Zarathushtra.

When, thousands of years ago, the ancient horsemen of the Russian steppes thundered southwards in a conquering horde, some of them wound up in the East, occupying India and imposing on the native population their own religion, which today we call Vedism. As you might recall from our first sermon on Hinduism, Vedism is the most primitive form of Hinduism. It is a native religion, with a vast pantheon of gods representing the forces of nature—Indra the god of thunder, Vayu the god of air, Agni the god of fire, and so forth. The *Rig Veda* is the holy book that survives from this time, and gives us a pretty good picture of Vedic beliefs and ritual.

But not all of the Vedics settled in India. Some of them veered West, and settled in the Middle East, in present day Afghanistan, Iran, and Iraq. They imposed their religion on the natives in what I will call these Persian areas as well. But just as in India, the priestly caste in Persia was corrupt. Just as in India, genuine people of spirit cannot tolerate a corrupt clergy for very long, especially when they set themselves at the top of the social ladder. But while Indian Vedism saw three different reform movements— Upanishadic Hinduism, Buddhism, and Jainism—Persian Vedism needed only one. The reformer that lead this movement was this same Zarathushtra.

His given name was Spitma, which has always hovored near the bottom of the baby names list in popularity, right down there with Derek and Uvula. By all accounts he learned his trade well, learning from childhood the sacred language of liturgy—a close relative to Sanskrit. He learned the complicated rituals Vedism demanded, and did all that was required of him.

But his heart was restless. He watched with increasing distress the corruption of the chief priests, who seemed more interested in pleasing the king than satisfying the needs of the gods. It became harder and harder for him to go through the motions when inside he knew something was deeply wrong. Then, in the depths of his moral struggle, he heard a voice that changed him forever.

The Creator himself visited Spitma, and charged him with a new ministry. He also gave him a new name, Zarathushtra, the meaning of which scholars are still debating. It could mean, "Owner of the yellow camel," but it could also mean, "the golden light." Feel free to pick the meaning that pleases you most. I like the one about the camel, myself.

The creator also revealed to him the error of the Vedic religious system. There were not many gods, as the Vedics had always supposed, but only One: Ahura Mazda, which means "the Wise God."

Ruling directly beneath Mazda were seven immortal spirits, which we today might name archangels. They were named Good Mind, Righteousness and Truth, Kingdom and Justice, Devotion and Serenity, Wholeness, and Immortality. Those are only six, I know, but the gender balance is exquisite—three of them are masculine, and three feminine. And above them all, second only to Mazda himself, was the Creative Holy Spirit, Spenta Mainyu, who is, apparently hermaphroditic, or at least androgynous.

In Indian Hinduism, the many gods of the Vedic pantheon were reinterpreted as many faces of one and the same god. But for Zarathushtra, these many gods were not gods at all, but spirits, servants of the One God. In other words, angels. It was revealed to Zarathushtra that there was, in fact, a vast hierarchy of angels in perpetual service to Mazda, who nevertheless govern the forces of nature in much the same way they used to do back when they were gods.

So God—or Ahura Mazda—might indeed be in his Heaven, but all was not right with the world. The Creator revealed that there were evil forces in the world as well. Just as Hinduism acknowledged the demons, Zarathushtra affirmed the reality of evil spirits. Mirroring the hierarchy of angels was a lowerarchy of demonic beings, led by the archangel of evil, Angra Mainyu, the "Evil Spirit." Now Angra is not really the evil twin of Ahura Mazda, as some have wrongly understood. Angra is the equal and opposite of Spenta Mainyu, the androgynous Holy Spirit.

For some reason which humans are still trying to suss out,

Ahura Mazda suffers evil to persist in the world, and presides over a great battle between the armies of the Holy Spirit and those of the Evil Spirit. And this is how Zarathushtra made sense of all the pain and suffering and evil in the world. This planet is not a paradise gone wrong, it is a battlefield, and always has been. This world is the field of blood where the arrayed hosts of armies both human and angelic are fighting it out to the bitter end.

This is our lot, we are born on a battlefield, and we must choose sides. Not to choose *is* to choose. We will either actively fight for the good, or we are against it. There are no neutral parties in this struggle. The weight of the world hangs in the balance, and every woman and man must choose his or her place.

Zarathushtra wrote a vast collection of hymns, or *Gathas*, most of which have been lost. Some of them survive, however, and they tell us some very important things about what Zarathushtra actually taught. But they also tell us that Zarathrushtra was a much better prophet than he was a poet—but perhaps if we could read it in the original Vedic we would feel differently. I'm willing to give him the benefit of the doubt, there.

As you might expect, Zarathushtra's reforms were not enthusiastically embraced. His fellow priests rejected his revelation—didn't you just know they would?—and sent him packing. So Zarathushtra fled into the wilderness with a motley band of disciples.

There they wandered aimlessly for some time, trusting that Mazda would lead them eventually to a new home where the new revelation would be embraced. Eventually they came upon the small kingdom of Balkh in modern-day Afghanistan. The king of Balkh gave Zarathushtra an audience, and was won over by the prophet's eloquence. He was also inspired by the new teachings that emphasized personal discernment and righteousness. He liked the way the heavenly hierarchy mirrored his own kingdom, for it seemed to support and validate his own kingship.

In spite of the vociferous protests of his own clergy, the king embraced Zarathushtra's new religion and imposed it upon his people. The old Vedic priests were not happy, of course, and swore they would have their revenge.

So Zarathushtra and his followers put down roots in Balkh and continued to develop their new religion, sending out missionaries and eventually finding more and more success. The old priests, however, did finally have their way—and Zarathushtra was murdered by one of them—but not before reaching the august age of seventy-seven.

It was only after his death, however, that Zarathushtra's teachings really caught on. Within a couple of hundred years it was the dominant religion in the middle east, reigning as the state religion of three Persian dynasties lasting nearly a thousand years.

One of the most interesting aspects of Zoroastrianism, however, was its influence on another middle eastern religion—namely, Judaism. About 700 years before Christ, the Jews were once again taken as slaves. This time they were not captive in Egypt, but in Persia, where they came into prolonged and intense contact with Zoroastrians.

Prior to their captivity in Babylon, the Jews did not have any developed ideas about angels. The tales in the Jewish scriptures prior to this time depict single angels, individual spirits sent by God as messengers. But the idea of hosts—armies—of angels had not occurred to them until they started living side by side with people who had such notions. Nor did they have any idea of demons or demonic hosts. Previous to the captivity, all evil spirits had their origin in God, just as the good messengers did.

The idea that God has a nemesis, too, is a gift from Zoroastrianism. Satan is just Angra Mainyu with a *bris* and a *bar mitsvah*. Likewise, Heaven and Hell were not ideas that had occurred to the Jews. They, too, were gifts from their Zoroastrian captors.

The Jews were also impressed by the *Gathas*, the collections of poems by Zoroaster. I like to think they were not so impressed with the poetry as they were with the mere fact that history could be thus preserved. It is only after contact with the Zoroastrians that the Jews began to write down their history, and to collect their scattered shards of memory into books.

The *Gathas* further inspired the Jews by introducing to them the literary genre that we today call "apocalyptic." Zarathushtra had originally written his apocalyptic vision of the battle between good and evil as a cosmic revenge fantasy when he was on the run for his life. Those who persecuted him were, of course, on the side of Angra Mainyu. But he took great pleasure in imagining how he and his followers would be vindicated when the angelic hosts invaded the earth and utterly defeated the powers of darkness.

This very same revenge fantasy would have an equal appeal to the Jews, who imagined themselves to be on the side of the Good God and those nasty Zoroastrians on the side of Satan. Daniel, writing in captivity in Babylon, was the first to turn Zarathushtra's own revenge fantasy against the Zoroastrians. He adopted the tale almost whole, simply changing the identity of the good and bad guys to favor their own people and their God. The Jewish apocalyptic took off as a genre of literature in its own right, inspiring many Jewish writers who eventually found their way into the canon, and many more who did not.

Rampant apocalypticism was like a dominant gene that Judaism bequeathed to both of its offspring religions—I am, of course, talking about Christianity and Islam. Think of what Christianity would look like if it had no concept of angels or demons, no Satan, no Son of Man, no cosmic battle between good and evil, no end of the world, no last judgement, and no Heaven and Hell. None of these are ideas original to the Jews, my friends. They are *all* Zoroastrian notions. One has to ask the question: if it were not for the Zoroastrians, would there have been a Christianity at all? And would that have been a good thing or a bad thing!?

I'll leave you to ask the same question about Islam, which also inherited all of these ideas. For it is the revenge fantasies of Zoroaster as understood and interpreted by Mohammad that is driving the terrorists' ideological agenda today. The cosmic battle may not actually be being fought in the heavens, but it sure as hell is being fought here on the earth.

Knowing the history of these ideas is important for us in the U.S. today, because so much of the rhetoric flying around concerning the terrorists and the war in Iraq is likewise being fueled by Zoroaster's revenge fantasies as understood and interpreted by Christian fundamentalists. The thing about prophesies is that sincere believers will twist the world inside out in order to make them come true. Apocalypticsim is rampant in our country today.

The *Left Behind* series of apocalyptic novels depicting the second coming of Christ, the cosmic battle between the angels of God and the hosts of Satan, the final judgment and the final reward of the faithful are the biggest selling phenomenon in the history of publishing. Over 80 million copies of these books have been sold in the U.S. alone, luring untold millions onto the bandwagon of the Apocalypse. And our current administration, for whom the *Left Behind* scenario is their operating paradigm, seem determined to make the battle of Armageddon a self-fulfilling prophesy.

Is it just me, or does it seem crazy to allow the revenge fantasies of an Afghani priest who lived 3000 years ago to dictate current foreign policy in the Middle East?

I believe we have had enough revenge fantasies. Revenge is the antithesis of the teachings of Jesus, who told us to forgive innumerable times, and to eschew judgment lest we ourselves be victims of that same judgment. That last admonition, it seems to me, is particularly poignant for us given our current plight.

So if these pesky Zoroastrians were so high and mighty and powerful, how come we don't hear too much about them today? Mostly it is because in the seventh century of the Common Era

148 | john r. mabry

the Persian empire fell to the Muslims. They were, in fact, defeated by enemy armies motivated by Zarathushtra's own revenge fantasy. It is an instructive warning for us to heed.

Some of the Zoroastrians rejected Islam, however, and fled to northern India. There they were called "Parsees," which simply means, "those people from Persia." When the British added India to their empire, they opened the way for Zoroastrians to come to England. The first known Zoroastrian to do so was in 1723, and they have been a vibrant part of British life ever since. In fact, the very first ethnic minority to be elected to Parliament was a Zoroastrian named Dadabhai Naoroji, elected to the Liberal Party in 1892. The first ethnic representatives of the Labor, Communist, and Conservative parties were also Zoroastrians.

There is a Zoroastrian temple in Fremont, California, and though Zoroastrians don't allow conversion, anyone is welcome to visit the temple. There are only about 150,000 Zoroastrians in the world today, but their influence far outweighs their numbers, having produced outstanding scholars, scientists, and statesmen in this century alone.

The Zoroastrians worshipped Ahura Mazda in the symbol of fire, and it is due to the eternal flame in their temples that the light of the presence was bequeathed to both Jewish synagogues and Christian tabernacles. That flame for Zarathushtra represented the fire of consciousness, the cathartic power of truth to cut through illusion and purify the soul.

May God grant us this same flame of discernment to sort the wheat in our traditions from the chaff, to know what is valuable to pick up and carry on, and what should be left behind as destructive and harmful. The world has had enough of revenge fantasies. The world has had enough.

God of the mighty hosts of Heaven,
whose arrayed splendor strikes fear
in the heart of demonic forces;

help us to see that those angelic and demonic armies
fight not in the heavens or upon the face of the earth,
but chiefly in our own hearts.
Help us to contain the fury of our internal battles,
and not to project them onto the world around us,
onto our neighbors, onto innocent people half a world away,
onto people who seem different to us, or strange.
Intervene, if you are able, and put a halt
to our misguided headlong plunge into self-fulfilling apocalypse.
Give us an ounce of the discernment
Zarathushtra esteemed so highly,
that we may see that the only demonic hosts
arrayed upon the earth belong to us,
that the preservation of the light of consciousness
is ours to save or damn.
Help us, O God, before it is too late. Amen.

⊕ *Preached at Grace North Church on July 17, 2005.*

17 | judaism

Imagine you are sitting down to a nice cup of coffee after dinner, getting ready to read the paper when a disembodied voice suddenly begins speaking to you from out of thin air. The voice claims to be a god—one that you've never heard of, by the way, and not part of any pantheon that you know of, either. The voice tells you that if you will do what it says, it will grant you your deepest and most secret desires. But here's what you have to do: you have to forsake your religion, swear off your old gods, pack up your family and hit the road for a location to be announced *en route*. Sound good? Or does it sound...a little psychotic?

Crazy or not, that's how Judaism begins, with an unassuming man named Abram. He lived about four thousand years ago in Ur of the Caldees, which is in the western part of the Sinai peninsula. God appeared to him, and with no more than a promise, gets Abram to pull up his tent stakes and move. "I am God Almighty," this new god told him. "Walk before me, and be blameless. And I will make my covenant between me and you, and will make you exceedingly numerous" (Gen. 17:1-2).

This new god wanted to make a covenant with him: if Abram would worship this new god, and this new god alone, he would be granted an inheritance of a land all his own, to be peopled by his own children, who would be "more numerous than the stars of the sky or the grains of sand" along the sea.

Now this had to sound pretty good to Abram, since he was past middle age and had no children. And who knows what the situation was like in Ur? Maybe he was being evicted, or prosecuted, or teased mercilessly for his childlessness. We don't know all of the reasons that made this such an enticing offer, but Abram went for it. When he did, the little voice told him to change his name, from Abram, which means "father," to Abraham, which means "father of multitudes."

So Abraham and his wife Sarah put everything they had on the backs of mules, and headed out into the desert. They passed through many lands, and had lots of close calls, but unfortunately, no children were forthcoming. Finally, Sarah just threw up her hands and said, in frustration, "Why don't you have children by my servant, Hagar?" We aren't told how Abraham received such a suggestion, but we do know he eventually agreed, and a child, Ishmael, was indeed forthcoming from that union.

It was then that Abraham got the sense that he was dealing with more than just a voice in his head. Three strangers stopped by their camp, and while Abraham and Sarah were tending to their hospitality, they announced that Sarah would soon be with child. Sarah considered this such a ludicrous assertion that she laughed out loud. She quickly stifled her rude outburst, but the strangers had heard. Imagine her surprise when, a couple of months later, she felt a baby stirring in her womb. When the baby was finally delivered, Sarah's sarcastic outburst was immortalized, for they named the boy "laughter," or "Isaac" in Hebrew.

Now Sarah did not know what to think. Sure, she had left her family, most of her belongings, and every shred of normalcy behind in Ur. But she was a dutiful wife, faithful to her husband even if he did hear psychotic voices in his head. And now, to her amazement, it seemed that this weird god was on the level.

Terror must have struck her heart when she realized that Isaac would not be the inheritor of Abraham's as yet unseen new country, as he was not the first-born. So, with all of the cunning and scruples of Lady MacBeth, she convinced Abraham to exile Hagar and Ishmael to the desert, where, with no food or shelter, they would surely die. Fortunately, the strange god had compassion on Hagar and Ishmael, who not only lived, but, tradition tells us, were the beginning of another new nation—the Arab peoples, the ancient and modern rivals of the Jews.

Things might have ended happily for Hagar, but now Abraham had a problem. The covenant he had made with his new god had been breached—by him. He had not trusted God, and because of this, Ishmael was born. The trust between Abraham and the new god had been damaged, and had to be restored. Today, perhaps, Abraham and God might have gone to a Marriage and Family Therapist to get back on track, but these were more barbarous times. God ordered Abraham to take his son Isaac up to the top of Mount Moriah, and there to sacrifice him on an altar of stones.

Who knows what Sarah made of this deal. My guess is Abraham did not tell her about it until afterwards—I mean, what mother in her right mind would allow it? At the top of the mountain, Abraham tied his son up, laid him on the altar, and prepared to strike. At the last moment, however, an angel caught his hand. "Enough," the voice in his head told him. Abraham had proven himself and the relationship between himself and God was restored.

God remained faithful to Abraham and his descendents, however imperfect or even devious they proved to be. Isaac's son Jacob was not the first-born, yet he masqueraded as his older brother, and stole the blessing of the first-born. After which, of course, he ran for his life. While Jacob was wandering around in the wilderness, a messenger of his grandfather's god appeared to him, and he did what any frightened person alone in the desert might do when confronted with a scary stranger—he fought. Jacob wrestled the divine messenger all night long, after which the stranger tried to leave. But Jacob held him fast and demanded a blessing. He was big on collecting blessings, this Jacob guy. But the messenger acquiesced, and Jacob walked away from the encounter with both a limp and a blessing. He also came away with a new name, "Israel," which means, "the one who wrestles with God."

Jacob was blessed, indeed. He had twelve sons, which were to become the patriarchs of the twelve tribes of Israel. One son, Joseph, was sold into slavery by his brothers, and after some hairy adventures of his own, ended up a prince in Egypt, saving that country from a dire drought.

Even though the Egyptians were grateful to Joseph and his kin, they didn't stay that way. Jacob's family flourished in Egypt, and the local people began to feel threatened by these fortunate foreigners. They seized their lands and treasures, and pressed them into slavery.

There they remained for many generations. While the Egyptians did their best to keep the Israelites down, they continued to reproduce at rates that were alarming to their captors. Eventually, the Pharaoh declared that all male children under two years of age were to be put to death. There was great sorrow amongst the children of Abraham in that time, and one mother refused to allow her child to be sacrificed. She hid him in a wicker basket and floated him on the Nile, where he was discovered by the Pharaoh's daughter. That little child was Moses, who was raised as a prince in the Pharaoh's court.

Moses would have had a cushy life, too, had the cruelty of the Egyptians not broken his heart. Seeing an Israelite slave being beaten senseless, Moses struck back at the abusive guard, and killed him. Knowing that the punishment for killing an Egyptian was death, Moses fled for his life, leaving Egypt behind for the wilderness.

Moses might have been demoted from prince to shepherd, but scripture does not relate him grousing about it much. Even though he fled without a shekel in his pocked, he did pretty well for himself. He married into the family of a pagan priest named Jethro, and lived a full and happy life with his wife, Zipporah.

Then something very strange happened. While out in the field with sheep, Moses came upon a bush that was burning all alone, as if lightning had struck it. But the odd thing was that, though burning, the bush was not consumed. And from that bush, Moses heard that same odd voice that had called to Abram so very long ago.

The voice told Moses to go back to Egypt, and to bring the Pharaoh a message: he must release the children of Israel. Moses was horrified. "I'm not a prophet or a preacher," he complained, "I don't do the public speaking thing." So God told him to take his brother, Aaron with him to do the actual talking. After a couple of unsettling miracles involving sticks, snakes, and leprosy, however, he consented.

Of course, the Pharaoh refused Moses' request. Moses was ready to pack up and go back to his ranch, but God counseled persistence. So Moses kept asking, and Pharaoh kept saying "no." So God sent a series of devastating plagues, the last of which paralleled the Pharaoh's own slaughter of the Jewish baby boys—the angel of death took the lives of the first born sons of the Egyptians. There's no payback like divine payback.

Overcome with grief, the Pharaoh finally assented, and the children of Israel leaped into action, moving *en masse* out of Egypt. But just as they reached the banks of the Red Sea, the Pharaoh had a change of heart and sent his soldiers after them to stop the exodus and return the Israelites to slavery.

Now imagine the panic of these people—they were fleeing slavery, and were trapped with a sea on one side and a fast-approaching army on the other. With the great burden of responsibility for his people weighing upon him, Moses uttered a prayer and raised his arms to heaven. In answer, we are told, the waters of the Red Sea rolled back on either side, leaving one small stretch of dry land in the middle on which they could pass to safety. Too overwhelmed to think logically about what they were doing, the Israelites poured into the seabed, trusting that the wall of water on either side would not come crashing down upon them and crush them.

As soon as the last Israelites had crossed to safety, the waters poured back down, right on top of the pursuing Egyptians. The children of Israel were finally safe, finally free, but after generations in slavery, had no idea what to do next, how to govern themselves, how to survive in the desert. They had millions of mouths to feed, after all, and had known no order but the lash. Naturally, they all looked to Moses for help.

Moses had no idea what to do next, so he climbed a mountain to meet with God and ask for further instructions. He got more than he bargained for. The covenant that God had made with their ancestor, Abraham, he now offered to them. Just as one man had stepped out on faith, forsaking all for the promise of a new land and a new tribe, God was asking them to do the same. He set before them a set of laws that guaranteed their survival. All they had to do was to honor these laws and keep them. In exchange, the strange deity would be their God, would keep them safe, and would show them a land for their very own, a land flowing with milk and honey, a land where they and their children could live in peace.

Moses returned from the mountain, with rays of light streaming from his countenance. And he set before his people the covenant, and said, "What do you want to do?" Overwhelmingly, the leaders of the tribes accepted the covenant and swore themselves and their families to it. And Jews down to the present day do their best to abide by this same covenant, from which they derive their identity, purpose, and sense of cosmic safety.

What exactly is a covenant, though? What does it mean that Israel and God had entered into a covenant?

The idea is similar to a contract, but with a major difference. Like a contract, a covenant describes the actions that two parties agree to do, each for the other. But the similarity stops there. A contract, once broken, is no longer binding upon either party. A covenant, however, remains in place even if one or both parties are unfaithful to it.

Think of a marriage. It is a covenant to which both parties swear. But if one of them is unfaithful, the other, by remaining faithful, can keep the covenant intact until the first party comes to his or her senses and makes amends. It is not dissolved until and unless both parties agree that it should be.

This concept became painfully clear to me several years ago when I was part of the Berkeley Celebration Circle, a gathering of people who felt the need to experience healthy spiritual community. We created our own interfaith ritual, and covenanted together to explore, worship, and be community for each other.

It was one of the most wonderful experiences of community I have ever had. Yet, after two years of meeting, I felt that I had accomplished what I had set out to do with the group. I felt like I had healed my own wounding around abusive spiritual communities, and discerned a need to turn my attention to the healing I needed to do around Christianity. So I announced I would be quitting the Celebration Circle, and was starting to do some theoretical work around how to apply what we had learned to specifically Christian worship. And of course, if anyone from the Celebration Circle was interested in that, they were welcome to join me.

Baaaad mistake. I was clueless at the time, but in simply opting out and setting my own agenda I was forsaking the covenant we had made to be community for each other and to make our decisions in a consensus manner. Instead of laying *my* discernment before the community for *their* discernment, I just said, "I'm taking my ball and going home. But if anyone wants to come with me, we can still play." It was not okay, and I am to this day deeply chagrined by the way I handled that transition.

That could have been the end of it right there and then, if we had had a contract. But because we were bound together by a covenant, something much more wonderful happened. The community sat me down and in no uncertain terms told me how they felt about my actions—which was not positive—and that they would be joining me in the new project of applying our interfaith learnings to Christian worship.

I had broken faith with them, but they did not break faith with me. Instead of jettisoning me and the horse I rode in on, as they had every right to do, they held me in love even though they were angry at me, even though I had acted like a jerk. And from this inauspicious beginning the Festival of the Holy Names was born.

The story of Israel is a similar one. Time and again, Israel disobeyed their God, and even turned to the worship of other gods. Yet God did not forsake them. When Israel could not uphold the covenant, God upheld it for them. Of course, covenants are a two way street. There have been times when God did not uphold God's part of the covenant, yet it endured because Israel remained faithful. Throughout the medieval ethnic cleansing, so often directed against Jews, throughout Hitler's holocaust, God was not faithful. Yet the Jews were, and the covenant continues.

Because one party has always been able to uphold the covenant, the other party is given the grace to return, repent, and repair the relationship. Of course, that doesn't mean that there isn't ever some chastisement involved, as I am painfully aware from my experience with the Celebration Circle. The history of the Jewish people is full of prophets preaching about what is likely to happen if God's people don't shape up and start abiding by the covenant. Contrary to popular opinion, prophecy doesn't have anything to do with predicting the future, and the Jewish prophets did not engage in such divinatory activities. Prophecy, then as now, simply means proclaiming the truth. Just as you can proclaim with relative certainty to your two-year-old that if she touches a lit stove she will burn her fingers, the Hebrew prophets in just the same way proclaimed the logical end of Israel's infidelities.

These dire warnings often went unheeded, however, and a great tragedy befell the Jewish people about seven hundred years before the Common Era. They were taken into captivity and forcibly removed to Babylon, which is modern day Iraq, where they once again found themselves slaves. While this was a terrible punishment, it also carried with it a great blessing. For previous to this time, the Jews were not monotheists. They were, instead, henotheists, which means that they believed that there were many gods, but that the gods had jurisdictions. So the gods worshipped by the Egyptians ruled Egypt, but had no power in Babylon. Similarly, the god of Israel had no power in Babylon, but ruled only within the borders of Israel. If you crossed the Jordan and entered Baal's territory, you were on your own. This is why when the prophet Elisha cured the servant of a foreign ruler of leprosy, the servant begged to be allowed to take a measure of earth back with him, so that the god of Israel would be with him at home as well. Gods, it seems, were inseparably bound to the land.

But all of this changed when the Jews were carried into Babylon. At first they were bereft, not only because their land and their freedom had been taken away, but because they were beyond the reach and help of their God who had sworn to protect them. But in Babylon they encountered those pesky Zoroastrians, who introduced to them the idea that there was only one God, who ruled the whole universe, and before whom all the other gods were mere wannabes. Of course, it was not a huge leap for them to wonder, "Hmm...what if it is *our* God who is the Lord of the universe?" Once they had made that shift, they discerned that their God was not bound by the borders of Israel, but was present to them even in their captivity in a foreign land.

He was faithful to them, even when they could not discern it. That's the magic of covenant, and that kind of magic is available to us even today. Think back on your own life, to the times when you had not been particularly faithful to God, but that God was faithful to you. Think, too, of those times when you hung in there with God, even when God seemed to have left the building. And here you both are. And here we are as a community, as well. God knows there have been times when I have not kept my end of the bargain with you—yet your love for me carried me, and our relationship has endured. Likewise, I reckon many of you can think of times when you have not been all that you might have been, yet here we are, in community with one another, with the good earth, and with the Holy One. For this, as the story of Israel demonstrates so well, is what covenant and community are all about.

Instead of a meditative prayer or special music, I'd like to close with a song by one of my favorite songwriters, Jane Siberry, which illustrates the concept of covenant very well indeed, *"The Life is a Red Wagon...."*

⊕ *Preached at Grace North Church on August 21, 2005.*

18 | judith

Several years ago, my band Metaphor had just wrapped up work on our first CD, the Gnsostic rock opera, "Starfooted." The masters had been shipped off and we were all waiting with baited breath to see the finished product. When it finally arrived, we were beside ourselves. We had worked so hard on it, and were so proud of the result. Just to hold a packaged CD, issued by a record label that was not, in some way *you*, was a great thrill, and we reveled in it.

I couldn't wait to get home and show off our new prize to my wife, Kate. During the long drive home from San Jose I fantasized what her reaction would be—what with the "oohing" and the "ahhing" I was sure would commence.

Boy, was I in for a surprise. I got home and brandished the new CD, grinning from ear to ear. Then the bomb dropped. Instead of being happy for me, her face screwed into a confused mask of irritation and contempt. "How *could* you?" she asked.

"How could I what?" I asked.

"Who told you you could *do* that?" She pointed at the CD.

"What?" I asked again, compelely flummoxed.

"Who told you that you could go out and make a CD? Who told you that you could write a book? Who told you that you could go out in the world and...do something? Because nobody ever told me I could do that! Who gave *you* permission to shine?"

But before I could think of a response she was off and running again. "What is it with men? They think they can just go out and conquer the world. But I'm not conquering anything—nobody ever told us girls we could go out and *conquer* anything. What gives you the *right*?"

By this time I had started to tiptoe backwards, out of the room whispering, "You know, maybe this is not a good time..." and wishing I had had some warning about stepping on her land mine that evening.

I've thought a lot about that encounter, and in fact, Kate and I have had a couple of very good conversations about it. There is something to her objection, that, when it was not catching me off guard, made a lot of sense.

One of my favorite bands, Marillion, has a lyric in which the singer says, "I was taught from way too young to shine and not reflect." Though men and women have the capacity to do both, we are nevertheless socially conditioned into these rather unhelpful roles. Men are encouraged to shine, and women are taught to reflect. This has led to disasterous stereotypes that diminish both sexes. Women are disempowered from childhood, and men are encouraged to be oafish and insensitive.

I am encouraged that popular culture has come to the rescue of girls. Kate never grew up watching "Power Puff Girls" or "Buffy the Vampire Slayer," or many of the other programs that feature strong female leads that are not afraid to shine, crack a little wise, or kick some serious butt. (Have you noticed that Buffy is invoked from this pulpit more than any other character on television? I have—I don't know what it means, but I'm just pointing it out.)

This morning we are focusing on a woman who, even without the reinforcement that television provides, took matters into her own hands, and kicked a little butt herself. I am, of course, talking about Judith, a story taking place between the closing of the *Old Testament*, and before the opening of the *New Testament*, and found in a collection known as the *Apocrypha*.

According to the story, King Nebuchadnezzar of Assyria had declared war on Arphaxad, the King of Media. Needing soldiers, he sent out a summons to all the territory under his command, as far north as Damascus and as far west as Egypt, and including Samaria and Judea. But to the King's great displeasure, no one responded. Have you seen that bumper sticker, "What if they held a war and no one came?" This is Berkeley, of course you have. It was kind of like that.

So Nebuchadnezzar went out against Arphaxad with only his local army, and victorious, then turned his attention to revenge against all those within his jurisdiction who ignored his summons. He put his armies under the command of a man named Holofernes, a great and fearsome general, and sent them out, saying, "March out against all the land to the west, because they disobeyed my orders. I am coming against them in my anger, and will cover the whole face of the earth with the feet of my troops, to whom I will hand them over to be plundered. Their wounded shall fill their ravines and gullies, and the swelling river shall be filled with their dead."

The *Book of Judith* then recounts several paragraphs of unpronounceable towns and villages that were destroyed by Nebuchadnezzar's armies. The Jews had just recently returned from Babylon, and had just finished rebuilding the temple in Jerusalem. They were terrified that the armies would not only raze their villages, but would also defile the temple again, something they simply could not allow. They all went into mourning and pleaded with the God of Israel to protect them.

Meanwhile, the armies of Nebuchadnezzar were approaching a little town called Bethulia. The people inside the town walls had stored as much food and water as they could, but they knew it would not last long. The approaching army could conquer them without shedding a single drop of blood if they wanted by simply staying put and starving them out. The people all knew this, and as they watched their stores decrease, they became more and more afraid.

It was at this dire time that a woman named Judith sent a message to the leaders of her town. Now, Judith was a very wealthy widow, with not a little bit of sway in local affairs, so they heeded her message. She told them, "I am about to do something that will go down through all generations of our descendants. Stand at the town gate tonight so that I may go out with my maid; and within the days after which you have promised to surrender the town to our enemies, the Lord will deliver Israel by my hand. Only, do not try to find out what I am doing; for I will not tell you until I have finished."

So Judith took off the sackcloth she had been wearing, and took a perfumed bath, and put on her most festive attire. She primped and preened, put on her most expensive jewelry, and topped it all off with a tiara. Then she wrapped up her remaining food, and accompanied only by her maid, Judith walked out of the town gates to meet the enemy.

Soon she was stopped by an Assyrian patrol, who took her and her maid into custody. When they questioned her, she told them, "I am a daughter of the Hebrews, and I am fleeing as we are about to be devoured. I am on my way to see the powerful general Holofernes, for I know a secret path by which his army can take the hill country with few casualties on either side."

That sounded reasonable to the men, but they were particularly struck by her beauty. They told her, "You have saved your own life by seeking out our Lord. We will take you at once to his tent. Do not be afraid, but simply tell him what you told us."

She was shown to a tent woven with gold and purple thread, covered with jewels. And lying in comfort within was Holofernes, the dreaded general. Judith and her maid fell on their faces before him, but the general said, "Do not be afraid, for I have never hurt anyone who serves Nebuchadnezzar."

Judith delivered her message, and Holofernes was so taken by her that he had a special tent set up for her, and she was treated very well. A few days later, Holofernes decided to have a private party, inviting only his most intimate associates. He told his servant to invite the Hebrew woman as well, since in his own words, "it would be a disgrace if we let such a woman go without having intercourse with her. If we do not seduce her, she will laugh at us."

When Judith entered, Holofernes was lovestruck and lustful. He told her, "Have a drink and be merry with us!" To which she responded, "I will gladly drink, my lord, because today is the greatest day in my whole life." But Judith had brought her own food and drink with her, and ate only these things, keeping both sober and kosher—a very important detail to this book's early Jewish readers.

Holofernes was so overjoyed at Judith's willingness that he really let himself go, and the text says, got more ripped than he ever had in his life. When the party was over, Judith helped Holofernes back to his own tent, and into bed. Then Judith, looking down upon the stinking drunk and snoring general, breathed a quiet prayer, saying, "O God of all might, look in this hour on the work of my hands for the exaltation of Jerusalem. Now indeed is the time to help your heritage and to carry out my design to destroy the enemies who have risen up against us."

Then she took Holofernes' sword in one hand, and grabbed the hair of his head in the other, and with two strong strokes, severed his head from his body. Then she put the head in the bag she had brought the kosher food in, and gave it to her maid to carry.

So then Judith and her maid, as they were accustomed to doing every morning, went out from the camp to pray. But on this morning, they just kept going, and when they got to the gates of

Bethulia, Judith pulled the general's head out of the bag and showed it to the sentries. They let her in immediately, and all the people were amazed. She said, "See here, the head of Holofernes, the commander of the Assyrian army, and here is the canopy beneath which he lay in his drunken stupor. God has struck him down by the hand of a woman. As the Holy One lives, who has protected me in the way I went, I swear that it was my face that seduced him to his destruction, and that he committed no sin with me, to defile and shame me."

Judith instructed them to take the head and hang it upon the city walls, and then to round up every able-bodied man. "Act as if you are going to attack them," she told them. "Then they will want to rush up here and crush us, and will rouse their leaders."

When the Assyrians saw that the Hebrews were about to make war against them, they said, "Quick, wake Holofernes, for these slaves are foolish enough to challenge us, and we must put them in their place."

But when they found the headless body of Holofernes, and realized what had happened, they flew into a terrible panic, and fled. The Hebrews pursued them, and as they ran, Jews from other villages joined in and the army was chased completely out of Judea.

The people rejoiced that God had delivered them, and blessed Judith publicly. Though many men came from far and wide to woo her, she lived out her days a widow, reaching the ripe old age of one hundred and five when she was finally gathered to her ancestors, and laid in her late husband's tomb, as was her wish.

What a ripping good story, huh? Now aside from the shallow and obvious moral of this story: "If you fall in love with a rich and beautiful widow, don't lose your head," there is a much more important lesson to be gained.

Nobody gave Judith permission to do what she did. She did not go to the town officials to ask for their blessing. She did not ask the priests their advice. In fact, aside from her maid, she told no one what she was up to. According to the record, she did not even ask God if this was a good idea. She just *did it*.

This reminds me of one of Fr. Richard's famous sayings whenever someone gets an idea for a ministry in the parish, "Don't ask permission, just *do it*." It is far easier to obtain forgiveness than permission, anyway.

Judith needed no invitation to shine. She needed no one's permission to take matters into her own hands. If she had felt within herself that she needed someone's blessing, she would not have had the courage to walk straight into the enemy's camp and cut the head from her enemy.

But hey, you might be objecting, this woman lied, snuck around, and murdered somebody, and you're holding her up as some kind of example? And I say to you, hypothetical objector, sure—haven't you ever seen a *Die Hard* movie or an episode of *24*? In dire circumstances, good people do things they would never dream of.

But hey, another hypothetical objector might say, this series is about mystics—how is Judith a mystic? Judith embraced her inner Buffy, and embodied the archetype of the warrior, which is typically thought of as a masculine archetype. In the *Gospel of Thomas*, Jesus said, "When you make the two into one, and the inside like the outside, and the outside like the inside, and the top like the bottom; and when you make the male and the female into a single one, so that the male is not male and the female is not female...then you will enter the Kingdom." I consider her a mystic because she balanced within herself both her feminine and masculine natures, and is therefore an image of human wholeness to which all of us may aspire, whether we be male or female.

In the story of Judith, we have a woman who did not ask anyone's leave to inhabit her full humanity, and that, by my standards anyway, is a variety of mystical intelligence. Judith was whole in a way that few of us will ever be whole, and who, when the time was right and she deemed it necessary, threw off the constraints of culture and propriety and let her inner Buffy shine forth.

So how about you? Would you have been able to sally forth to meet danger as Judith did? Just in case no one gave you permission, I'm going to give it to you right now. By all the authority invested in me by heaven and earth, by the dubious power of the apostolic succession, and the intermittent authority of the state, I hereby give you permission to go forth and shine, regardless of what you have been told in the past.

If there has ever been anything you felt you were here to do, but somehow felt you were not allowed to do it, or that it might offend or upset someone, or that you just might not be up to the task—I say take the bull by those horns and give them a good twist. It's high time you stepped out of the shade and into the full light of day. It's time you shone rather than reflected. It's high time you reached beyond your grasp. It's time you stopped worrying about how it might look, or whose feelings might be bruised, or whether or not you might fall flat on your face.

It might be necessary, or it might not. It might be something great, or something small, but whatever it is that you are here to do, it is the birthright of your full and true humanity to do it—fail or succeed, right or wrong. If you are here to do something, and you know in your heart of hearts what that something is, then by God do not go to your grave with that thing undone.

You don't need my permission, but my dear friends, you have it. Go forth and kick some righteous butt.

In the Gospel of Thomas, Jesus also tells us, "When you bring forth that which is within you, that which you bring forth will save you. If you do not bring forth what is within you, what you fail to bring forth will destroy you."

God, give us discernment
to discover our purpose in this life.
And once we have uncovered it,
grant us the courage to do it,
just as you gave to your servant, Judith.

Help us to bring forth the gifts
that are within us for the good of the world,
and for the cure of our souls.
For we ask this in the name
of the one who brought forth all things
and saves all things, even Jesus Christ. Amen.

⊕ *Preached at Grace North Church on September 4, 2005.*

19 | hillel

Back in High School, I was a leader in the youth group at Berea Baptist Church in the suburbs of Chicago. Berea was a Southern Baptist church, but in name only, because the theology we taught was considered far too fundamentalist for most Southern Baptists at the time. Our pastors were influenced by the Independent Baptist tradition of Bob Jones University, beside which the teaching of most Southern Baptist churches seemed downright liberal.

Naturally, our youth group had some pretty extreme rules. We were taught to mortify the flesh by taking icy cold showers in the middle of winter. The girls in our youth group were not permitted to wear pants or shorts at any time—at church, school, or at home. When the girls at Berea Baptist School went to gym class, they wore dresses. When the girls in the youth group went tobogganing, they wore dresses. When they went swimming, they wore dresses.

We men were to be in three-piece suits every time we attended a church event, especially those of us who were aspiring preach-

169

ers. All of the boys in the youth group had to keep our hair short. In fact—and remember this is the era of Saturday Night Fever and big hair galore—we had to shave up over our ears every day. If any hair even touched your ears, you could be called into the youth pastor's office for what was euphemistically known as "a chat."

Rock-and-roll music was considered to be demonic, especially that 4/4 beat that placed the emphasis on the third beat of the measure—-ooh, that was the worst. The messages were mixed whether this dread syncopation originated with the pagan rites of the Druids or with the dark spirits of Africa, but our leaders were terrified of it, and we were forbidden to listen to it.

But I loved my high school radio show, and with the support of my father, in an act of open rebellion, of civil disobediance, I refused to stop playing the demon music. (Even though it was "Christian rock" which was even more suspect since it was seen to be a kind of pagan Trojan horse, promising edifying lyrics but delivering the demon beat just the same.)

Thus it was that my family found itself excommunicated from our religious community, which was a very painful thing for me, since all of my friends were in that youth group. But then something marvelous and grace-filled happened. My radio teacher was himself a committed Christian, according to him—I was leery because he was a white man with a sizable afro. Anyway, Mr. Moore invited me and my family to worship at his Methodist church for the month or so before we moved out to California.

To my great surprise, my mother agreed immediately, and the next Sunday we found ourselves amongst the Methodists. I thought the service very strange, the sermon suspiciously short, the vestments surreal, and the creed, with its affirmation of the "one holy catholic and apostolic church" frightening in the extreme. But what really made my head want to explode was the youth group.

It was a healthy, sizable youth group, and they invited me to participate in their car wash the next Saturday. When I arrived I was positively scandalized—the girls were all wearing pants, some of them even wore shorts! The boys had hair hanging down to their shoulders, and some of them wore Black Sabbath t-shirts, and other apparel advertising the Devil's music.

And the youth director! He was an early-thirties, unemployed slacker living with his parents, embodying the hippie dream as long as he possibly could, all the while encouraging us to do all these hippie things like love each other and not judge people. "What?" I asked myself. "Was this guy completely nuts?"

To put it mildly, I was horrified and confused. What confused me even more, however, was how they treated me. Instead of being aloof until they figured out whether I had an acceptable holiness factor or not, they *just loved me*. They welcomed me in with open arms, made me a part of them without a moment's hesitation or consideration, even giving me responsibility, for I found myself playing guitar at many events.

It rocked my world. The gift that the youth director and his motley little band of youth disciples gave me is inestimable, for he showed me that there was another way to hold my religion— a way that saw all people as equal and equally beloved of God, regardless of their behavior or manner of dress. They loved me without condition, and professed that they did so because that was how God loved them. I dare say that I stand in this pulpit today because of the ministry of these righteous heathens. For they showed me that what God was interested in was not how tenuously I held to the rules, but how willing I was to love people without condition or distinction. They utterly unmade my understanding of Christianity, and rebuilt it on an even firmer foundation—that of Jesus himself.

For in fact, as I learned much later, many of the teachings of Jesus were not original to him, but part of a very influential school of religious philosophy. Jesus was not an anomaly among

172 | john r. mabry

rabbis in his time. Instead, he stands in a line of Pharisaical rabbis influenced by the philosophy of a truly radical teacher, Hillel the Elder.

Hillel was born in Babylon, about seventy years before Jesus, and like Jesus, was descended from the house of David. He came from a reasonably well-off family, but left his wealth behind when, as a young man, he traveled from Babylon to Jerusalem to study Torah with the greatest teachers of his day.

He was so poor that he could not afford to pay the modest fee required of Torah students, and so he climbed up on the roof and listened at the window to the lecture and discussion, even though it was snowing hard. It was the evening of the Sabbath, and he must have fallen asleep there, because the next morning the teachers noticed that the room was dark even though the sun was out. Eventually they discovered Hillel perched on the roof, covered with five feet of snow! Even though it was the Sabbath, they brought him down from the roof and built up a roaring fire so he could get warm.

I like to think that this was Hillel's own epiphany. Just like the youth group turned my world upside down, it must have shocked Hillel to discover that there were revered teachers in Israel who considered his health, his lowly life, to be worth more than the sanctity of the Sabbath. For his sake, they profaned that most holy of days. That one act of kindness reverberated through Hillel's teaching for the rest of his life, and influenced his entire approach to Jewish Law and life.

Now, don't get me wrong, Hillel was as devoted as any Pharisee to the law and the ardent study of Torah. His famous seven rules are still held up as the hermeneutical plumbline for interpretation and argument. He fixed the norms of the midrash and halacha, and exhorted other teachers of the law not to esteem themselves above those they teach, but to be active members of their congregations.

In fact, he denied the distinction between the sacred and the profane, and insisted that every part of life was to be infused with the awareness of God's presence. "God says, 'If I am here, then everyone is here; if I am not here, nobody is here.'" Everything and everyone was sacred in Hillel's teaching. Once, when an honored guest was coming to his house for dinner, Hillel's wife made a special, elaborate meal for him. But then she saw a beggar outside the window. Being of the same heart and spirit as her husband, she took the dinner outside and gave the meal to him instead, trusting that God, her husband, and her guest would understand.

Hillel extended that kind of grace to himself as well. Once, after classes, he walked for a while with his students toward the center of the city. "Where are you headed, rabbi?" his students asked him.

"To perform a religious duty."

"What duty is that, teacher?" they asked.

"I'm going to soak at the public baths."

"*That's* a religious duty?" his students asked incredulously.

"Indeed," he told them. "Look, if the statues of kings that we find in the theaters are washed by the man appointed to watch over them, then how much more am I bound to keep this body clean, which has been fashioned in the image of the most high God?"

Hillel was not without his enemies and rivals, however. Another revered teacher at the time was Shammai the Elder, who played Confucious to Hillel's Lao Tzu. Shammai was a strict legalist, and was unwavering in his adherence to the letter of the Law. Hillel, in contrast, based his teaching on the *spirit* of the Law. The distinction between these two approaches really began with the rivalry between these two teachers. It is, of course, an argument that is still underway, but even in that day, the sparks flew when Hillel and Shammai clashed.

Shammai taught that there will be three groups on Judgement Day: the utterly righteous, the utterly corrupt, and those that are in between. The righteous, he taught, will inherit eternal life. The wicked will descend into Hades, and those in between will go to Hades but will cry out for redemption.

But Hillel had a different teaching, which infuriated the students of Shammai. Hillel taught, very simply, that the One who is the master of grace always tends towards grace.

In what is probably the most famous and oft-repeated tales, it is said that a Gentile came to Shammai and told him, "I will convert to Judaism if you can teach me the whole Law while I stand on one foot." Shammai was so incensed that he chased the man out into the street, lashing at him with a ruler.

So the same man went to Hillel and made the same offer, "I will convert to Judaism if you can teach me the whole Law while I stand on one foot." Without batting an eye, Hillel replied, "Do not do to your neighbor what you do not want done to you. That is the entire Law. The rest is commentary. Now go and learn."

One story says that once, when many of the great rabbis were gathered together at Jericho, a voice rumbled from the heavens, saying, "Among all those present here, there is one upon whom the Holy Spirit would have rested, if the time were ripe." And every man there looked right at Hillel.

Thus, it is not surprising that when Hillel was forty years old and his teacher died, all the other faculty of the school where he was studying resigned their posts so that he could step up and take his teacher's place as the head of the school. He continued in this position until his death, forty years later.

There are many parallels between Jesus' teaching and that of his predecessor, Hillel. It was Hillel who first formulated the golden rule. Hillel may have stated it in negative terms: "What you hate, do not do to others" and Jesus, in positive terms, "Do to others as you would have them do to you," but the point is the same. Hillel also said, "He who wishes to raise his name, lowers it," and "My humiliation is my exaltation; my exaltation is my humiliation."

This is very close to Jesus' own "Whoever exalts himself will be humbled and whoever humbles himself shall be exalted."

Hillel was called "the peacemaker," and Jesus, "the prince of peace." And whereas Jesus said, "Judge not lest you yourselves be judged," it was Hillel that originally said, "Do not judge anyone until you have walked in their shoes."

In fact, it is much more likely that Jesus was a Pharisaical rabbi of the school of Hillel than he was a savior come down from Heaven or an Essene or even some kind of rabbinical lone ranger. His emphasis on the spirit of the Law, rather than the letter, puts him squarely in the school of Hillel.

The school of Hillel and the followers of Jesus would continue to cross paths. When the early Jewish Christians were hauled before the Sanhedrin to defend their rabbi and his teachings, it is Hillel's grandson Gamaliel that advised caution, in case Jesus and his followers were indeed blessed by God and divinely guided. There is even evidence to suggest that this same Gamaliel was the teacher of a promising young student named Saul of Tarsus who would one day become St. Paul.

Clearly, Rabbi Hillel was a most remarkable man, and Judaism today would not be the same without him. Nor would Christianity; indeed, one must ask if there would have been a Christianity had it not been for the teaching of Hillel. For here is a man who taught that God's mercy is greater than God's justice, that people are more important than religion, that human beings have a responsibility to love and care for one another, and that there is no difference between the mundane world and the sacred, for where God is, there indeed is everyone and everything else.

I have come a long way from that teenager who was shocked when a Methodist boy with shoulder-length hair and a Black Sabbath T-shirt proclaimed, "Jesus rocks," for I can now say with a whole heart, "Yes, Jesus rocks, but only because Hillel rocked first."

God of mercy and love,
we thank you for the witness of thy servant Hillel,
and for the wisdom that he bequeathed to the House of Israel,
to Jesus, to us, and indeed, to the whole of the world.
Grant us the courage to love with as big a heart,
to seek after wisdom with even half as much fervor,
and a portion of his good humor and patience.
For in our love for our neighbors we see the true test of faith.
Help us to not be found wanting,
but abounding in every good thing,
for we ask this in the name of our rabbi, Jesus. Amen.

⊕ *Preached at Grace North Church on September 25, 2005.*

20 | kabbalists

When Leonard appeared for his spiritual direction appointment, he seemed to be carrying more than his share of heaviness. He didn't seem so much depressed as sad. The water in the kettle was hot, and I invited him to fix himself a cup of tea. He waved my suggestion away and just sat down, staring blankly into space.

I locked the door to the church office and lit a candle. "This is to remind us that there are three of us here," I said, and then we sat in silence for a while as we sought and found our center.

"How are you doing?" I opened the session.

"He's gone," he said.

"Who's gone?" I asked.

"God," Leonard answered. "I feel like he's just *gone*. I feel abandoned."

"Say more," I prodded.

"Well, when I was a kid, it seemed like God was everywhere. God was *real*, you know? And then, when I was in college, I became an Episcopalian. And God was even more real. I felt his

177

presence whenever I got up before the sun, whenever I stepped foot into church, whenever I said Compline in my study at night. I felt so...held, so loved, so cared for. But that was twenty years ago. Now, when I try to feel God, I just feel tired. Where did God go, John? It's like I got up one morning, and God had just *moved*, and didn't leave a forwarding address. I miss the intimacy I used to feel. I miss feeling cared for and loved. I *miss* God."

Almost every client I have in spiritual direction who has had a regular spiritual practice grounded in a specific tradition has uttered some variation on Leonard's complaint. Most of us have had experiences of incredible intimacy and grace, and then somewhere along the line it feels like we took a wrong turn, and suddenly God and us are walking separate roads. We feel bereft of a sense of primal safety and warmth that was precious to us, and we do not know how to get it back.

This experience is so common as to be archetypal. Every religion has a memory of a time of divine union that has somehow been lost. In the Jewish and Christian traditions, we symbolize this experience with the story of the Garden of Eden. We all knew what it was like to be in Eden in the womb, in early childhood, and in times of spiritual ecstacy and intimacy. But the hard truth of human life is that we cannot live permanently in the Garden, and we will all be cast out into the world of tears where we must earn our keep by the sweat of our brow, and bring things to birth only through our own suffering.

But that does not stop us from wanting to regain that paradise lost. Indeed, one can see every religion on earth as humankind's attempt to rattle the gates and gain entry once again. No tradition has made this promise of paradise regained quite so explicit as the Jewish mystical path known as the Kabbalah.

According to legend, the Kabbalah was first taught to the angels before the foundation of the earth. Then God made the Garden, and placed within it the two trees: the Tree of the Knowledge of Good and Evil, and the Tree of Life. God made Adam and Eve, and gave them the gifts of every plant in the Garden, with the single exception of the Tree of Knowledge. If one ate of the Tree of Knowledge one would become as wise as God, if one ate of the Tree of Life, one would be immortal, and would in effect *be* God. Since God is a jealous god and cannot countenance rivals, this could not be allowed. So when Adam and Eve disobeyed God's command not to eat of the fruit of the Tree of the Knowledge, they were cast out of the Garden before they could eat of the Tree of Life. But as they were leaving the Garden, the archangel Raziel gave Adam a crash course in the Kabbalah, so that through great effort, he might yet one day eat of the Tree of Life and regain his place in the Garden.

Adam did not pass this knowledge along to his children, but the secret knowledge was given to Abraham thousands of years later. Abraham taught it to his children, but once again the knowledge was lost when the Israelites were in slavery in Egypt.

But it was God's will that the Kabbalah not be lost to the children of humanity, so it was given once again, this time to Moses. The first time Moses climbed Mt. Sinai, he was given the Ten Commandments—the outer, exoteric teachings of Judaism, which could be written down. But then Moses ascended the mountain again, and this time God gave to him the Kabbalah, the inner, esoteric teachings of Judaism, which could only be passed on by word of mouth.

This time the secret wisdom was not lost, but cherished, tightly guarded, and dutifully passed from one generation to another. The word "Kabbalah" literally means "that which is revealed," and was named by the Spanish mystic, Solomon Ibn Gabriol, during the height of the Spanish enlightenment in which Jews, Christians, and Muslims alike shared their intellectual heritages with one another, and science and philosophy took hold as never before in Europe.

Though it was for a very long time an oral tradition only, people inevitably started writing the secrets down. The first major

Kabbalistic text is the *Sepher Yetzirah,* the "Book of Creation," which is attributed to an early Kabbalist named Rabbi Akiva, and was probably produced sometime in the fifth century of the Common Era.

According to legend, four pious men were experimenting with the early Jewish system of Merkobah mysticism, from the foundation of which the Kabbalah later arose. Merkobah mysticism was concerned with triggering out of body experiences during which the spiritual pilgrim would behold the chariot and the palace of God, and visit the various heavens, divining in the process the inner workings of the universe.

During one of these spirit journeys, these four men each gained access to paradise. One of them lost all desire to live in the world, and died instantly. Another of the men beheld paradise and was so overcome that his mind snapped and he went stark raving mad. The third man beheld a great shining light in which he clearly saw not one God, but two, and was exiled as a heretic. Only one man, Rabbi Akiva, entered into paradise safely, and returned again intact.

A fourteenth-century mystic named Moses de Leon claimed to have found scrolls written by a student of Rabbi Akiva. These scrolls became the second great text of Kabbalistic lore, called the *Zohar*, also known as the "Book of Splendor." Now, scholars agree that the text is probably not the product of Rabbi Akiva's pupil in the third century, but a glorious forgery penned by Moses de Leon himself.

In all fairness to this medieval Moses, he was probably compiling many oral sources of great antiquity, doing everyone a great favor by putting them all in one place. Furthermore, we cannot be too hard on him for attributing his work to someone of authority in the history of Judaism, as this was a very common practice. Many of the books of the Bible, in fact, were not written by the people to whom they were attributed. Saying that someone famous had written a book was a sure-fire way to give it instant credibility and assure it a wide readership. Moses de Leon was simply following a great and ancient tradition.

So just what are these secret teachings that the Jewish mystics have so carefully guarded and faithfully transmitted from one generation to the next?

The secrets all revolve around one of the central symbols in the Garden of Eden story: the Tree of Life. Instead of an actual tree with branches and leaves, however, the Kabbalists viewed it as a metaphorical tree, a mostly vertical map of the various universes, their properties, and how they interpenetrate one another. Finally, it is a teaching about how these worlds intersect and inform our own world, and how knowledge of the properties of these worlds can aid our journey into spiritual and psychological maturity until we find a place of renewed innocence, gaining entry once more to Paradise.

The Kabbalists saw these worlds as being emanations of God, called *sephiroth*, each being the embodiment of a cluster of related divine attributes, ranging from the highest and most abstract realities to the lowest and most material spheres, which is where we live.

Rabbi Isaac Luria led one of the most celebrated Kabbalistic schools in the sixteenth century in a little village in Gallilee. He taught that God is evolving along with creation, and in fact, needs creation in order to grow. All of nature, including and especially humankind, are necessary for God's self-realization. We have the choice to either oppose God's evolution, or to cooperate, participate, and assist God in the task of evolution, for without our help God cannot find fulfillment.

Luria taught that there are three stages to creation: the first stage is Limitation. In order for God to evolve, God must have an "other" to relate to. So God emptied a region of the universe of the divine Presence, creating a pocket of dualism in which a universe of distinct things could emerge.

Then came the second stage: into this pocket of duality God

placed ten lights, or realms of being called *sephirot*. Into these spheres God poured his creative energy. Unfortunately, this creative force came out too forcefully, and six of the ten spheres burst, and many of them fell. The sphere that fell the lowest was the one that contained the physical universe. But it was strong—though it fell the farthest, it did not burst, and into it fell uncountable shards of divine light from the broken vessels.

According to Luria, there is a shard of that divine light in every human being. We are now in the third stage of creation: known as *Tikkun olam,* or the repair of the world. The sparks of divinity in each of us long to be once more reunited, to be joined once more in unitive bliss, to return to the Garden, if you will. It is our job to repair these broken vessels, to reunite them within ourselves, and in so doing, put the universe back in its proper order. We do this by a process of painstaking psychological and spiritual work. The main jist of this work is the reunification of the feminine and masculine aspects of our psyches—remember Judith? She embodied intuitively what the teaching of the Kabbalists made explicit. Thus, Kabbalism is a kind of interior Tantra that facilitates our own healing, the healing of the world, and ultimately, the healing of God.

This work of healing is effected by the exploration and integration of the powers dominated by each of the *sephirot*, the original worlds of light. Working with them in reverse order, the seeker eventually climbs up the Tree of Life from the world of dualism and matter to the womblike unitive consciousness of the highest realm. Just what are these powers, these hidden universes? Make sure you've got film in your camera and a good supply of sunscreen, for we are about to take a whirlwind tour of these various worlds.

At the top of the Tree is the *sephira* called Keter, which means "crown." This is the highest, most spiritual emanation, which is beyond all being. It is no-thing, the great nothing, and yet it contains all things. It is the ultimate—and ultimately unknowable—

source of all things. To experience Keter is to be one with all things, one with God.

Descending the tree we come to the second *sephira*: Hokhmah, which means "wisdom." This *sephira* is the masculine divine principle. In Taoist terms we would call this the *yang* energy, the active, creative force that produces all things. Hokhmah is pure generativity.

Opposite Hokhmah is Binah, the third *sephira*. Binah means "understanding," and it embodies the passive, feminine divine principle. The Taoists would call this *yin*, and for the Kabbalists it provides containment for the unbridled creative force of Hokhmah, creating balance between active and passive forces, between chaos and order, movement and rest. Binah provides boundaries and limits, without which the creativity of Hokhmah cannot be productive.

The fourth *sephira* is called Hesed, which embodies divine love and mercy. This world is the source of the compassion and generosity of God. This is the face of divinity that is the God of love, the one we like to focus on, and the properties it generates are likewise positive, such as pleasure and joy.

As you might expect, this world is linked to another that provides balance. For the fifth *sephira* is Gevurah, the world of justice, judgement, and severity. Once again the expansion of one *sephira*, the generosity of Hesed, is restrained by another, the limitation of Gevurah, because the buck has to stop somewhere. Psychologically, Gevurah represents our conscience, which provides appropriate limits for pleasure and the epicurean excesses of Hesed.

Ensuring that the mercy and judgement are kept in more or less equal measure, there is between them a whole universe devoted to balance, called Tiferet. For when mercy and judgement are held together, beauty, compassion, and health can be assured. Tiferet is the center of the tree, it might even be seen as the center of gravity for all the worlds, holding them all in their proper place. Psychologically it represents our higher self, the abode of both our guardian angel and our inner child.

These are all pretty abstract worlds, but when we get near the bottom of the tree we enter into the realms of human experience. The seventh *sephira* is called Nezah, which embodies passion and victory. This is the abode of the procreative energies of the worlds, it is from this realm that creativity is generated. It is the seat of sexuality, the place where poetry, songs, art, and puppy love all come from.

Balancing the passion of Nezah is the eighth *sephira*, Hod. This is intellect, the realm of thought, of splendor and majesty. If Nezah represents the emotional energies of humanity, Hod represents the cool clarity of the mind and its discernments. It is from this sphere that communication emerges. This being the age of information, Hod is a very happening place, these days.

The ninth *sephira* is Yesod, which is the place of the imagination and dreams. If Jung's collective unconscious has its origin in any one of the *sephirot*, it is probably this one. The Kabbalists also call this realm foundation, for as scripture says, "without a vision, the people perish." Yesod is the realm of visions, the non-rational repository of images and ideas that inform and inspire all beings.

Finally the last *sephira* is Malkhut, which represents the body on a personal level, and "the Kingdom" as a collective reality. Malkhut is the gate of manifestation, it is the phenomenal universe, the world of matter and form, of earth, air, fire, and water in which we make our home. This is the world we live in physically, but which is informed and shaped by the archetypcal forces of all the higher *sephirot*.

Got all that? Are you ready for a pop quiz? This all seems very complicated, I know, but in fact it is merely the tip of the iceberg. It actually seems to me that the strategy of the Kabbalists is to so utterly overwhelm the spiritual seeker with excruciating minutia that they break down in mental exhaustion, and in the momentary absence of all thought induced by this breakdown, enlightenment either exalts the seeker into the presence of the Holy One, or dissolves the sanity of the seeker altogether.

It sounds baroque, incomprehensible, arbitrary, and yet the Kabbalah has stood the test of time. It has withstood pogroms and persecution, and it will withstand the indignity of Madonna hawking her magical "Kabbalah Water" as well. The mystical insights of this system have influenced not only Jews, but Muslims and Christians as well, becoming the backbone of western occult theory. The entire western mystery tradition is beholden to this system, and it is impossible to understand any of the movements of western esotericism without a firm grounding in its sublime and complicated theory of reality. In it we see the beginnings of scientific speculation, the first forays into process theology, and the first conscious exploration of transpersonal archetypes.

But more than any of this, it is, in its essence, a desire to return to a place of peace and safety that we once knew, and know no more. It is the sentimental longing for the innocence of childhood that we cannot recapture. Arthur Deikman describes this longing in his book *The Wrong Way Home* as the feeling of being a child in the back seat of your parents' car coming home from a late night visit to friends. Mommy and Daddy are in the front seat, all is right with the world, and the sleepy lull of motion creates in us a feeling of dreamy euphoria and safety that most of us would do anything to feel again.

But the truth is you cannot go home again. The gates to Eden are shut, and we will never be that blissfully ignorant again. We have eaten from the Tree of Knowledge, and we are familiar with the taste of betrayal, bitterness, and toil.

Yet the Kabbalah promises that such peace and communion is not an ever-receding goal, but that a new intimacy, a new peace, a new Eden may be discovered. Like Blake's *Songs of Innocence and Experience,* the Kabbalah promises that a new innocence is possi-

186 | john r. mabry

ble; one that does not turn its back on all we have learned, but instead teaches us a new way of holding our experience that eschews cynicism and resentment, and creates a space for wonder and joy to be born anew. We can become, as Jesus admonished us, as little children once more. In working the Tree of Life, we gather up the splintered shards of our lives and find a way to become whole again. And in healing the dualities within ourselves, the Kabbalists promise us that we are healing the world—that indeed, we are healing God.

Baruch hata, Adonai, sovereign of the universe,
who set the spheres of the heavens in their places,
and in thy infinite wisdom, made of them teachers for us,
for that by means of study and contemplation,
we may find a way to return to innocence.
Help us to pursue this not only for our own redemption,
but for the redemption of the world,
as we seek to find those parts that are lost,
heal those that are wounded,
and befriend those who are alone.
For you are God beyond beginning,
who has set in our hearts the divine spark
that will not rest until it is gathered
once more into paradise.
Blessed be the name of God, now and forever. Amen.

⊕ *Preached at Grace North Church on October 23, 2005.*

NOTE

Information for this sermon from *The Practical Kabbalah Guidebook* by C.J.M. Hopking (New York: Sterling Publishing Co., 2001).

21 | jesus

Not long ago, I was lunching with an acquaintance who shot me a look full of distaste and bewilderment. "Why Jesus?" she said.

"What do you mean?" I asked.

"After all the horrors done in the name of Christianity—hell, even you have suffered from its abuse! How in the world can you call yourself a Christian?"

And I laughed at her. Not because she had said anything foolish but because it is a question I have often asked myself. She eyed me quizzically until my amusement passed and made it clear that the question still held. "Well?"

I carefully considered my answer. There were lots of ways I could go with it. I decided the simplest was the best. "I guess it's because I'm in love with Jesus."

She had to chew on that one for a while. So did I. It's a hard one to argue with, because love is not rational, it's obsessive, compelling, and sometimes utterly insane. It was, I decided, a good answer. It didn't occupy her for long, though.

"Okay, fair enough. But why? Why Jesus and not Buddha or someone else even mildly more palatable?"

"Well, first of all, let's make a distinction between Jesus and Christianity," I said. "They are not the same thing. I'm in love with Jesus, Christianity has problems."

"Okay, forget Christianity. Why Jesus?"

It's a very good question, and I'm not sure my answers to her were my best, or definitive. So I'd like to take this sermon to answer them in a way that makes sense for me right now.

First of all, who was this Jesus guy, anyway? Our best guesses are that he was born to a poor family in Nazareth, that his father was a carpenter, and his mother was very young at the time of his birth. His uncle was the high priest of the Temple in Jerusalem, and Jesus was probably reared in the pietistic tradition of the Pharisees, so he would have been steeped in the Jewish faith from his earliest days.

There are lots of legends, of course—the whole virgin birth thing, and the whole "Word come down from Heaven" thing. But the earliest records of Jesus' life, the gospels of Mark and Thomas, do not know these stories, or they do not consider them credible enough to relate.

We know little about his childhood, other than the legends of his ability to impress the socks off of his elders at the Temple when he was twelve. The real stories about him begin when he goes to his cousin, John, to be baptized.

Now John was a wild man and revered by many in Israel as a prophet. The people were suffering under the military occupation of the Romans. The Jews, who, like most people, tended to interpret the present in reference to their past, remembered the other times they had been an enslaved or occupied peoples. They remembered Egypt and Babylon, and their tradition told them that these evils were visited upon them because they had been unfaithful.

Many in Jesus' day pointed to the Temple hierarchy, to their corrupt collaboration with the Roman occupiers, and proclaimed this was the cause of their situation. Others interpreted the problem as a more personal and internal one. The hearts of the Jews, they said, were hard and not properly submissive to God. Others said that God would help them only if they acted to liberate themselves, and they waited for a messiah, a new king, to lead them into the fray.

Many people looked to John the Baptist as the harbinger of this messiah. "Make straight the way of the Lord!" he cried, and invited any who would hear him to be baptized, to be washed of their sins, to ready the Jewish people for their deliverance.

When Jesus came to be baptized it was his personal way of saying "yes" to God. The gospels tell us that many people recognized him as the one they were waiting for right there and then, and began to follow him. He did not dissuade them, and he taught them. But the content of his teaching was difficult for any of them to swallow, for it was not at all what they wanted—or were prepared to hear.

For Jesus was not merely a prophet, nor was he a military leader or a king. He was, quite simply, a mystic. He understood that he was in God and God was in him, and he called those around him to a similar awareness.

And the great thing about Jesus was that he called *everybody*. Not just the people who were, in some way or another, *worthy*. "Worthiness" did not seem to be a word in Jesus' dictionary. Either everyone was worthy or no one was. So when the religious leaders of his day insisted that there were people who were acceptable and people who were unacceptable, he defied them and refused to acknowledge any such distinctions, welcoming into his company the self-righteous and the criminal with equal hospitality.

The great symbol of this was his practice of eating dinner with people. In Jesus' day, a rabbi would only share a table with someone he approved of, and thought that God approved of. So Jesus outraged many of his contemporaries by breaking bread not only with holy men and women, but equally with prostitutes and political traitors.

This shows the profound mysticism of Jesus' insight. He saw his followers and friends as God saw them. He viewed them through the lens of God's outrageous generosity rather than through the lens of religious propriety. And when he did that, when he embraced those who had always been told they were unlovable, something truly miraculous happened—people believed him. They received his love and felt *lovable*, perhaps for the first time in their lives. In loving them he restored to them their dignity, their hope, their humanity, and just as important, their sense of relatedness to God.

In the *Gospel of Mark* we are told of a time when Jesus was preaching to a packed house, and four friends tried to figure out a way to get their paralyzed friend close enough to Jesus to be healed. So they cut a hole in the roof and lowered him down, right in front of the teacher.

Jesus was amazed at the love and devotion of these men, and at their faith in him. He said to the paralyzed man, "Your sins are forgiven."

But there were some other Pharisees, teachers of Jesus' own religious movement, who were outraged. "He can't say that!" they cried. "This is blasphemy! Only God can forgive sins!"

This seemed to amuse Jesus because he said to them, "So what's easier, forgiving sins, or making the paralyzed walk?" Then he turned to the paralyzed man and said, "Get up and walk." And according to the story, that is exactly what the man did.

Traditional Christianity interprets this to mean that Jesus can forgive sins because *he is God*, but I believe something much more radical is going on. Jesus didn't tell this man his sins were forgiven because he, Jesus, in that moment, forgave the man's sins. Instead, I believe he was telling the man the simple truth: "Your sins *are* forgiven. God holds nothing against you. Never has.

Never will. No tally is being kept of your misdeeds. No one is holding anything against you but you."

The same thing is true of us. There is no need to confess, there is no need for absolution. God holds nothing against you, nor ever has, nor ever will. Your soul is free. That, my friends, is the Good News of Jesus. That and only that. Anything less than that is not good news and is not worthy of your attention.

Of course, this is just as shocking a message to religious people today—especially Christians—as it was in Jesus' own time. Religious people somehow feel like they've worked hard and deserve to be God's favorites, and it pisses them off when upstart teachers like Jesus deprive them of their pride of place. But that's just one of those things I love so much about Jesus.

Jesus didn't deny the reality of sin. Sin is real. Sin happens when people hurt each other, and we do it to one another all the time, with varying degrees of severity. But sin is not an indelible stain on the soul. Instead, the pain that results from sin leaves behind something else much harder to eradicate: a grudge.

Traditional Christianity teaches us that human sin separates us from God because God holds a grudge against us as a result of our sin. In St. Anselm's theory—the Roman Catholic theory of the atonement—human beings, because of our sin, have robbed God of the honor due him, and because he holds a grudge against us for that, "he" cannot embrace us until Jesus comes along and restores his honor. In Calvin's theory—the Protestant version—human sin has violated God's sense of order and imperiled the justice that God insists must be in place. As long as human sin goes unpunished, God's justice is unsatisfied, and God nurses a grudge against humankind until Jesus comes along and agrees to bear the punishment for the sins of the world.

Note that in both the Catholic and Protestant versions of this theory, the grudge that separates humankind from God resides in God. Because God holds this grudge against us, "he" cannot embrace us or in any way be in communion with us.

This is baloney. It is completely contrary to Jesus' teaching. Remember the Prodigal Son? A young man begs his father to give him his inheritance early, and he goes off and squanders it all on wine and women. Once he has blown every penny, he spends months eating out of garbage cans because his pride will not allow him to return to his father and say, "Wow, I really blew it. I don't expect you to treat me as your son any more, but could I just, like, have a job?"

Eventually, however, things get so bad that he swallows his pride and walks back to his father's farm. His dad misses him terribly, and is always scanning the horizon for some sign of his long-lost son. Then one day, he can barely believe his eyes—his son is walking up the road!

The old man drops whatever it was he was holding, and runs with every ounce of strength to his son, whom he embraces. He kisses him and nearly sops the lad in his tears of relief and joy. His son was not expecting this kind of welcome. He tries to apologize, to ask for a job, to be treated as a servant, but the old man will have none of it. He puts fine clothes on the boy and orders a party to be held in his honor.

This is not a man who is holding any grudges. The only thing stopping the young man from returning to his father's embrace was his own internal sense of guilt and shame. And so it is with us. The grudge for human sin does not reside in God, *it resides in us.* God holds nothing against us. God cannot wait to run to meet us, to catch us up in wild and loving embrace. It is we who cannot forgive ourselves. It is we who feel unworthy of such love and communion. As Meister Eckhart once wrote, "God is at home. It is we who have gone out for a walk."

This is the powerful mysticism of Jesus. We are in God, and God is in us. God does not hold us at arm's length because of our sin—we hold God at arm's length because of our shame. Jesus shakes his head, says, "Silly humans—can't you just let yourselves be loved?" And then he just *loves us.* And in doing this, he shows us God.

And there are no strings attached to this love, much as those "religious" people might insist otherwise. You don't have to *do* anything to earn God's love, you don't have to *believe* anything, you don't have to pray any particular prayer, perform any particular rituals, or join any particular organization. You don't have to do *anything*. God *already* loves you. Wholly and completely. Without reservation. Now and forever. No ifs, ands, or buts.

And *this* is why I love Jesus. As the old Sunday School song put it, "O, how I love Jesus, O how I love Jesus, O how I love Jesus—because he first loved me." That is why I follow Jesus. That is why I call myself a "Christian." Not because I believe any of the stuff ordinary, orthodox Christianity teaches, because I don't. Most Christians would not consider me a member of their club. But that doesn't matter to me one little bit. It is not their opinion of me that matters. It is Jesus' opinion of me that matters, and of that, I have no doubts whatsoever. Jesus ate dinner with whores, priests, traitors, and thieves. And today, at this very table, he eats dinner with me, and with you as well.

And in so doing he gives my life back to me: my dignity, my wholeness, and my humanity. He says, "I hold nothing against you. God holds nothing against you, either. And if you can let go of the grudge you hold against yourself, you can experience the same unity with the Divine that I do. Your sins are forgiven you. Now get up and *walk*."

Jesus, how we have tortured your teaching,
how horribly we have twisted it
from the simple thing of beauty you delivered to us,
and turned it into a weapon with which to oppress and enslave
both one another and ourselves.
For this we are sorry, but we know
that you do not hold it against us,
nor does God.

Help us to forgive ourselves for our abominable past,
help us to remember where we have gone wrong,
and to do it differently in the future,
Help us to forgive ourselves even the most heinous crimes,
so that we can start again,
and have a chance to know ourselves to be
worthy of your unstoppable love.
And if we cannot, help us to trust that you will not stop loving us,
even when we cannot love ourselves. Amen.

⊕ *Written specifically for this collection.*

22 | hildegard of bingen

My friend Megan was a very successful businesswoman. She used to do organizational development work—big clients, big accounts, big stress. She made a *lot* of money, very fast, but it did not come without a price. She literally worked herself into the ground, and she got sick.

It was one of those mystery illnesses that the doctors couldn't quite put their fingers on. She took rounds and rounds of tests, but the upshot of it all was that she couldn't get out of bed for six months. Now this was not a case of a *prima donna* deciding she was tired of working. It was a case of an extreme workaholic pushing her body to the point where it simply said, "Enough!" and refused to cooperate any further with her success-driven insanity.

It was during those long months of illness that it occurred to her how precious her life was, how very short it was, and how she had just one shot to do something worthwhile in this world. She began to view her body as a source of wisdom rather than an uncooperative mule, and realized that what she had been granted was not so much a sickness as a revelation.

195

And as she surrendered to the wisdom of her body, as she embraced her exhaustion, something shifted inside her, and the life began to return. It came slowly, slowly enough that she did not forget what she had just learned, and instead of leaping back into the rat race, she went to the Mercy Center instead and trained as a spiritual director.

That was where we met, and we became fast friends. Like me, she had come from an abusive Baptist background, and also like me, she was determined to do something meaningful with her "one wild and precious life" (to quote Mary Oliver).

She didn't abandon organizational development work, but as she recovered, she returned to it as a different animal, and with a different focus. Her objective now was not productivity at any cost, but the cost of productivity—specifically the toll it takes on the soul. Jesus said it best: "What will you gain if you win the whole world but lose your soul?" Megan began to ask this question wherever she went, and of everyone with whom she worked.

She began to teach CEOs and organizations how to tend to the "soul" of a corporation, to do values clarification, and to train employees in spiritual sensitivity and deep listening. She now goes into Fortune 500 companies and "feels out" the spiritual and emotional health of their environment, making observations and recommendations to the powers-that-be. And she routinely has one-on-one spiritual direction sessions with CEOs, standing toe-to-toe with them and challenging them to do the right thing with both the financial and human treasure entrusted to them.

Megan is one of the people I admire most in my life. She's also one of the most fun to hang out with. She reminds me an awful lot of our mystic today, and in many ways, I believe she is carrying on the legacy of this noble woman, Hildegard of Bingen.

Hildegard was born in 1098 to a noble family in Germany. She was the tenth child, and so according to tradition, she was "tithed" to God and handed over to the nuns when she was only eight years old. Hildegard was entrusted to a very popular spiritual teacher named Jutta who took her under her wing and raised her, teaching her to read, to sing, and to pray the hours.

Jutta quickly saw that Hildegard was anything but an ordinary child. She was, in fact, a seer of visions from as early as she could remember. Hildegard later wrote about her experiences of receiving visions—it was like a white sheet was pulled over her eyes, and pictures appeared in her mind, accompanied by voices that interpreted them.

At first she told people about them, but she soon realized that not everyone could see visions, and that they looked at her strangely when she spoke of them. She realized how dangerous this could be for her, and for years she refused to speak of them. Instead, she labored tirelessly for the abbey. She was loyal to Jutta for all the old nun's days, and when her mentor finally died, Hildegard was elected abbess.

In the medieval Catholic system, to be an abbess is as high in the hierarchy as a woman could go. To be an abbess, in fact, is to hold the same rank as a bishop, and Hildegard bore the responsibility with determination and grace. She worked hard, but she kept quiet about her visions, even as their intensity increased. The voice that accompanied the visions began to demand of her, "Write what you see," but she refused, and as a result of this great inner conflict, she fell ill.

The voice in her visions berated her, and even threatened her, demanding to be spoken aloud. Finally, she collapsed beneath the weight of them, and confessed everything to her spiritual director. Her spiritual director was no slouch, and quickly put two and two together. He went to his own abbot, and with the support of Hildegard's community, she was ordered to obey her visions, and to write down what she saw.

So write she did. She was given a scribe to help her, and she began the first of her nine books, *Scivias*, which means, "Know the Way!" She was forty-two years old when she began to record her visions, and though she occasionally fell ill, it was never like her great illness, and the good she did in the second half of her life is truly remarkable.

She was, to put it mildly, a genius. In addition to her visions, she wrote on pharmacology and biology, morality and ethics, and kept up a hefty correspondence with some of the most powerful and important figures of her age. Her cause was championed by St. Bernard of Clairvaux, who presented a copy of her first book of visions to the Pope, who declared them divinely inspired and urged her to continue God's work.

Amazingly, however, she is best remembered today as a composer. A trip to any music store with a halfway decent Classical section will yield a whole slew of Hildegard CDs. She wrote liturgical music for the use of the nuns in her own abbey, and what music it was. It was ethereal and strange. Similar in some ways to the plainsong being sung by the male monks in the next abbey over, they were nevertheless completely unlike anything ever heard before—or since for that matter. If you have never heard a CD of Hildegard's music, do yourself a favor and rush out in a buying frenzy. You will not be sorry you did. It is amazing stuff—strange, angelic, uplifting, and unsettling, all at the same time. Her music falls squarely into the "not to be missed" category.

She was a wild woman. She was brave. And most of all, she was prophetic. She wrote letters to the Holy Roman Emperor and chastened him for his abuses of power. She wrote to the Pope and told him that the church was too corrupt and that he needed to work harder to reform it. She wrote bishops and kings, and people from every strata of society. One biographer dubbed her "the medieval Dear Abbey," and indeed, she dispensed advice and correction to anyone who asked for it.

Don't get the idea that she was negative, though. Behind all of her exhortations was a profound faith in veriditas, the "greening power of God," that courses through all things and renews them. Bavaria is a lush country, and it is easy to see how, surrounded by such potent verdancy, someone as spiritually sensitive as

Hildegard could actually perceive the unstoppable *élan vital*, the life force that grew and regenerated everything she saw. What is interesting is that she universalized this force, and saw it as an aspect of God. *Veriditas* is at work not just in plants, but in humans, in animals, in society, in any thing and place where God is creating, healing, and growing.

Late in her life, she decided to take her show on the road, and traveled Europe as its most celebrated preacher. This was unheard of for a woman at the time, but she preached to packed cathedrals throughout Germany and as far as Switzerland and Paris.

She had one last little political tussle to deal with at the end of her life. Apparently she had allowed a young man who had been excommunicated to be buried on the abbey grounds. Her bishop censured the abbey and shut down the singing of the daily prayers. Hildegard mounted a fierce defense, and said that the young man had repented, had been given last rites and communion, had died in the arms of Holy Mother Church, and had every right to rest in its grounds.

Hildegard was a woman who got her way, and she stared down the bishop this time, too. The Daily Office was restored to the abbey and Hildegard died soon after, on September 17, 1179.

Hildegard's mysticism is a profound one for us, because it emphasizes the importance of creation, not in terms of "natural resources" but in terms of a holy ecology, supporting and supported by human beings living in community and harmony with all that God has made. How can you not think of our current ecological crises when you hear her say:

> Now in the people that were meant to be green, there is no more life of any kind. There is only shriveled barrenness. The winds are burdened by the utterly awful stink of evil, selfish goings-on. Thunderstorms menace. The air belches out the filthy uncleanliness of the peoples. There pours forth an unnatural, a loathsome darkness, that withers the green, and wizens the fruit that was to serve as food for the people. Sometimes this layer of

air is full, full of a fog that is the source of many destructive and barren creatures that destroy and damage the earth, rendering it incapable of sustaining humanity.... God desires that all the world be pure...the earth should not be injured; the earth should not be destroyed. As often as the elements of the world are violated by ill-treatment, so God will cleanse them. God will cleanse them through the sufferings, through the hardships of humankind.[1]

That's prophesy, folks. And in a time when women were routinely burned at the stake for being uppity, Hildegard was, to my way of thinking, one of the gutsiest women in human history. She told off Popes, and if our current powers-that-be would listen, she's be telling them off, too.

But that's where we come in. Hildegard is not a prophet because she foresaw the ecological disaster that has befallen us. Prophesy has nothing to do with seeing the future. Prophesy is the willingness to stand up to the powers-that-be and tell the truth. None of the Hebrew prophets foretold the future, they just spoke the truth about the consequences of human evil: "If you do that, this is what will happen."

Hildegard is an important mystic for us not only because she saw the holiness of creation, and our interdependence with it, although she did that. She is important because she insists that we have the courage to stand up to those who would wither the holy things of this earth, and say, "Enough! Not on my watch!"

And she insists that we do this not only for creation, not only for God, and not only for our fellow creatures, but for ourselves—because as she and my friend Megan so aptly illustrate, when we are not doing what God has put us here to do, when we do not stand up and take our place in the great scheme of things, when we refuse to live into our potential, *we get sick.*

And Hildegard is all about calling us to health. She struggled with sickness in herself, and it was illness that led her to a far more profound healing than simply the alleviation of her own symptoms. Her illness led her to act for the healing of the earth. May we be so foolish, so wise, and so bold as she.

Let us pray in the words of Hildegard:

O Holy Spirit, clear fountain,
in thee we perceive how God gathers the perplexed
and seeks out what has been lost.
Bulwark of life, thou art the hope of oneness for all that is separate.
Thou art the girdle of propriety, thou art holy salvation.
Shelter those caught in evil, free those in bondage,
for the divine power wills it.
Thou art the mighty way in which every thing that is in the heavens,
on the earth, and under the earth,
is penetrated with connectedness,
is shot through with relatedness.
Fire of love, breath of all holiness,
thou who art so delicious to our hearts,
infuse us deeply with the good, green smell of virtue. Amen.[2]

⊕ *Preached at Grace North Church on October 29, 2006.*

NOTES

1 Gabriele Uhlein. *Meditations with Hildegard of Bingen* (Santa Fe: Bear and Company, 1983), pps. 77-9.

2 *Ibid.,* 40-41.

23 | thomas merton

I was talking to my mother on the phone the other day, telling her about a recent visit to a favorite synagogue, and she said to me, "You know, I always had a feeling that you would convert to Judaism one day."

It was a very odd thing for my mother to say, and it was especially odd to hear a note of wistfulness in her voice as she said it, as if to say, "Ah, if only you'd become a Jew and not what you are—a Catholic!"

Perhaps I am being too sensitive and inferring what is not there—but I know my mother, and I think it is not my imagination. In my own defense, I longed to blurt out, "Hey, at least I'm still a Christian!" But either the Baptist mind is actually synaptically different from other minds, or the prejudice against Catholics is so huge as to border on the irrational. I'm tempted to argue for the former position, but I think the latter is probably true. As Mike Warnke once said, "When Catholics die they just put them in the basement and send them straight off to Hell—do not pass 'Go,' do not collect $200."

I suppose I should have some compassion for my mother's horror at my conversion, but I don't. What I remember most about the period when I first started delving into Catholic theology was my own outrage at discovering that almost everything I had been told as a boy about what Catholics believed was a lie. Catholics do not, for instance, actually worship saints; nor do they believe you have to earn your salvation; or that the host will bleed if you bite it; or any number of other ludicrous things I was brought up to think about them.

Instead, what I discovered, when I actually started to investigate it for myself, was a treasure-house of human depth and spiritual wisdom. Through the ceremonial worship I learned that spirituality was more than simply an exercise for the mind, but one into which my whole body was invited. Through its saints and scholars I learned about the deep mysticism that dissolved the absolute wall between Creator and creation. In its art and architecture I learned that beauty and sublimnity transformed the soul and spoke to it of its true nature.

But the most important thing Catholicism gave me was history. Growing up in the evangelical church, there was this odd sense that somewhere about one hundred years after Jesus the true church winked out of existence, only to magically reappear 1,700 years later with the establishment of the first Baptist congregation on American soil by Roger Williams in Rhode Island.

But an amazing thing happened to me when I started reading Catholic theology: it occurred to me that the whole of Christian history—the art, the music, the saints, the scholasticism, the mysticism, the heretics, the theology, the ceremony, and the magic—that it all belonged to me! That this was my heritage!

It was almost too much, this revelation. I felt drunk. I felt like I had won the lottery or stumbled upon a cache of buried treasure. This was *my* history, these were *my* people, this was *my* culture!

It was during this time that I read a book by a man named Thomas Merton titled *The Seven Storey Mountain*. It was an earth-shattering experience for me. It is an autobiography written by a man who was only twenty-seven at the time—which was exactly my own age when I read it. It is also the story of this man's conversion to Catholicism. As you might imagine, I found much to resonate with in this work.

The Seven Storey Mountain was published in 1948, and became an instant best-seller, which seems unlikely given its content. In it, Merton describes his early life, how he was orphaned at an early age, and was shuffled from one boarding school to another. He also describes how, as a young man, he sowed his share of wild oats, leaving Cambridge under a cloud as he abandoned the young woman he had gotten pregnant.

He came to America for a fresh start, and at Columbia University he came under the influence of a teacher named Mark Van Doren, a Catholic whose approach to the faith Merton found both unsettling and intriguing.

Merton was far from an instant convert, however. He was a man who lived large, and his appetite for novelty, literature, free jazz, and sheer animal sensuality seemed insatiable. The thing was, it seemed this way not just to the outside observer, but to himself as well. He realized that the more he fed his appetites, the greater his craving became; that there was a gaping hole in the place where his soul should have been, and that all of his scrambling after pleasure only brought pain to himself and, he realized with profound shame, to those around him.

And it was with that realization of emptiness that he discovered God in the void. He converted to Catholicism and felt instantly attracted to the life of the monastery.

This is, of course, classic addict behavior. An alcoholic must have complete abstinence in order to maintain his sobriety, and usually transfers the addiction to more acceptable substances—like donuts, cigarettes, and coffee, as anyone who has ever attended an AA meeting can attest.

Merton had traded sensuality for "the God Donut," and sought total abstinence from the world of sensual temptations in order to maintain his precarious spiritual equilibrium.

I'm not saying this is a bad thing. Just very human, very normal. And that is part of the appeal of Merton. The sense one gets in all of his writing is of a profoundly flawed man; one who nevertheless seeks to be more than he is, to discern what is his own true and God-given nature from what society has piled on top of him and insists he carry. His search was, when you come right down to it, one of identity and integrity.

He first applied to the Franciscans, but they rejected him because of the whole knocking-a-girl-up-in-Cambridge thing. A little later he took a retreat at the Abbey of Gethsemani in Kentucky, and fell in love with the place. It was a Trappist monastery, which is a pretty strict order. Trappists make great beer, but they are not allowed to actually talk.

In my twenties, I think I would have wrestled quite a bit with that trade-off. Beer—or talking, beer—or talking...hmm. If I'm honest, I think the beer would have won out, and so it was with Merton. The glories of the Trappist life—which included a great deal more than beer, mind you—outweighed the strictures imposed by the austere life, and he felt a call to the monastery resonating deeply within himself.

The Trappists were apparently more forgiving than the Franciscans, and he became a Trappist, withdrawing completely from the world and entering a medieval life of prayer, chant, and study.

Sounds like kind of a happy ending, doesn't it? Far from it. Merton wrote *The Seven Storey Mountain* while he was still in his honeymoon phase with monasticism, but not long after, this man of appetite began to chafe under his self-imposed bonds. His abbot refused to allow him to go out, and at times Gethsemani felt like a prison. He alternated between wanting more contact with the world, and wanting to withdraw even further into seclusion.

206 | john r. mabry

Trappist life allows neither option. It is a sequestered life, but fiercely communal. The monks may not talk to each other, but they are always together, working hard in their fields, singing together in the choir, worshipping together at Mass god-knows-how-many-times-a-day. It was, probably, exactly the right mix for his personality, but Thomas, like any wild animal, could not help but to pace his cage.

His abbot encouraged him to write, recognizing in Merton a rare intellectual talent, and seeing it as, perhaps, a kind of acceptable form of therapy for the disaffected young man. And write Merton did—almost more than anyone could read. He published books, articles, poetry, reviews, and editorials in journals and magazines both religious and secular, world-wide. He once said that he entered the monastery to escape his ambition to become famous, but it seemed a fate unavoidable. The sequestered monk in Kentucky was, all throughout the 1950s and '60s, nothing short of a household name.

And ironically, he discovered the world as well. He was one of the first Christians to write forcefully and convincingly against the Vietnam war. He cherished his collection of Bob Dylan records, entertained visitors like Joan Baez, and hid monastic contraband such as *Time* magazine under his mattress like a teenage boy hides copies of *Playboy*.

He was, simultaneously, one of the greatest intellectual giants of the twentieth century, and a very naughty little boy, in more or less equal measure. And this, too, is why people love him.

It was around this same time that he discovered a profound spirituality beyond the Catholic tradition. He had begun to explore Zen Buddhism, and was struck by the parallels to the mysticism of his own tradition. He dove in deep, examining not only Buddhism, but Taoism and Hinduism as well, and finding in these other traditions a wisdom that he could not only not deny, but which illuminated aspects of his own tradition in ways that delighted and inspired him. He became, perhaps to the horror of his religious superiors, a pioneer in interfaith scholarship.

And just as the story of his early conversion to Catholicism moved me as a convert myself, it is his approach to interfaith work that continues to inspire me today. His approach, I find, is especially meaningful, and I think, appropriate for what we are building here in this parish.

A few weeks ago, I was talking with a friend and found myself crowing with pride about Grace North Church—as I am wont to do—especially about how we are moving more and more towards an interfaith orientation.

"Oh!" my friend said delightedly, and with a little surprise. And then she asked, "So when are you going to stop doing all that Christian stuff?"

I felt my head cock to the side the way my dog's does when she encounters something truly puzzling, and it occurred to me that my friend and I were not at *all* on the same page.

"Um…we're *not*." I said. And as I watched the wheels turning in her head, I imagined she was wondering how we could worship as Christians and consider ourselves as being in any way interfaith, while I was wondering how we could be in any way interfaith without being rooted in *some* faith to begin with.

And this is where Merton's work is so appealing. The more he plumbed the depths of the Eastern traditions, the more he discovered about his own. In the very same way, being an interfaith parish doesn't mean that we are not grounded in a tradition, only that we do not hold that tradition to be in any way superior to any other, and are, in fact, eager to learn from the wisdom of our sister faiths.

Being part of a tradition is very much like being part of a family. Every family provides some essential things we humans need to live healthy lives—such as love and belonging—and every family is dysfunctional in its own ways, too. But just because I love my family does not mean that I think it is somehow better than your family.

Just so with religion. I don't in any way think that Christianity is a better religion than Judaism or Hinduism. But it is *my* family, it is *my* home, it is *my* heritage, and *my* culture. And I *love it*. I see no reason why I must reject my own family in order to affirm the worth of another. I do not need to forsake Jesus in order to affirm Mohammad or Buddha, or to love them, or to learn from them.

In our parish, I think we have struck a marvelous balance of celebrating our own religious heritage, while at the same time opening our ears and minds to the great wisdom that God has granted to other traditions as well.

And just as I consider myself a human being first and a Mabry, second, I consider myself a person of faith, united to all other people of faith of every tradition around the world, first and foremost, and secondarily, a Christian. I think I have my priorities straight, but I don't think I would if I simply rejected my heritage altogether in the name of some nebulous "interfaith" ideal. For how can we be "interfaith" if we hold none for ourselves? The Sufis say that if you dig a bunch of shallow holes, you will never ease your thirst. Pick one spot, dig deep, and you will hit water.

And so in this parish, we dig here, in the Christian tradition, and we own all of it—the whole 2,000 years of both Catholic and Protestant history, the orthodox and the heretical, the good, the bad, and the ugly. Because this is our home, and dysfunctional as it often is, it is the family into which we were born and to which we belong. This is *our* heritage and it belongs to us, love it or hate it—and most of us do, sometimes in more or less equal measure. And that's just the way it is with families sometimes. They're not better than other families, they're just *yours*.

And it was in that spirit that a new abbot finally let Thomas Merton out of his cage to travel the world and—in very un-Trappist fashion—to *speak*. In December of 1968 Merton was addressing one of the first-ever conferences for both Buddhist and Christian monastics in Thailand. After his lecture, he retired

to his room for a nap, and afterwards took a shower. As he exited the shower, he reached for the base of a large electric fan to
steady himself, and died of electrocution.

Those prone to conspiracy-theories have maintained that he
was murdered by the CIA for drumming up protest to the war in
Vietnam. No doubt he had an FBI file of some heft, but the truth
is probably the simpler, and more banal version of the story.

It is ironic that Merton, who wrote so forcefully against military
bombers, should take his final journey in one, as the military
returned his body in one of them. He was laid to rest at the Abbey
of Gethsemani, where to this day, thousands of visitors make their
pilgrimage; people who have been touched by his writings, by his
humanness, and by his refusal to be caged.

You, O God, are the sovereign of wild men, and of gentle,
and in Thomas Merton, you have given us
an example of one who was both, and yet still a saint.
Help us to embrace those polarities within ourselves,
and to have the courage to root ourselves
in that place that is our true home,
even if it is not a comfortable place at times.
Help us to embrace that which is ours,
while at the same time humbly honoring
and seeking wisdom from others.
For you are the God of polarities,
of light and dark, of chill and fire,
sinners and saints, belief and doubt, and yet you are one,
and bid us be one through your precious son,
the wild and gentle Jesus Christ. Amen.

⊕ *Preached at Grace North Church on October 22, 2006.*

24 | islam

Whenever I go to visit my parents, I am obliged to attend church with them. I cannot always arrange to be there when it does not involve a weekend, after all, and since my parents' social life revolves around their Southern Baptist church, it is important for them to show their friends on occasion that their eldest child is not, in fact, a fiction.

A year or so ago, while I was gritting my teeth and doing my best to enjoy an adult Sunday School class, I was delighted—in an evil way—by an ironic diatribe by one of the women in the class.

It was an almost hysterical monologue on the corrupting influence of American society on her children. She talked about how Hollywood was bombarding people with images of corrupt sexuality, making them think that "anything was okay as long as it felt good." She decried the dissolving of the traditional family, the selfishness that permeated American culture, the constant messages of individualism, especially when individuals were valued over the family unit or the church. She lambasted the godless philosophies of Satan, filling her children's heads with nonsense about relativism and evolution. "How can we expect our children to know the right way to live," she cried in near desperation, "when there are so many voices out there saying different things?"

I'll come back to the ironic import of what this woman was saying in a minute, but for now, suffice it to say that she might be surprised to learn that a young Arabian man named Mohammad was just as perplexed by all the conflicting voices that clamored and claimed to be the truth in his own time.

He didn't have the structure of the Southern Baptist Mission Board's lesson plans to guide him, however, and so Mohammad's slide into religious despair was a solitary one.

It was the eighth century in Saudi Arabia, and Mohammad was surrounded by contradicting religious claims and a society in an advanced state of internal turmoil. First, there was no government to speak of. Arabian culture was fiercely tribal, and blood feuds were the order of the day. It worked like this: Someone from your family steps on someone from my family's toe. Someone from my family is then honor-bound to kill your dog. Your family is then honor-bound to kill my goat. My family is then honor-bound to kill the guy from your family who killed my goat. Your family, of course, is honor-bound to kill the guy from my family that killed the guy from your family. So someone from my family, of course, has to kidnap, rape, and leave your sister for dead. So someone from your family has to take out three of my wives and all of their children. And…so on.

The really tough thing about this system of alleged "justice" is that there is no end-point to it. It just escalates. And since any given town might have a hundred families with blood feuds with half of the other families at all times, well, it just doesn't make for many Fourth of July picnics without bloodshed, wailing, and revenge on the menu. And the heads of the various families is about as complicated as the municipal government got. In other words, infrastructure, as such, did not really exist.

212 | john r. mabry

Add on top of this the fact that most Arabian families were followers of the native religion of the region, with local nature deities representing air, water, fire, and no doubt, sand. These local deities, of course, were supplemented by private, family deities, each of which must be appeased by safeguarding the family honor. Thus, the blood feuds also had a religious dimension to them.

But these were not the only voices in the marketplace. There were Jews, who insisted God was One, not many, which really rubbed the local nature-worshipping Arabs the wrong way. Plus, there were those seen as traitors, the Hanif, Arabs who accepted the Jewish revelation and strove to serve the One God as the *other* children of Abraham. These "Arabic Jews" would deeply influence Mohammad's understanding of his own revelation.

Then, of course, there were those pesky Christians, who, like the Hanif, also saw themselves as non-Jewish followers of the One God of the Jews, led by the teachings of a divine prophet named Jesus. Then there were the Zoroastrian traders, who also worshipped the One God, as articulated by their prophet, Zarathushtra.

Mohammad suffered horrible nightmares and found that he had trouble concentrating on running his wife's businesses because of his extreme and emotional agitation. His wrestlings led him to hole up in a cave by himself for extended periods of prayer and meditation. His society, he realized, was a mess—so much chaos, so much bloodshed. There was no common law to bind them into a people, no device by which the endless cycle of blood feuding might be interrupted. He saw no hope for peace for his people.

And then there was the religious piece. The Jews were just as tribal as the Arabs were, but their tribes worked together, not against each other, because the One God the Hanif honored had sent them a prophet, Moses. The Christians were not just composed of different tribes, but different peoples and different races scattered all over the globe. Yet they lived in peace because the One God had sent them a prophet, too: Jesus. And the Zoroastrians were very much like the Arabs in many ways, yet they were able to band together to such a degree that they conquered the world under one throne, and all because the One God had sent them a prophet, Zarathushtra.

Mohammad fell on his face in the cave atop Mount Hira and cried out to the One God, saying, "Why have you abandoned us? Why have you sent every people a prophet but us? Why do you not care about us? Why do you not love us? Why do you allow us to suffer so, to live in such a state of wretched violence and despair?"

On one of these visits to the cave, in the midst of his urgent prayers, Mohammad was gripped by an unseen hand that threated to crush him. "Recite!" a voice said to him.

"But I can't read!" protested Mohammad.

"Recite!" the voice said again, more urgently.

"I can't recite, because I can't read!"

But the voice was having none of it. "Recite!" it commanded. "Tell your people that the God who formed you from a single drop of semen, that God is most generous."

Shaken, Mohammad rushed down off the mountain, went straight home and into the arms of his wife, screaming "Hide me! Hide me! I am scared for my life!" He was shaking, and was sure that he had been possessed by a demon or was turning into a *sahir*, one of those ecstatic prophets that roamed the desert, whom nobody thought very highly of but other *sahirs*.

His wife took Mohammad to her cousin—a Christian—who listened carefully to what he said, and far from warning him away from this vision, counseled him to make himself available to the voice, since it may very well be the voice of God.

So Mohammad agreed to try it. He continued to go up the mountain, and nearly every time, the voice would speak to him another word of wisdom. This was almost always a physically painful ordeal for Mohammad, and it is a testament to his devo-

214 | john r. mabry

tion to the One God that he endured it again and again for the rest of his life. Each time he came down the mountain, he repeated what he had heard to a small group of supporters, but he declined to go public with the revelations for fear of what would happen to him.

Eventually, however, he was emboldened, and he began reciting the revelations publicly. There was an enormous public outcry against the heretical teachings. Yet the revelations were couched in such outrageously beautiful poetry that people found they could not help but listen to them, if only for the artistic merit and not the content. But this is part of the genius of great art, as any revolutionary artist knows. Pete Seeger has nothing on Mohammad. Get them tappin' their toes, and then hit them with the radical message. It was a winner, and before he knew it, whole families were forsaking their traditional deities for the One God as revealed to Mohammad.

Then a terrible thing happened: Mohammad's uncle died. Remember, this was a tribal culture, and without a strong clan leader to protect him, Mohammad was fair game for anyone who felt his teachings were endangering their traditional way of life.

Then something completely unexpected happened. A group of representatives from a neighboring city called Yathrib approached Mohammad and made him an offer he could not refuse: come to our city and be our leader. "We have heard your teachings," they said, "and we are tired of these bloody feuds that tear our city apart. Come, lead us, and teach us a new way to live."

Let's see, stay here and be beheaded by my enemies, or go with these guys and be king...hmm...hard decision, eh? Mohammad went, of course, and hundreds of families went with him. When they reached Yathrib, the city greeted him as a hero, set him up in a palace, and pledged themselves to his leadership, even over their tribal loyalties.

This was a radical position at the time. It was, in fact, heresy, and lots of folks in Mohammad's home town of Mecca criticized him and even led armies against Yathrib to retaliate against what they saw as Mohammad's betrayal of his own family and the entire tribal system.

They were quite right, of course. It was a betrayal of the tribal system, for it insisted that there was something more important than the tribe, and this something became the cornerstone of Mohammad's teaching.

For the revelations he had been receiving were indeed radical, and they went against everything the Arabians held dear. Mohammad taught that it was pride—this insane compulsion to save face and restore honor—that kept their society captive to endless conflict. In order to break this pride Mohammad engaged upon an aggressive re-education campaign.

In order to combat the relentless pride of the Arab peoples, Mohammad commanded them to lose face publicly by bowing their heads to the ground in submission to the One God right there out in the open where everyone could see it. Not once a week, not once a day, but five times a day. How proud could a man be on his belly, after all, before his wives, his slaves, his children, and his neighbors?

Second, Mohammad insisted that those who joined their swords together under his would never again turn them against one another. Together, all of the tribes that put themselves under Mohammad's protection were an unstoppable force, but only at the price of relinquishing all claim to the kind of family honor that demanded revenge. This again, was a humbling of the Arab spirit that paradoxically made them stronger and more noble than they had ever been.

Third, no one was permitted to strive for personal gain at the expense of others. A tenth portion of all of one's profits must be given directly to the poor in the form of alms, so that widows, orphans, the elderly, and the handicapped would all be cared for. Furthermore, women, who had previous to this time been seen as mere property, were raised by Mohammad to the status of human beings, and were granted the right to sue, to divorce, and to inherit property. (The wearing of the *berkah*, by the way, is an Eastern Orthodox Christian invention, and a corruption of Islamic teaching.)

Everything in Mohammad's teaching was oriented towards one thing, the one thing that the One God was trying to bring about: the formation of the *Ummah*, the Just Community—a place where one need not fear murder for the sins of one's father, where all peoples that honored the One God would find safe haven, whether Muslim, Jew, Christian, or Zoroastrian; a place where no one exploited another, and none would go hungry or homeless; a place where a man's pride was sacrificed daily on the altar of the common good in a ritual and visible way; a place where every day one was reminded that he or she was not the center of the universe, that the good of the Just Community was more important than any private concern, more important than pride, and more important than material gain.

This was the vision that was revealed to Mohammad, and it is still the vision that guides the Muslim world today. And this is what I find so ironic about what the woman in my parents' Sunday School class was saying. Because every one of her complaints against Hollywood, against the cultural assault on the traditional family, against the godless ideologues, against the attacks on Christian morality, were, word for word, the complaints of the Muslim world against the West.

It is no surprise that the Muslim world is angry at the West, but it isn't envy that drives them, as we like to imagine. For the vast majority of Muslims, what drives their fury is completely invisible to us—it is our unconscious attack on the foundations of the Just Community. Because we in the West have refused to humble ourselves before the One God, we have set ourselves up as gods with nearly omnipotent power over the earth and over one another, wildly destructive power that is evident to whoever has eyes to see it. In our drive for profit, we are bombarding the world—

including the Muslim world—with images of a society that values the individual over the good of the community, and are thereby undermining the fundamental purpose of Islam. We are infecting the world with narcissistic selfishness that they fear will destroy everything that the Prophet sought to build. Our moralistic relativism, another symptom of our refusal to submit our own will to Allah's, threatens to corrupt the sons and daughters they hold so dear, exposing them to such Western maladies as sexually transmitted diseases, babies born out of wedlock, sexual promiscuity, and divorce.

What was so deeply ironic about what this woman was saying, however, was that in the very next breath she started a whole new diatribe against the Muslims and their attack on "the American way of life." I wanted to take this clueless woman and shake her, to make her see that every one of her complaints against the prevailing culture would be shared by the vast majority of Islamic mothers who were as deeply religious as she. That if she were but willing to humble herself, forsake her religious imperialism, stop turning her sword against her sisters, they could stand together shoulder-to-shoulder against the tide of rampant greed, individualism, relativism, and immorality that they feel are so assaulting their traditional way of life.

A lot of what Muslims see as important to the Just Community seems to us a little extreme, but we must be careful of chronological snobbery. We must remember that what the One God proscribed for Mohammad's followers was an extreme solution to an even more extreme situation. And who is to say that we are not facing another? Although I would certainly take issue with some of what the Islamic faithful find wrong with American culture, much of it is right on target. Our business model is unashamedly dot-eat-dog. Our corporations don't care who they have to roll over to make a buck. Where is the commitment to the good of the whole? Where is the commitment to the environment? Where is the commitment to the poor, the oppressed, the powerless?

I think Mohammad was onto something. Perhaps we need to humble ourselves. Perhaps we need to fall on our faces and confess that we have exploited others in our mad dash for wealth and glory. Perhaps we need to admit that the desires of the individual are not more important than the needs of the people around us.

Certainly, we need to set aside the cartoonish portrayals of the Islamic world, and attend to the true words of wisdom that they are speaking—sometimes calmly and moderately, sometimes desperately and hysterically. The extremists are only expressing in a morally reprehensible way an agitation that is felt at every level of Muslim society. It is a *just* irritation, for we have forsaken the pursuit of the Just Community. It's not like it hasn't been preached to us, too, after all. Jesus commands us to bring about the Kingdom of Heaven here on earth, a command we have conveniently ignored or spiritualized to the point that it no longer has any earthly relevance. And this is to our shame.

Mohammad calls all peoples who profess faith in the One God to stand together in one body and bring about the Just Community—not just Muslims, but Christians and Jews as well. He adds his voice to those of Moses and Jesus and Zarathushtra and all the other prophets who have guided humankind throughout the ages. Will we listen? Can we set aside our petty differences, put an end to our blood feuds, and stand as one people of faith in the service of the Just Community? Only if we are willing to humble ourselves, to forsake our pride, to submit our will to that of the One God, who commands us to put the good of others ahead of our own material gain.

In the name of God, the beneficent and merciful,
let us set aside our prejudices
and see Mohammad in the context of his time.
Let us hear his prophetic voice with new ears,
and be willing to be moved,
to humble our spirits,

to submit our will to the will of the One
who calls us to create a truly Just Community,
where none are exploited or used,
where none are deprived of justice,
where none go hungry or homeless
—not because the Muslim world has done this perfectly,
not because we have brought it about either,
but because we have all failed desperately to achieve this goal,
and because God commands it.
For there is no God but God,
and Mohammad is his prophet.
Will you hear him? Amen.

⊕ *Preached at Grace North Church on June 11, 2006.*

25 | rabia

While I was at California Baptist College, I went through a major crisis of faith. The catalyst for this was, actually, a poem we read in Margaret's English Lit class. In Robert Browning's "Caliban Upon Setebos," Caliban, the monster in Shakespeare's *The Tempest*, is soliloquizing on Setebos, which is what he called his god.

Because Caliban is quite an evil creature who delights in killing little beasties, and he knows that compared to Setebos he is himself a wee beastie, Caliban cowers in fear of his god. Of course, he assumes that his god is just as bloodthirsty and uncompassionate as he is himself. His sense of fear in the poem is overwhelming.

This poem hit me right between the eyes. For it made me confront the spectre of the monster god I myself had been given as a child, and question my own motivations for serving him. After many nights of fitful sleep, I came to the conclusion that religion borne of fear was invalid. I was no different than Caliban, cowering before Setebos, begging not to be squashed like a bug or eaten.

My faith, I discovered, was based on an invalid proposition: that if I didn't serve God, I would burn in Hell. End of story. I realized then that love of God was the only valid basis for faith, and that if I could not find a way to do that, then I was barking up the wrong tree, and I should just give up on God altogether. No God, after all, is better than Setebos; to worship no God is preferable to groveling at the feet of a monster.

What I didn't realize at the time was that I was not the first one to have such thoughts, or to come to such conclusions—far from it. Oh, I'm sure that for my own spiritual development it was important to come to these realizations for myself, but our mystic of the day, Rabia al Basri, went even further.

She said that not only is fear of Hell an invalid foundation for faith, but hope for the reward of Heaven is likewise invalid. That idea would have really blown my Southern Baptist elders out of the water, since this carrot and stick approach was pretty much all there was to my childhood faith.

Rabia called this hope of reward "selfish love." To her credit, she admits that she has it, but she also sees the consequences. When she loves God with selfish love, she is incapable of seeing the needs of those around her. But when she loves God with the kind of love that is worthy of God, her veil is lifted so that she can see others clearly.

This remarkable woman was one of the first Sufis, and was, in fact, courted by the founder of the Sufi sect, Hassan al Basri. But in typical Sufi style, Rabia had eyes for none but her Beloved, Allah. The Sufis were—and are—a deeply devotional sect of Islam. Carrying over mystical traditions of the native Iraqi peoples, the Sufis infused Islam with a renewed sense of commitment and Divine intimacy. Mohammad had outlawed monasticism, but the Sufis embraced the closest thing to it in Islam. Eschewing the kind of Islam that they considered to be insincere, or "for show" in the busy cities, they embraced an ideal of poverty and complete dependence upon Allah. They got into a lot of trouble because their mystical practices, like turing around in circles until they reached an altered state—often left them babbling about how they and Allah were one, or that they *were* Allah! This, of course, did not go over well with the mainstream Muslims, and although Sufis have always had a place within Islam, they are simultaneously regarded by most Muslims with both suspicion and reverence. The Sufis are also known as the whirling dervishes, and are often referred to as dervishes in Islamic literature.

Rabia is one of their greatest, and oldest, saints. She was born around the year 715 of the Common Era in Basra, Iraq. Her parents were the poorest of the poor, and the night she was born her parents did not even have oil for their lamp. Her father, worried over how he would provide for his new daughter, fell into a disturbed sleep. The prophet Mohammad came to him in his sleep and told him that his daughter would be a great saint. He also commanded the poor man to send a letter to the Amir the very next day, reminding the Amir that every night he was committed to saying one hundred prayers, but last Friday he had neglected to do it, and as a punishment the Amir must pay to you four hundred dinars.

When the Amir read the letter, he was so struck in conscience that he not only sent the money to Rabia's father, but he personally came and rubbed his beard upon their doorpost, and gave two thousand denars to the poor. (Look, gentlemen, if you ever want to apologize to me for anything, money is fine, but please rub your beards on your own doorframes if you feel so compelled. Thank you.)

This was indeed a boon for Rabia's family, but it was only a brief respite, for soon the young girl was orphaned. One night, she and her sisters were so hungry that she decided to brave the cruel streets of Basra to see if she could find some food for them. While she was out, she was kidnapped by a slave merchant and sold into slavery.

She worked dutifully in her master's house, fasting by day and standing upright all night long in prayer. One moonlit night, her master, unable to sleep, looked out of his window and saw her praying. He strained to catch her words and was just able to make them out. "O Lord," she prayed, "you know that the desire of my heart is to obey you, and that the light of my eye is in the service of your court. If it were up to me I would not cease from praising you for a single hour, and yet you have seen fit to make me subject to a man, a creature...."

Her master saw a lamp hovering over her head, floating in the air, unconnected to any chain, and the light from it illumined the whole courtyard. This sight disturbed her master even further, and when morning came he summoned her and granted her freedom.

She went directly to the desert to spend her days in prayer and devotion. Eventually she felt moved to follow Mohammad's command to complete the *hajj*, the pilgrimage to Mecca. But while she was traveling, her donkey keeled over and died. The other people in her caravan said, "Let us help—we'll carry your baggage," but in true Sufi style, she declined, saying, "I don't need anyone's help but God's."

After they had gone on their way, she kind of read Allah the riot act. "So, is this how a king deals with a woman, weak and a stranger in these parts? You called me to visit your house, and then you abandon me in the desert? Is that any way to treat your servant?"

No sooner had she finished praying than her donkey gave a loud snort and rolled over onto his feet. Apparently unsurprised, she fastened her baggage to the beast and continued on her way.

So repentant was Allah, that when she was not yet halfway to Mecca, as legend has it, she saw a huge black building floating through the air towards her. The Ka'ba, the holiest shrine in all of Islam, had come to meet her halfway. Now, whereas most of us would fall over at such a miracle, Rabia was an odd duck, as mystics are wont to be, and merely said, "It is Allah I need, not his house. I want to meet him who said, 'anyone who moves a foot toward me, I will move toward them a yard.' What joy does the Ka'ba bring to me?"

At the same time, a man named Ibrahim, who had been on pilgrimage for fourteen years, prostrating himself and praying at every step, arrived in Mecca only to discover that the Ka'ba was missing! He was furious, and even more so when he saw Rabia arriving with the Ka'ba floating behind her as if in tow behind her donkey.

"Woman," he wailed, "why have you brought such woe to the world?"

"What are you talking about?" she said. "It is you who have brought trouble to the world because you have taken fourteen years to get here!"

"Yes," he said, "but I took so long because I was praying all the way."

"You prayed rote prayers and made a show of it," she scolded him, "you did not pray in your heart." And having completed her pilgramage, she returned to her life in the Iraqi desert.

Like many Sufi saints, Rabia was a poet, and left behind some startlingly beautiful and profound mystical poems. In Islam, so greatly is she revered, that her status as a woman is entirely ignored and she is counted "an honorary male," which, insulting as this sounds today, was, I think, intended in her time to be a compliment.

Her legacy is a deeply meaningful one, for her genius was in discerning true worship from false, divining the motivations of the heart, which many people would just as soon keep secret. But just as to God, "to whom all desires are known and from whom no secrets are hid," Rabia was likewise not fooled by anybody. Her example invites us to examine our own lives of faith and to ask of them some hard questions: What are our real motivations? Why are we really here? Do we worship God because we are afraid of what will happen if we do not? If so, our religion is nothing but a response born of fear. Do we serve God because we want to go to Heaven some day? If so, then our religion is nothing but a response born of greed. Are we here because of something we want to get, or is it because of something we want to give?

Only you can answer these questions for yourself, and the truth is probably much more complicated than a single answer can indicate. We humans are relentlessly complex beings, and our motives for worship are likewise complicated.

I did my own inventory for why I am here this morning:

20% of my motivation is my gratitude to God for my life;
30% is the community of friends and loved ones
   around this table;
20% is the fact that you are all counting on me
   to be here, and I'll be in big trouble if I'm not!;
20% is that this is my profession—I am paid to be here;
5% is a feeling of obligation to God
   to be in worship once a week;
and the other 5% is a weird mix that I have yet to sort out.

While looking at this list, I am relieved to discover that not a bit of it is fear of God, or of Hell; and considering where I have come from, I see that as progress indeed.

But what about you? What are your percentages? Not only why do you come to worship here, but why do you pay attention to God at all? I invite you to do your own inventory. You might surprise yourself. You might find yourself a little embarrassed. But it is good information to have, for it can serve as both a corrective and an encouragement on our journeys.

May we all, like Rabia, seek after God, rather than God's house. May we all, like Rabia, seek the true worship of the heart, rather than rote prayers and rituals. May we all, like Rabia, seek a love worthy of Allah, alongside the selfish love that we will always have just because we are humans. And may that worthy love grow.

Blessed be God, the beneficent, the merciful,
who has honored the poor and the weak, like the Sufi Rabia,
and has given to them the secret of true devotion.
Help us, Allah, to seek you with our whole hearts,
with true and undisguised devotion,
that we may love you with a love that is worthy of you,
and keep you before our eyes in every moment of every day. Amen.

⊕ *Preached at Grace North Church on June 18, 2006.*

26 | rumi

ast winter while Flavio and I were on vacation we went to the movies and saw the new film version of *Rent*, the 90s stage revival of *La Boehme* set during the height of the AIDS crisis.

Now I saw *Rent* on the stage, and I enjoyed it, but I didn't really clue into the cult-like following it achieved back then. I still haven't. But from the moment that movie started, something inexplicable happened to me. I started sobbing. I cried more during that damn movie than I've cried in the last ten years put together. It was embarrassing.

I don't really understand it. I didn't know anyone that was lost to AIDS. I was never in the thick of the gay community back in the heyday of the AIDS crisis. I mean, I love musicals, but none of them ever affected me like this. It even freaked Flavio out a little. Not only that, but the effects endured. I bought Flavio the CD for Christmas, and every time he puts it on, here come the waterworks. It's the craziest thing. I bought the DVD when it came out,

228 | john r. mabry

but truth be told, I simply haven't had the strength to put it on. I know it's going to be a workout.

These days I consider this reaction a little quirky, an inexplicable emotional oddity. As a younger man, I would have found it an insufferable source of shame. "Big boys don't cry," was the creed I was raised on, and I believed it. And since I've always been such an absolute emotional mess, I always felt really bad about myself. Emotion has always trumped reason for me, and as a child, the quick leap to tears, the wrenching twist in the gut of unstoppable feeling was always a source of shame. As an adult I have made my peace with it, because, like today's mystic, I have come to discover that the inexplicable and uncontrollable leapings of the heart are as reliable a guide to the divine as many other august paths can be. And for those of us predisposed to deep and relentless feeling, perhaps the best path.

Jalaluddin Rumi was born in 1207 in Balkh—yes, the very same city in Afghanistan where Zoroaster first found refuge. Maybe it was something in the water that attracted—or grew—great mystics. Whatever it was, Balkh has always had more than its share. Rumi's father was an Islamic theologian and a Sufi mystic of some renown, and he brought Rumi up to be a scholar and teacher of the faith.

When Rumi was only 12 years old, the Mongols invaded Balkh and Rumi's family fled west to Konya at the invitation of its king. It was a good thing they left when they did, because not long after, the Mongols came back through for another sweep and mercilessly slaughtered everyone in the city. The Mongols, you may be chagrined to learn, were Christians, intent on spreading the love of Jesus in their own special way. The name Rumi, by the way, refers to one heading towards Rome—Romi—and was a nickname gained during the family's exodus.

As the family approached their new home, a Sufi saint named Attar saw the boy trailing behind his father, and uttered the prophetic words, "Here comes a sea, followed by an ocean." He gave the young Rumi a copy of the *Book of Mysteries*, a Gnostic Islamic treatise on how the soul is entrapped in the material world. This book meant a great deal to Rumi, and he seems to have been inspired by the encounter.

Once resettled in Konya, Rumi's father was put in charge of a seminary there, where he taught until his death. Rumi continued his studies under one of his father's disciples and eventually succeeded his father as the head of the school.

Meanwhile, a wandering Sufi named Shams Tabriz was praying to Allah, pleading with him, "Won't you please send me someone who can endure my company!"

Allah felt compassion for Shams, and said to him, "What will you give me in return?"

Shams replied, "I'd give my head!"

And the voice of Allah said to him, "The man you seek is Jalaluddin Rumi in the city of Konya." Shams set off straightaway for the city and sought Rumi out.

And thus began one of the greatest love stories the world has ever known. From the moment they met, they were inseparable. While most scholars think they were probably lovers, there is no doubt that they were soul mates and that the relationship had a profound effect on both of them. Shams and Rumi were not two peas in a pod, they were one pea in two pods, and Rumi rejoiced and praised God for sending him such a marvelous and soulful companion.

Rumi saw in Shams the perfect reflection of the divine. His friend embodied Allah just as Allah embodied him, and in gazing upon his beloved, Rumi felt he was gazing upon Allah. And the great passion and love that welled up in his heart for Shams he understood to be a love for God. In being in love with Shams, Rumi fell in love with God. Wheras before he had only taught about the infinite mystery and mercy of God, in the company of Shams, Rumi *experienced* God in a way that utterly changed him forever. Shams brought him not knowledge, but *gnosis*, the unmediated experience of union with the Divine that is the goal of all mysticism.

Unfortunately for Rumi, he seems to have been more deeply in love with Shams than Shams was with him, for about two years into their partnership, the wanderlust hit Shams, and he hit the road. Rumi was, as you might imagine, utterly bereft. He couldn't sleep, he couldn't eat, he couldn't teach. One night as he lay tossing and turning, he had a dream in which Shams was in a small tavern just outside Damascus, playing dice with a Frenchman, and completely winning the shirt off the man's back. The Frenchman was so angry at having been beaten that he jumped up and struck Shams across the face.

At that moment, Rumi awoke and dispatched one of his disciples to Damascus with a bag of gold, urging him to "fill Shams' shoes with money, and point him toward Konya and beg him to return to us." As soon as the disciple entered Damascus, he found Shams at the tavern just as Rumi had said, being beaten nearly to a pulp by an angry Frenchman. The disciple intervened and implored Shams to return, which, to Rumi's great relief, he did.

Shams and Rumi had another blissful couple of years together before the jealousy of Rumi's disciples undermined the partnership. Shams was called to the door one night, and he never returned. Rumi's heart broke, and he wandered the country for two years searching for his lost love. Then one night, while in Damascus, Rumi had an insight. He later wrote about it, saying, "Why should I keep looking for him like this? Shams and I are the same person. His spirit still lives in me. I have been looking not for Shams, but for myself."

This notion comforted him greatly, and he returned home and took up his teaching once again. But he was a changed man. He began writing an amazing stream of poety, and employing dance and ecstasy in his teaching and spiritual practice in ways that were entirely novel. People came from near and far to sit at his feet, for they discovered in him a man who had truly encountered and merged with the Divine.

He seems to have truly taken to heart his insight about Shams and he being one soul, for from then on, the name he signed to all of his poetry was not Rumi, but Shams. He and Shams were one, and since it was Shams who had truly shown him Allah, he and Allah were one as well.

He was a prolific writer, and produced an astounding amount of poetry. His *Mathnawi* is a poem that runs six volumes and is commonly referred to as "the Persian Koran." It is often said of him, "He was not a prophet, but he did bring forth a scripture." Rumi's works are some of the most translated writings in the world, and in the West the translation and publication of Rumi poems has turned into something of an industry in its own right. It's not hard to understand why. Rumi is addictive. One taste of his poetry will leave you wanting more, not only because of its beauty, but because of its profound humanity.

Though it is true that some of the early Sufis were ascetic in their practice, asceticism is alien to Islam, and in Rumi's order it certainly had no place. For theirs was not a way of renunciation, but of embracing. Rumi's way is not, like the Buddha's, an eschewing of desire, but the cultivation of it. For it was desire that led him to Allah, it was passion that opened his eyes to the essential oneness of all souls, and it was emotion and ecstasy and pleasure that taught his spirit to dance.

Rumi's followers are still dancing. One of his innovations was the practice of spinning around and around until one reached a state of undifferentiated union with Allah. These are the whirling dervishes, and Rumi was the first.

In looking back on my inexplicable reaction to the film version of *Rent*, I believe it shook me so deeply because I saw so much of myself up there on that screen. Almost every character was a mirror reflecting to me a poignant and vulnerable part of my own soul, and the emotion was simply too much to hold. I saw myself in those characters, and for a time, I was transformed.

Rumi's experience with Shams was similar, in a way, except that it was much more profound, and it seemed to be permanent. I eventually recovered my equilibrium a couple of hours after leaving the theatre, but Rumi never did. His encounter with Shams left him so drunk on reflected divinity that he just never sobered up. He took it all in, filtered it through his heart, and gushed it all out again in his poetry. In my heart of hearts, I am still a little ashamed of the depths of my own emotions, but Rumi never was. They were in no way a source of shame or an impediment to his spiritual progress, or the self-image of his manliness, or any of the other negative messages we men are given about our feelings. They were, in fact, the fingers of God, drawing him into an embrace that was both divine and everlasting.

Merciful Allah, you who are the lover of our souls,
who fashioned within us the strange engines of our hearts,
capable of producing feelings through which you call to us
as a lover to her beloved.
Help us to heed your call, to see you in the faces of those
whom you have sent to companion us in both good times and bad.
Help us to see you in one another,
and to recognize every soul as our own.
Help us not to eschew our feelings, but to utterly embrace
your gift of humanity in all of its messy glory,
for it is in being who we really are that we discover you. Amen.

⊕ *Preached at Grace North Church on July 16, 2006.*

27 | hafiz

S t. Ignatius of Loyola, the founder of the Jesuits, was a true
spiritual innovator, and a pioneer in the field of spiritual
direction. He developed a system of spiritual discernment
that went directly against the collective wisdom of his day, or
ours, even. He told his students not to deny their desires, not to
ignore their emotions, but instead to listen to them, since they are
the very voice of God.

This is what he told them: Pray for what you want. Pray for it
with all your heart, because if you do you will discover something
astounding—that what you want is not *really* what you want. If
you truly pray for what you want, what you *really* want will reveal
itself, and what is more, will be given to you. In this way, prayer
is not simply a quaint obligation, it is a powder keg that can utterly lay to waste your illusions, your self-concept, and can bring life
as you know it to a screeching halt.

There, I've said it: Prayer can ruin your life. Are you happy,
now? You've made your priest say something that would have
gotten him burned alive three hundred years ago. Not that that's

anything unusual in this parish! Still, a truer thing was never spoken from the pulpit. If done correctly, prayer *will* ruin your life. But the good news is, it will also give it back to you again, stripped of your conceits, masks, and self-delusions. You have to give up your fake life to get a real life. So be careful what you pray for—you may not get what you think you want, but you will most assuredly get what you *really* want, which is not always a comfortable bargain.

No one knows this difficult truth better than today's mystic, Hafiz. He was born in a beautiful garden city called Shiraz in southern Iran around the year 1320. His given name was Shamseddin Mohammad, and he was the son of a coal merchant who died when he was a boy. But before he died, Shamseddin would sit at his father's feet and listen while he recited the *Koran*. So closely did the boy listen that he memorized the entire text, thereby earning the name we know him by today. *Hafiz* is Arabic for "guardian," and is bestowed only upon those who have committed the *Koran* to memory.

After his father passed away, Hafiz had to go to work, as the family was very poor indeed. He apprenticed at a drapery shop, and later at a bakery. All the while, though, he had a keen interest in the life of the intellect, and he audited classes at a nearby college until he had mastered every subject.

One day, while he was working at the bakery, one of the regular delivery men fell sick, so Hafiz was pressed to cover for him. Hafiz took his measure of bread out to a rich neighborhood that he rarely had occasion to visit. He was delivering the bread to a mansion, and just before he reached the door, he looked out and saw a stunning maiden on the balcony. Of course, his heart melted in his chest, and he desired her with everything that was in him. In fact, he nearly passed out on the spot.

He discovered that her name was Shakh-i-Nabat, which means, "branch of sugarcane," and indeed, the sweetness of her image haunted him for weeks to come. He could not eat, he could not sleep. He could not do anything but dream about her. He wrote several poems about her, many of which still survive. One of them goes,

> My love is a bright candle
> —tell me, O Lord, whose house does she illumine?
> My soul burns when I ask of you, "Whose sweetheart is she?"

He was soon to discover the answer to that question—she was betrothed to a prince, and so the pauper Hafiz realized just how foolish his desire for her heart would be. Then he had a hairbrained idea—which is the only kind worth having if you're going to be the subject of any story worth telling. He recalled "the promise of Baba Kuhi," who was an enlightened teacher several hundred years ago right there in Shiraz. According to the legend, anyone who could keep vigil for forty consecutive nights at his tomb—without falling asleep once—would be granted a great boon: the gifts of poetry, immortality, and best of all, the thing he or she wants most in the world.

Of course, Hafiz, that crazy guy, decided to try it. So every night after work, Hafiz dragged his exhausted butt off to the shrine of Baba Kuhi, which had the added advantage of being located not far from the house of the girl he was in love with, which served as a ready reminder to him every day of just why, exactly, he was putting himself through all this.

Now, Hafiz was already a pretty well-respected poet, and some of his poems in praise of his beloved had found their way to Shakh-i-Nabat, and as she watched him round the corner every day on his way to the shrine, and saw how determined he was, and how, as day succeeded to day, he looked more and more haggard and wild-eyed, she guessed what he was up to, and her heart melted.

On the fortieth day, the very last night of his vigil, she met him in the street and declared her love for him, crying out to anyone who cared to hear that she preferred the love of a genius to even that of a king. But, oddly, Hafiz took no notice of her. She was, at that moment, a distraction he could not afford. The man was on auto-pilot, fearing that if he faltered now, all would be lost.

So for the last night, he sat vigil. And what should appear to his blood-shot eyes at first light the next morning but the angel Gabriel, the very being that had delivered the *Koran* to Mohammad. He greeted Hafiz, and gave him a cup that contained the Water of Immortality. He bid him drink it, and then informed him that he had also received the gift of poetry. Presumably, this excellent poet was to be, after his month of vigils, and even better one. Then Gabriel asked Hafiz what his heart's desire was.

But Hafiz found he could not answer. He was transfixed by the beauty of the angel, and the strangeness of what was happening. It was all so surreal that he momentarily forgot all about Shakh-i-Nabat and the whole purpose of his vigil. Instead, he thought, "If Gabriel is this beautiful, God must be even more beautiful still!" And so, when Gabriel pressed him, asking once more what his heart desired, Hafiz blurted out, "I want God!"

The angel smiled and gave him the address of a man in Shiraz who could help him with that. The angel walked with Hafiz a while as he made his way to the city, but before long, Hafiz found himself alone, standing in front of a fruit and incense shop owned by a humble man named Mohammad Attar, who was, Gabriel had told him, an enlightened master.

Just as Hafiz was beginning to wonder if he had done a very foolish thing in trading the beauty of his beloved for the hovel of a wizened old merchant, Mohommad Attar rushed out and embraced him. "I've been expecting you!" the old man said, and ushered the poet inside. He congratulated Hafiz on his vigil, and informed him that he would gladly accept him as his disciple, all without Hafiz, apparently, uttering a word. Suitably impressed, Hafiz submitted to Attar's tutelage, and remained devoted to him for the rest of the master's life. The old man made him promise to keep his identity a secret, and indeed, although Hafiz mentions his master many times, it is never by name.

Apparently, Shakh-i-Nabat forgave Hafiz for slighting her on the eve of his final vigil, and true to her word, married the poor poet. He loved her deeply, and they had children together, though how many they had is a matter of some dispute. He outlived his wife and at least one of his sons, as there survive several poems of grieving presumably written at their passing.

Hafiz was never a "safe" poet, and he regularly wrote poems that alienated the princes of his city. His career had the trajectory of a yo-yo as he bounced in and out of favor with the ruling elite. For much of his adult life he taught theology and poetry at the local college. He was, as you might expect, a very popular teacher, and had many devoted students.

Hafiz was a dedicated Sufi, did everything his master asked, and yet was extremely frustrated when, after forty years of sitting at his master's feet, he had yet to attain divine consciousness. He wanted to be enlightened, to experience that same union with Allah that Rumi had described in his poetry. It was certainly not for lack of effort, or desire, or even holiness. Hafiz might have been politically and even poetically scandalous at times, but he was a religiously sincere man.

Finally, in a fit of frustration, he confronted Attar, "What have I gained by hanging in there with you for forty years?"

"Hang in there a little longer, and you will find out," his master said.

"Why did I know you were going to say that?" said Hafiz, and stormed out of Attar's shop.

In his desperation, he began another vigil. He went home and drew a circle on the ground. He then sat down inside the circle and swore that he would not leave it for forty days. For there is a legend that if a believer does this, God will grant his or her request. Hafiz was kind of crazy when it came to being determined, as you have probably gathered by now. Of course, he was successful in sitting in his circle for forty days. And at the end of the fortieth day, the angel Gabriel once again appeared to him. "What do you want, now?" the angel asked with a wry smile.

Just then Hafiz realized how foolish it was to be impatient, that he didn't want to be powerful, but obedient. So instead of saying, "I want to be enlightened," he simply said, "I only want to wait upon my teacher, and to tend to his wish." Gabriel nodded, and at this Hafiz rushed to the shop of his master, where Attar was waiting for him with a bottle of aged wine, which, as you know, is forbidden to Muslims. Hafiz gulped at the wine and as he did so, the veils were lifted from his eyes, and he saw all things as God did. He and his soul's maker were one. He and his master were one. He and all things were one.

In both of these incidents, Hafiz discovered that what he thought he wanted were only fingers pointing to the object of his true desire. His passionate craving for Sugar-Cane girl, no matter how sweet she actually was, led him to a deeper place, a place he was not even aware existed. His love for his beloved led him to the true Beloved, who desires a union with us that goes beyond the joy of human companionship or even sexual union.

In fact, we speak of marriage as a sacrament in Catholic Christianity specifically because the love of two people points to and foreshadows a much deeper and more profound union, that of the soul with its God. This is the Beloved that Hafiz would write about for the remaining eight years of his life. Not of the God of the academic, viewed from afar, and subject to endless speculation, but the God of his own passionate experience, that Beloved that wooed him and taught him, and united with him with an intensity that the poet, try as he might, could never quite articulate.

But his failures to communicate the ineffable are nothing if not poetic triumphs. Few poets from any culture are as profound or as beloved as Hafiz. Many people use the *Divan*, the collection of his poetry, for divination. People will pray a question, and then open his book at random. The poem that they light upon will speak to them its answer.

The very first time Hafiz' poetry was used as an oracle may well have been at his death. The poet died in 1391, but the clergy refused to allow him a Muslim burial. Upon hearing this proclamation, the common people revolted and demanded that Hafiz be given his due honor. They were at an impasse until someone made a suggestion that they ask the poet through the vehicle of his poetry. They wrote a bunch of his couplets onto little strips of paper and put them into a jar. Then they asked a small child to reach in and grab one of the strips. The poem that resulted was this one:

Neither Hafiz' corpse, nor his life deny,
That for all his faults, Heaven awaits him.

This seemed to settle the matter, and Hafiz was laid to rest in due and proper form in a garden in his beloved city.

I have seen a bumper sticker around that says, "Be careful what you pray for, you just might get it," but like most bumper stickers, it is a little too simple. Both Hafiz and Ignatius of Loyola bear witness to a more subtle truth: "Pray for what you want, and what you really want will be yours." But beware just the same!

Allah, you are the Beloved to whom all human love and desire points.
Help us to heed you when you woo us,
help us to see through the veils of our desire,
to discover the love our hearts truly pine for.
Liberate us from our illusions
that we may embrace you in our very souls
and discover that your heart and ours are one and the same.
For you are the merciful and beneficent one,
you are the lover of our souls and the end of all our desire. Amen.

⊕ *Preached at Grace North Church on July 30, 2006.*

28 | guru nanak

I have preached many times about the spiritual epiphany I had in my early twenties, when I saw a vision of the universe as a great cosmic dance, in which all of creation knows the steps except human beings, who have forgotten. I saw that our religious traditions were merely our feeble attempts to learn the steps and join back in, in our own clumsy way. But I have never told you what happened after that.

Since I saw in my vision that all religious traditions were more or less arbitrary, all metaphorical fingers pointing to the moon of Divinity, I returned to the practice of Christianity because it is my culture, and because the Trinity is the metaphor for the Divine that looms largest in my imagination. Since I'll never escape these images, and since they're more or less of equal value with those of any other tradition, why start from scratch? I became, for the first time in my life, what I considered to be a "real" Christian. By that I mean not knocking myself out to fit into somebody else's mold of what a Christian was supposed to look like, but simply following Jesus as I understood his teachings.

So I went back to church, and hitched my wagon to the entourage of a young evangelical preacher named Andy. Andy and his wife Maggie had just been kicked out of the church my parents went to. So I thought, "Hey, my kind of people." They weren't kicked out for any kind of bad behavior, but for their novel ideas about worship through the arts, and also, I think, because Andy's charisma threatened the pastor. The pastor, by the way, resigned after cheating on his wife with the church secretary, and Andy, bless him, still pastors his church out in Pleasant Hill, and it is a vibrant parish with many hundreds of members.

Anyway, I got involved in forming this new church. We would worship in Andy's living room—I'd sing original songs, Maggie would dance, and sometimes we'd just watch a video and then discuss it. It was a pretty cool Baptist church, even if we didn't have a building or a lot of people. It was intimate and meaningful. One day as Andy and I were at the pub drinking beer and throwing darts, I described my vision. "Oh," he said, "you're a universalist."

"I am?"

"Yeah, you believe everyone is saved, or that all religions are valid."

"Yeah, I guess I do."

Andy nodded. "It's not my opinion, but it certainly has a long history in Christianity." Andy was a great teacher, and I learned a lot from him, not only about theology, but about pastoral skills.

Not long after, I went away to Riverside to go to California Baptist College and joined the Episcopal Church. After three years there, I returned to Oakland to do a master's degree in Creation Spirituality, a Christian theology of a decidedly universalist bent.

I went to visit Andy and Maggie, and when Andy was in the back yard tending to the barbeque, Maggie asked me the subject of my master's thesis. "It's on the *Tao Te Ching*, and how in line it is with Jesus' teaching."

Her face went white, and she struggled with what to say. "Jesus is the only way to Heaven, John," she finally spat out. "What you're doing is demonic. If you really believe there is any truth in this Tao thing, then you are *not* a Christian." She shot me a look that could have melted lead and pretty much ignored me for the rest of the visit.

My heart sank. I loved these people, and I was sure that Andy wouldn't have treated me like this, even if he didn't agree with me. But I was surprised that he had never shared the fact that I was a universalist with Maggie. Or perhaps they had both changed. Why was it okay for me to have been a universalist five years ago, but not now? I drove away feeling very sad indeed, for I had lost my friends. As I did so, her words reverberated in my head, *"You are not a Christian."*

Guru Nanak had a vision similar to mine, and it similarly rocked his little world. And likewise, people had a variety of reactions to it—some outraged and alienating, like Maggie; and some enthusiastic and embracing—like you folks!

Nanak was born in 1469 in a small village in what is now Pakistan. His family were Hindus, but his father worked for local Muslim businesspeople. There was a very large Muslim population at the time, and then, as now, there was a fair bit of conflict between the Hindu and Muslim communities.

Nanak had always been a spiritual child, but he eschewed the rituals of Hinduism and abhorred the caste system. He even dabbled with Islam for a while, but decided it was no better. He was also a terrible student, and his father, desperate for the boy to be of some use to the family, sent him out to herd cattle.

He was a gentle cow-herder for about fifteen years—much like Krishna—and then one day he simply disappeared. He had last been seen heading toward a river to bathe, and it was assumed that Nanak had slipped on a slimy rock and drowned. His family searched for him, but to no avail. Then, just as they were resigning themselves to their loss, Nanak emerged from the wild, lost in rapture and mumbling about the beauty of the Name.

When he was coherent enough to communicate, he told his family that while he had been bathing he was ushered into the Divine presence. In a vision, he was given a cup filled with nectar to drink. A voice like none he had ever heard resounded in his head, saying, "Nanak, this is the cup of the adoration of my Name. Drink it. I am with you and I bless you and I raise you up. Go forth and rejoice in my holy Name. Teach others to do the same, for I have given you the gift of my Name. This is your life's purpose."

When Nanak exited the water, he uttered what were to be his most famous words: "There are no Hindus, there are no Muslims."

What did Nanak mean by such cryptic words? He was surrounded by Hindus and Muslims! He meant, I believe, that neither religion has a monopoly on the truth, that the Divine is not Hindu or Muslim, and that if you strip away the trappings of either religion, you are left with the soul naked before God, the light and its reflection, the essence and its emanation. The love affair between the soul and its Beloved, the Divine, was the only real truth, and that our various religions are like the languages in which the courtship between ourselves and the Divine is carried out. Necessary, but of human origin, and ultimately no more than metaphors steering us toward the truth but in no way defining it.

He started to dress in a very odd way, combining Hindu and Muslim styles of clothing, and he took to the road with a Muslim musician. For most of the rest of his life, he and his friend traveled from village to village, singing love songs to God. In Hindu villages, he exhorted the people to be good Hindus. In Muslim villages, he encouraged them to be good Muslims. In Christian communities, he preached the importance of following Jesus. But everywhere he went he sang his simple, catchy melodies about the love affair between his own heart and God's.

He met some opposition, of course, but for the most part, people were overwhelmed by his passion and obviously heart-felt devotion. And they loved his music and poetry. Soon people all over India were singing Nanak's love songs to God, and good will between rival religious communities seemed to follow in his wake.

People began to follow after Nanak, of course, traipsing after him from town to town, just like people did with the Grateful Dead in the 1980s. They started calling themselves "Sikhs" which means, simply, "follower" or "disciple."

Like the Jews and Muslims, Nanak eschewed the worship of images, and instead steered the devotional life of his community toward poetry and song. His followers loved not only Nanak's songs, but his teaching as well. He told them that the Name of God was not something that could be pronounced by the mouth, but only something that could be discerned and adored in the heart. The Name of God resided in the heart of every creature, not just humans, not just Hindus, not just Muslims, and not just Christians. The Name of the Beloved is written on every heart, and the Beloved calls all beings into the Divine embrace.

This Name is similar to the Tao, which, as Lao Tzu says, "cannot be described in words." It is similar to the Hebrew Tetragrammaton, the unpronounceable name of God. It is similar to the Greek *logos*, the Word through which all things were made, an idea adopted by the early Christians and applied to Jesus. It is like the secret name of Christ written upon his arm in the *Book of Revelation*, and known only to him. It is the Name, ineffable, indescribable, yet inseparable from every creaturely soul.

The Name is no respecter of persons, either. Nanak preached against the caste system, against the notion that any religion was better than any other, and against the notion that men were superior to women. In Nanak's community of followers, everyone was equal, regardless of their origin, their sect, or their gender. For the Name resides in the heart of every creature.

Nanak taught his followers that the biggest impediment to full union with the Beloved was the mistaken notion that we are in any way separate from divinity, or for that matter, from one another. "I," "Me," and "Mine" are all fictions that serve only to perpetuate the illusion of separateness that is the cause of all self-ishness, suffering, and folly.

Nanak was the first interfaith minister, and his followers comprised the world's first true interfaith movement. No one who followed him left his or her religion behind, instead they celebrated all faiths and were devoted believers. Nor did they any longer denigrate the faith of others, but discovered in them more of the beauty of the Beloved.

They called Nanak their guru, after the Hindu fashion, and just before he passed away, after a long and fruitful ministry, he called out one of his disciples, a man named Lahina, to succeed him. On his deathbed, he changed Lahina's name to Angad, which means "a part of my own body," and indeed, it seemed that Nanak's genius was somehow transferred to Angad.

The new guru picked up right where Nanak had left off, composing new poetry and songs so close to Nanak's own style and skill that people were amazed. Angad even signed his compositions "Nanak" since he believed that it was the spirit of his old master flowing through him.

In 1603 the fifth Sikh guru, Arjan, took up the task of compiling the poetry of the previous Sikh gurus. It was a huge task, as all of them had been prolific poets, and all wrote in Nanak's name. The poems were organized according to the music they were sung to, and arranged into thirty-one musical sections. Within each section, the songs were put in the chronological order of their composition, with Nanak's poetry first, and the current guru's last.

The community rejoiced when the project was completed and built a beautiful shrine to house the book: the Golden Temple, so called as it was indeed gold-plated. On August 16th 1604 the holy book of the Sikhs, the *Granth*, was installed in the Golden Temple, where it is still enshrined and revered. The last surviving original disciple of Guru Nanak carried the book on his head in procession, with the current guru walking behind him.

Soon after this, the Sikhs met with their first real taste of oppression. As they grew in number and prosperity, the Muslim rulers of the Punjab began to feel threatened, and they threw Guru Arjan in prison, and executed him in 1606. The martyrdom of their guru set off a firestorm in the Sikh community, and the sixth guru took the community in a decidedly militaristic direction. At his installation, the new guru arrived for the ceremony dressed not as a holy man, but as a warrior. The Sikhs began to fight back, and soon made a name for themselves as fierce warriors.

The tradition continued and the ninth guru stood up to the Muslim elite, and defended local Hindus against coerced conversion to Islam. For this act of defiance this guru was also put to death. But his son succeeded him, and continued to lead the Sikhs with resolve.

This was the tenth guru, Gobind Singh, and he began a special religious order, the Khalsa, the Order of the Pure. Members of the Khalsa all took the name Singh, which means, "lion." The guru gave the men five symbols to wear, which all begin with the letter "K" in the language of the Punjab. First was uncut hair, worn in a turban. Second was a comb to keep it tidy and to symbolize their engagement with the world, unlike the Hindu recluses who also grow their hair long but do absolutely nothing with it. Third was a steel bracelet, symbolizing might. Fourth was a pair of short pants, the kind worn by warriors in that culture, and finally, a sword.

In joining the Kahlsa, a Sikh man and his family left behind the caste system and all restrictions as to the kind of work he was permitted to do. He also left behind his religion of origin, and his right to his own life. From now on, he was a soldier fighting for the rights of the defenseless against all oppressors.

And with this shift, the genius of Sikhism, in my opinion, met its end. For in forming the Khalsa, the Sikhs ceased to be an interfaith movement, and became just another religion, with its own scripture, its own lineage, and its own doctrine.

It is a cautionary tale for those of us doing interfaith work. I cannot tell you how many times people have taken me aside and entreated me to articulate a theology for the interfaith movement. But I resist the temptation, for to do so would turn the interfaith movement into just another dogma for people to reject. I may yet work on an interfaith systematic theology, but it will be an entirely comparative approach, not a synthetic one.

The Sikhs have, as a religious group, nevertheless had an amazing history. When the British empire moved into India, the Sikhs were world-renowned for their dependability and ferocity in battle. They have been amazingly successful in business, and are respected the world over as moral and loving people, in spite of their fits of militarism now and then.

The *Granth*, their holy book, is one of the least-known books of mystical poetry, and yet it contains some of the most beautiful examples of it the world has ever seen. Find a copy in translation—you will not be disappointed.

Finally, regardless of the fact that later Sikhs evolved into their own tradition, the original vision of Guru Nanak remains for us a revelatory inspiration. It hurt my feelings when my friend Maggie accused me of not being a Christian. But if being a Christian means being mean-spirited and exclusive, if it means I must embrace a spiritual manifest destiny that denies the value of other religions, then I guess she's right: I'm not a Christian. I don't believe in Christianity, or Catholicism, or any other "-ism." I just follow Jesus. And since the word "Sikh" simply means follower, I am not too proud to wear that label.

For in truth, there are no Hindus, there are no Muslims, there are no Christians, there are no Jews, there are no Buddhists, there are no Wiccans, there are no Zoroastrians. There is only the

Beloved, and we are all its lovers, no matter what kind of clothes we wear, what we call ourselves, or what our history might be. Like Guru Nanak, I'm not interested in joining anyone's club, I just want to be in love.

As Guru Nanak once prayed:
Air is our guru, water our father,
and the great earth our mother.
Day and night are the female and male nurses
in whose laps the whole universe plays.
Good and bad deeds are all disclosed in the presence of Righteousness.
Our actions take us near or far.
Those who remember the Name earn true success.
Nanak says their faces shine,
and they take many with them to liberation. Amen.[1]

⊕ *Preached at Grace North Church on August 6, 2006.*

NOTE

1 Information for this sermon was derived from Nikky-Guninder Kaur Singh. *The Name of My Beloved* (HarperSanFrancisco, 1995). The prayer was adapted from this source as well.

29 | baha'i

When I was a very young boy in Sunday School, I thrilled to the stories of Moses calling down the plagues upon the Egyptians, Elijah challenging the prophets of Baal to a divine duel, of God raining fire down upon the sacrifice, and then Elijah single-handedly putting the hundred or so prophets of Baal to the sword. "Prophets rocked!" I concluded, and in between my fireman and my cowboy phases, I wanted to be one.

I imagined myself roaming the desert in my flip-flops and coat of many colors raining fire down upon bullies and grouchy people. But when I announced my vocational ambitions in Sunday School, I was soundly rebuffed. "Oh, Johnny, you can't do that!" the Sunday School teacher said with a bit of a giggle. "There aren't any prophets any more."

I was horrified that my perfect life-goal had suddenly been swept away from me. "Why not?" I asked.

"Well, honey, because God doesn't talk to us like that any more.

The prophets heard God talking like I'm talking to you, but nobody can hear God that clearly any more."

Looking back, I wish I had defied her. I wish I had said, "You just wait and see if God doesn't talk to me!" But I was a good little Baptist boy, and I took my disappointment in stride.

The Christian faith isn't the only one that denies the viability of further prophets. Islam, too, says that after Mohammad, none need apply for the prophet trade. Fortunately—and unlike me—there was a man who didn't listen. That man was called the Bab.

His given name was Ali-Muhammad, and he lived in Shiraz, the same city where Hafiz did his thing. The Bab means, "the Gate," and he was a profound spiritual teacher. In 1844, he said that eighteen disciples would each find him independently, coming from far and wide, and when they did so, his real ministry would begin. Sure enough, eighteen young men sought him out and sat at his feet as his disciples.

His message was an unusual one, however. The Bab was not a messiah or a prophet, but instead he was a forerunner, and his chief message was to tell people to get ready for the one who was to come after him. With this message he sent out his eighteen disciples, and they roamed the Middle East, spreading the mystical teachings of the Bab, and entreating them to prepare themselves to receive the One who was yet to be revealed.

The Bab's fame grew, and his wisdom and insight were renowned. The King of Persia even heard of his teaching and sent one of his most trusted advisors to investigate. His advisor, however, never returned. So moved was he by the Bab's teaching that he resigned his post at court and became a disciple.

The Muslim clergy were in an uproar, however, for the message the Bab was spreading—that another prophet was on his way—was heresy. Mohammad is, in Muslim teaching, the "seal of the prophets," the last and final word given by Allah. Anyone claiming to have heard another word after him was a heretic and declared anathema.

So the clergy denounced him from the pulpit, and whipped up the ire of the people against the Bab. Thousands of his followers were imprisoned and tortured, and the Bab himself was put to death in 1850, when he was only thirty years old.

But as any observer of martyrs can tell you, that did not put an end to the Bab's movement. In fact, it only made it stronger—and angrier. In retaliation for the Bab's life, some of his followers, who called themselves Babis, made an attempt on the life of the king.

The entire movement was blamed, and a great wave of persecution began. Many were slaughtered, and thousands of Babis were imprisoned. One of those was a man who came to call himself Baha'u'llah.

Baha'u'llah was born in 1817 in Tehran, the son of a nobleman and governor of two Persian provinces. Though he never had any formal schooling, even as a child he could be found contending with the imams in the mosques, and as a young man was a tireless advocate for the poor. When his father passed away, he was offered the opportunity to succeed him, but Baha'u'llah declined. The Prime Minister was heard to remark, "I am not surprised. Such a position is unworthy of him. I am sure he is destined for some great career. His thoughts are not like ours."

Baha'u'llah had become an enthusiastic follower of the Bab, and bore his imprisonment patiently. And it was there, in an underground dungeon in Tehran known as "The Black Pit" that Baha'u'llah had a vision of a maiden from God who visited him and announced that he was to be a messenger and prophet of God, and that he was, in fact, the one whom the Bab had prophesied would come. He was horrified by this revelation, and he told no one about it for many years.

Eventually he was released from prison and banished from Persia. He headed to Baghdad, and became the chief teacher in the Babi community there. But the person selected to succeed the Bab, a man named Mirza Yahya, felt threatened by Baha'u'llah's charisma and began speaking against him behind his back. This poisoned the Babi community from within, and the movement began to decline.

Baha'u'llah wanted nothing to do with such a negative environment and he went off to live by himself in the mountains of Kurdistan. But even there, the many sheiks of the Sufi orders discovered him, and flocked to hear his teaching. Soon the news of a new sheik teaching in the mountains reached Baghdad, and Baha'u'llah's family recognized the teachings and pleaded with him to come home. They were greatly relieved when he did indeed return to them.

In his absence the Babi community had degenerated to an appalling degree. Twenty-five people had claimed to be the promised prophet, and Mirza Yahya had had most of them murdered, and had, in fact, coerced the Bab's wife into marrying him. He also hatched another plot to assassinate the Shah of Iran.

Baha'u'llah did not intervene. Instead, he continued to teach the Bab's revelation, and published many books on theology and mysticism. Soon, however, his fame caught up to him again, and he was once again exiled, this time to Constantinople. On the eve of his departure, he gathered his closest followers together and revealed to them for the first time that he was the prophet that the Bab had foretold. His followers kept this secret for eleven years, a time that Baha'is today call "the Days of Concealment."

In Constantinople he found no more peace than he had in any other place. Before long he was exiled again to Andrianople, where he finally revealed his true identity to the world. And when he decided to do it, he did it big. He wrote to Pope Pious the IX and announced the he himself was the second coming of Christ. He wrote to Napoleon, the Czar of Russia, Queen Victoria, and the President of the United States, and announced that since the Prophet of God had come, the need for warfare and division was at an end. All of them should turn their faces toward him and inherit the paradise that God promised all peoples.

Amazingly, every single one of the dignitaries ignored the self-proclaimed Persian prophet, despite the dire warnings his letters indicated would befall the nations if they did not hear him. In fact, he so annoyed the Ottoman Empire that he was once again exiled—this time to a prison in Akka, in Palestine.

At first, life for Baha'u'llah and his disciples in the Akka prison was very hard. But soon he gained the trust and respect of his jailors. They were so impressed with his wisdom and the amazing degree of equanimity with which he met every setback that soon they were coming to him for counsel. After a couple of years, the prison authorities had purchased a mansion for Baha'u'llah and his followers a short distance from the prison, and even though they paid lip service to the authorities and assured them that the self-proclaimed prophet was under guard, he was permitted to live out the balance of his days in relative luxury.

There he received visitors from around the world, including the British orientalist Edward Granville Brown, who wrote of him, "Those piercing eyes seemed to read one's very soul; power and authority sat on that ample brow…. No neeed to ask in whose presence I stood, as I bowed myself before one who is the object of a devotion and love which kings might envy and emperors sigh for in vain!"

Finally, in 1892, Baha'u'llah contracted a fever that took his life. He was buried in Akka, in modern-day Israel, which is today one of the chief places of pilgrimage for Baha'is.

He left behind a huge body of work, much of which has been translated into English. Even though his story may seem to us full of folly and hubris, the content of his teaching was amazingly ahead of its time, and may indeed constitute a new revelation worthy of our consideration.

Baha'u'llah taught, as Mohammad had, that all the prophets were sent by God, and that all of their revelations were valid ones. But although Mohammad limited the legitimate prophets to those from the Hebrew tradition and Zoroaster, Baha'u'llah widened the scope saying that Abraham, Moses, Krishna, Zoroaster, Buddha, Jesus, Mohammad, and many others were the "Manifestations of God" for their times, and all brought the same basic message, which he called "The Greater Covenant." Their messages, however, were all uniquely tailored to the specific cultural needs of the peoples to whom they were delivered, and thus the differences in their teachings were referred to by him as the "Lesser Covenants."

As human cultures grew and matured, further messengers were sent by God to give us a more and more complete revelation. That ongoing revelation continues, as Baha'u'llah proclaimed that even more prophets would come from God as humankind was ready to receive them.

Baha'u'llah proclaimed not only the oneness of all religions, but also the oneness of God, the unity of all humankind, the complete equality of men and women, the elimination of all forms of prejudice, the equal validity of religion and science, the free access of education for all peoples, the cooperation of all governments, the eradication of all war, and the elimination of extreme wealth and poverty.

There are approximately five million Baha'is in the world today, and they are found in nearly every nation on earth. They are everywhere revered as upright citizens, except in Islamic countries, where they continue to be persecuted as heretics. The repression of the Baha'i movement in Iran has been particularly bloody and merciless. Between 1978 and 1998 more than 200 Baha'is have been executed, and to this day they live in continual fear.

Baha'is do not meet in churches, but in study circles in private homes. They keep a private liturgy of devotional prayers instituted by Baha'u'llah, and are forbidden to vote or hold public office. They are nevertheless tireless advocates of the United Nations, and are among the few non-governmental agencies that hold offices in the United Nations building in New York.

Though formal worship is not part of Baha'i spiritual life, nevertheless enormous temples have been erected to bear public witness to the teachings of Baha'u'llah, one on each continent. There are seven such temples—and no, there is not one in Antarctica. Inexplicably, South America gets two. I have been to the North American Temple in Chicago, and I declare to you, if you ever have opportunity to visit it, do not pass it up. It is a breathtakingly beautiful monument and a great educational experience.

There is a lot to love in Baha'u'llah's teachings. They speak of things that were shockingly controversial a hundred years ago, but which seem to us today almost common sense. For all of his self-proclaimed glory, Baha'u'llah did not claim for himself a unique revelation, but only that he was one among many speaking the divine truth to the world. He affirmed the teachings of those who had come before him, and his revelations all called for peace, tolerance, and equality amongst peoples and nations. I do not know if God truly spoke to him, but many of the things he spoke I believe to be true. And this, too, I believe: God is still speaking, regardless of what the imams, or even my own Sunday School teacher may say.

There is one God, one earth, one people,
one truth spoken to the children
of humanity through many prophets.
Help us, O God, to discern the true voices of your prophets,
and to not eschew a new voice just because it is new.
Speak to us today, speak to us tomorrow,
and do not cease in sending us prophets,
those who listen closely to the whispering of your Spirit,
and are not afraid to speak it, even in the face of oppression.
For your truth is never a popular thing,
and we are not good at hearing.
So give us ears to hear, and voices brave enough to speak it.

For we ask this in the name of one who spoke the truth,
even unto death, and made for us a way of life,
even Jesus Christ. Amen.

⊕ *Preached at Grace North Church on August 20, 2006.*

30 | the alchemists

As many of you know, in addition to my pastoral work here in the parish, I also see clients for spiritual direction. This is a precious and holy calling, in which about once a month, a person comes in to sit in the quiet of the sacristy, to meditate upon the candle we light to represent for us the presence of the Divine, and to talk about what is happening—or not happening—in his or her spiritual life.

Usually, this happens without incident, and to be quite frank, I think I often get more out of the session than they do. But every now and then it will become clear to me that a person has something going on in his or her emotional or psychological life that is interfering in the spiritual process. One woman—I'll call her Francine—simply could not focus on her relationship with God because she was too freaked out about what people were thinking about her. We had not been meeting very long, and I had begun wondering if she was ever going to be able to sink in and get down to business.

One day she launched in to a monologue that could only be

described as paranoid. Finally, I stopped her. "Francine, I believe that you really care about your spiritual health." She nodded, wondering where I was going with this. "But I think you are struggling with emotional issues that are getting in the way. I'd like to continue working with you, but you are bringing in a lot of things that I am not trained to help you with. I think you need to see a therapist as well."

Well, she hit the roof. "What? You think I'm crazy? I don't need a shrink!" And that was the end of our session and our professional relationship. I'm not sorry I recommended this to her—in fact, it was the professionally responsible thing to do.

And, I don't think she was crazy, either. I am a great believer in psychotherapy. Heck, I've been in therapy for twenty years running! And it's not because I'm crazy, but because I am committed to doing my inner work.

Inner work is precisely what the alchemists were concerned with, as well. Now, when you hear about alchemy, what do you think of? I think of the prototypical mad scientist, of a distinctly medieval variety, laboring away in a dank laboratory with wet, mossy stone walls, working with putrid-smelling elixirs, attempting to turn lead, or dirt, or feces into gold. Probably, this is not so far off base.

Alchemy arrived in Europe in the twelfth century, along with higher mathematics and ancient Greek philosophy, among other gifts of the Muslim enlightenment taking place in Spain. From there it became the favored pursuit of philosophically- and metaphysically-minded men and women with the leisure and means to spend the majority of their time procuring expensive and rare books, studying incessantly, and performing dangerous experiments in their laboratories.

Since most people could not read and had to work for a living, alchemy was largely a noble gentleman's occupation, and indeed the history of alchemy is full of noblemen of note, probably the most recognizable among them being Roger Bacon.

But just what were they doing in those rank, dank labs? The cover story—and thus the story most people know—is that they were trying to turn some lesser substance into gold. And indeed, a good many alchemists worked hard towards this goal. Jim Melodini tells the story of Alexander Seton, a Scotsman and alchemist who traveled around Europe in the early seventeenth century performing public displays of alchemical transformations.[1]

Right there, with a whole crowd of onlookers, he wowed the public by transmuting base metals into gold. Sometimes, he stood afar back and gave detailed instructions to the city officials, so that they themselves performed the transmutations, much to everyone's amazement and delight.

As you might expect, Seton's success attracted both welcome and unwelcome attention. The Elector of Saxony, Christian II, summoned Seton and demanded that he divulge the secret of the Philosopher's Stone—the magic ingredient necessary for successful transmutations. Seton said, "No way," and Christian II threw him into prison. Seton eventually escaped, but died soon after from the rough treatment he had received.

Cash-strapped rulers were often lured by the alchemists' promises of easy gold, and thereby some alchemists found royal patrons. But just as many found themselves running for their lives when, like Seton, they did not produce what the authorities demanded of them.

Whether or not any of the alchemists could actually transmute worthless metals or other worthless substances into gold remains an open question. Mercury and gold sit next to one another on the periodic table of elements, with only one "pound" of atomic weight differentiating them, so it is perhaps not inconceivable that some hapless medieval alchemist might have stumbled upon just the right conditions to make the transformation happen, but this is highly unlikely.

What is far more likely is that all the lab work was simply a cover for a far more dangerous process. Dangerous because beneath all the test-tubes and beakers and incomprehensible recipes and formulae was shrouded a mystical teaching so heretical that if anyone dared to speak it openly, it would surely bring down upon them the wrath of holy mother church.

This is the real alchemy, not just a physical process involving a bunch of stinky lab work transforming lead into gold, but in addition to this an interior, spiritual and psychological process designed to transform the alchemist into an immortal being.

The alchemists taught that all things were alive—not just plants and animals, but minerals and other "inanimate" substances as well. All things, they taught, consisted of three basic substances: sulphur, salt, and mercury. Sulphur, in this system, was analogous to the emotional, mental, or psychological kind of life possessed by all things. Salt was the physical nature things possess, while mercury indicated the spiritual aspect of things. All creatures, then, whether animal, mineral, or vegetable, contain sulphur, salt, and mercury, or mind, body, and spirit.

In the lab, the alchemist tried to separate these elements from one another. He then attempted to refine each of these separated elements, making them purer and more potent. Finally, when the refining process was finished, he recombined the purified parts, which, he believed, resulted in a substance of great power, such as the famed Philosopher's Stone.

On the symbolic level this process represents the discernment by the alchemist of the three parts of him- or herself—the physical, psychological, and spiritual natures common to us all. Then, the alchemist works on refining each of these, toning the body, sharpening the mind, and purifying the spirit, for only when this is complete can a whole and healthy person emerge.

The refinement process itself was highly symbolic as well. The first stage was "blackening," which represented the fact that a part of the Divine was trapped in base matter. By "cooking" the blackened subtance, the alchemist attempted to purify it, to reveal its divine essence and to release it from matter. The next stage was "reddening" where the divine subtance once again was introduced to the earth for the healing of creation. In some texts, yet another stage follows, "yellowing" which looks like gold and represents *gnosis*, or the divine knowledge that is itself the Philosopher's Stone.

Like the ancient Gnostics, from whom much of the alchemists' philosophy is derived, they believed that immortality was not an innate quality. The divine spark in all matter must be identified and purified if the consciousness of the alchemist is to survive the death of the body. Alchemy, then, is the art of soul-making, shrouded in the obfuscatory language of science.

Divinity in all things? This is indeed heresy to medieval Catholicism. A soul does not survive death unless one makes an effort? More heresy! And heresy it is, indeed, but one of a decidedly sublime nature, from which we still have much to learn.

The image of the lonely alchemist toiling in his laboratory, seeking noble ends from ignoble toil reminds me of my own grandfather. He was a blue-collar worker—I'm not sure he ever graduated from high school. He worked for most of his adult life for the Southern California water company. All of my memories of him are in the khaki shirts and pants that he wore to work every day. This was not educated work, some would say that there was nothing innately noble about the manual labor that was his daily lot. And yet that base work wrought in him one of the sweetest and most noble of spirits I have ever known.

I long to be like him, and believe me, I'm working on it. I recognize that my body, mind, and spirit all need attention if I am going to be a whole person. I go to my own spiritual director once a month to hold me spiritually accountable and keep me on the straight-and-narrow, and I go to see my therapist twice a month to continue working on those things that still "trigger" me emotionally. I've done these things for a long time, but tending to my body has always been my short suit. But now, with Judy, the new dog in my life, I am going on numerous walks each day, and I'm beginning to feel the benefit of that.

I'm not finished, of course. My doctor just told me I have to give up nightshades, and I am now faced with the terrible question: "Is there life after tomatoes?" I'm sure I'll do it, but I have to psyche myself up for that one. With St. Augustine, I am praying, "Lord, make me chaste, but not yet!"

So yeah, I have a long way to go. I can still hear my grandmother's voice sounding through the house on days when I was being particularly obnoxious, "Put that boy in the oven, he ain't done yet!" We could all use a bit more cooking. We all have some refining to do. We all begin life as a lump of base matter, and it is up to us to find and cultivate the spark of divinity within. No one can do it for you. You and you alone can decide whether you will begin this great work of separation, purification, and unification.

The alchemists' work is not the domain of a crazy bunch of medieval heretics, shrouded in secrecy. The alchemists' work is before each and every one of us. What are you going to do with the lump of coal that is your life? Will you let it just lie there, or will you make it into gold?

Like the medieval alchemists, you are in a privileged position. You have the leisure, the time, the money, the education, and the intelligence to take what you have been given and to create of it a thing of beauty; to take your brokenness, and make it whole. And, according to the alchemists, when you become whole, you contribute to the wholeness of the world, even the wholeness of God. The Philosopher's Stone is within your grasp. Now, get cookin'!

Blessed are you, source of life,
for you have placed within us
a part of your own self,
and have given us the power,
the intelligence, and the means,
to discover it, recognize it as our true selves,
and with it given us the ability to heal ourselves and others.

Let us not neglect this work,
but tend to each of the sacred dimensions of our lives,
striving for health in body, mind, and spirit,
that we may be the people you have intended us to be,
enjoying the wholeness that is our birthright
as creatures of matter, mind, and divinity.
For we ask this in the name of the one
who wrought great transformation in himself
and in everyone he encountered,
and who continues his work of transformation in us,
even Jesus Christ. Amen.

⊕ *Preached at Grace North Church on September 17, 2006.*

NOTE

1   "The Age of Gold," *Gnosis*, Summer 1988, p. 8. Much in
       this sermon is indebted to information from this issue of
       Gnosis.

31 | the masons

You wouldn't think that studying religion at a hard-core Christian school like California Baptist College would shake up your faith, but that is exactly what happened, not just to me, but to lots of folks. My Introduction to New Testament class is just one example. For it was there where we were told—for the first time ever—that the accounts of the resurrection recorded in the four gospels all contradict each other. They are utterly irreconcilable testimonies. I invite you to try it some time. The pieces just do not fit together—they are not part of the same puzzle.

I was shocked. I was far from a fundamentalist at the time, but I was nevertheless astounded by this fact. And as I studied the four accounts, there was no getting around it. These were not the writings of four guys who had their story straight.

Or did they? They didn't have their facts straight, certainly, but what about the *story*? The stories were in agreement, while the details of those stories were not. It was then that it began to dawn on me that the story was more important than the facts. That it was the story, the myth, if you will, that was salvific, not the history.

And what is more, the more people focused on "facts" the more likely they were to be dogmatic. Myth liberates us from dogma, because we can enjoy the drama and apply its symbolic import to our lives as seems fitting, rather than trying to fit into the mold of those who have it all figured out, nailed down, and defined. And more often than not the folks who have it all figured out are hostile to those who take a more relaxed approach to their spirituality.

This is something that our mystics today, the Masons and their antecedents learned the hard way. Yet they were way ahead of their time in their honoring of story over dogma. Not surprisingly, their story begins with a myth:

Hiram Abiff was the chief architect for King Solomon, and building the temple was primarily his responsibility. As a builder, he was a wonder, and his constructions dazzled and amazed people to such a degree that some were envious of his talent, and longed to learn his secrets.

One day three men conspired to attack Hiram and to wrest from him the secret of his success: the secret of the chief stonecutter, the master mason. As he attempted to leave the construction site of the Temple, he was met by one of the ruffians at the south gate. The man threatened him with a makeshift weapon, a mason's rule, and demanded to know his secret. Hiram refused him, and the man struck him on the right side of his head.

Hiram fled to the west gate, where another of the ruffians set upon him. This man wielded a level, and again demanded the architect's secret. But Hiram was not telling, and suffered a blow to the left side of his head.

He fled again, this time to the east entrance, where the last of the evil men awaited him. This man was armed with a stone hammer, and when Hiram once again refused to divulge his secret, he was brutally murdered.

The thugs tried to hide their crime, and buried Hiram in a pile of construction waste at the Temple site. Then they thought better of this and reburied him under a tree at some distance from the Temple.

Solomon, as you might expect, was desperate to find his wonder-worker, for without him, how could the Temple ever be completed? He sent a platoon of soldiers out to find him, and was deeply grieved when they did. They exhumed the body, and gave it a third and final burial beneath the Holy of Holies on the site of the Temple itself.

Hiram's secret went with him to the grave, and thus, the Temple could never be completed. It could be finished, wrapped up, but it would ever be a shadow of its potential brilliance.

Now, even though this is a myth, there must have been some sort of actual secret buried beneath the Temple site, for in the Middle Ages, a mysterious religious and military order formed following the Christian conquest of Jerusalem. They made their home on the Temple site, and surreptitiously excavated it. No one knows what they found beneath that ancient rubble, but it must have been profound. It must have been some secret so threatening to the "official" account of Christianity taught by the Catholic Church that this fledgling order of militant monks quickly became Papal "favorites."

They called themselves the Knights Templar, or the Knights of the Temple. Their numbers swelled to the thousands, and they became one of the most wealthy and influential groups in Christendom—perhaps *the* most powerful, second only to the Papacy itself. When Jerusalem fell to the Muslims in 1291, the Templars relocated to Europe where they owned vast land holdings, and invented banking as we know it today, for one could deposit a sum at a Templar vault in France and withdraw it again at a Templar estate in Italy.

The Templar's success was widely envied, and it will not surprise you to learn that one particularly wicked king, Philip the

Fair of France, plotted their downfall. Philip already had an impressive resume of horrors by this time: he had expelled most of the Jews from France, had kidnapped and murdered Pope Boniface VIII, and subsequently poisoned Pope Benedict XI for good measure. He had set up a puppet Pope of his own, Clement V, and in collusion with this Pope, plotted the destruction of the powerful Templars.

On the morning of Friday the thirteenth, 1307, sealed orders sent previously all over France were opened, and the King's soldiers simultaneously raided over five hundred Templar monasteries. Over 3,000 Templars were rounded up and brought to trial before the Inquisition. They were accused of heresy, idolatry, and black magic, and many of them, including the head of the Order, Jacques de Molay, were put to death. As he surrendered to the flames, de Molay prophesied that within a year both the King and the Pope would have to answer to God for their crimes. Sure enough, a year later, both were dead.

But not all of the Templars were murdered. Those in Germany and other places were exonerated, even though they were forced to disband by Papal decree. Even some of the French Templars escaped, and this is where the story gets *really* interesting. For it seems that someone tipped off at least some of the Templars to the coming persecution, and a fleet of Templar ships laden with the Order's treasure—and presumably, the secret documents they took from the site of Solomon's Temple—eluded the King's forces and fled to safety on the cold and inhospitable shores of Scotland.

The fleeing Templars must have seemed like an answer to prayer to Robert the Bruce. His war against the English was not going well, but with the arrival of the rich and talented warrior-monks from France, his cause was resuscitated. The Templars tried to blend in with their new Scottish neighbors. They shaved their trademark beards, but the red Templar cross they formerly wore over their armor was adopted by the Scottish army, and renamed St. Andrew's Cross. They appeared to the casual observer to simply be Scottish knights, but they identified themselves to one another by special handshakes and symbols known only to themselves.

Since they could no longer call themselves Templars, they needed a new name, a new organization through which their secrets could continue to pass on to those worthy of them. For this they looked to the mythical builder of the Temple, and recast themselves as a professional organization, a guild of stone masons, or Freemasons.

Freemasonry flourished in Scotland, and when King James took the throne, he brought the order with him to England, where it spread like wildfire. It wasn't long before there were Masonic Lodges on the Continent, and soon, in America as well.

Now, the "official" version of the origin of the Masons put forward was that the English Guilds of actual stone masons gradually evolved into the theoretical, or "speculative" Masonry of the Lodges, but that is highly unlikely. First of all, there is no doubt that Freemasonry developed in Scotland, where there is no record of medieval Masonic Guilds. Secondly, as Richard Smoley points out, it is highly unlikely that "a group of nobles, kings, and lords" approached the Stone Masons and said, "Hey, good fellows, do you mind if we use your tools and ceremonies for our own betterment?"[1] That doesn't really fly.

The Templar origin of the Masons is fast becoming the scholarly consensus, for, unlikely as it is, it is not as improbable as the alternative and "traditional" origin story.

Because of their experiences with King Philip and his puppet Pope, and due no doubt also to the influence of the Scottish antipathy for the English King, the Masons developed a fiercely republican ethos, and were very critical of sovereigns and prelates. When the tyranny of King George made things unbearable for the American colonies, the democratic leanings of Freemasonry led many to suggest that the "grand experiment" of democracy might take root in this new land.

As is widely known, a great many of the architects of the "American Experiment" were Masons, and indeed, Freemasonry was nearly ubiquitous in the colonies. George Washington was a Mason, so were Benjamin Franklin, Thomas Pain, John Hancock, Paul Revere, and many, many others. The majority of generals in the Continental army were Masons, and field Lodges kept the troops' spirits up by supplying camaraderie and values important to the fledgling nation.

Masonic symbolism is rampant in American history. It is stamped on our money, and even the layout of the streets in Washington, DC is patterned after Masonic designs. America is itself a Masonic experiment, an attempt to complete the Temple begun in Solomon's day.

But in what way can we say that Masons are mystics? This history is all very interesting, but why are we talking about them here, in church? Because mysticism is the very foundation of Freemasonry, and much of the spiritual heritage of the West, especially the western occult heritage, is indebted to it.

To understand how, we must return to the myth of Hiram Abiff, who is for them the archetypal Mason. He alone has the secret needed to complete the Temple, which he took to his death. According to Smoley, Hiram represents consciousness, and the Temple he is working on is the true Self, the whole and realized human being. The three thugs that thwart him represent thinking, feeling, and doing, which, because they are unintegrated, can succeed only in preventing the completion of the Temple, but they cannot erase the memory of the Builder or his Secret. Solomon sets up a memorial to this man and his secret, yet the secret of the completed Temple—the whole human being— remains a mystery.

But the Masons hold that while that secret cannot be spoken in words—as it is, like all mystical knowledge, ineffable—it can be grasped symbolically. The Masonic rituals attempt, through sacred ritual and archetypal symbol, to provide its members with the means to discover for themselves the secret of the Master Mason, the necessary *gnosis* required to complete the building of the spiritual Temple of their own lives.

This is not a building made of stones and wood, but the fulfilment of a person's own spiritual potential, the discovery of the True Self, the return to the primal wholeness lost in the expulsion from Eden.

Although it started out as a Christian order, Freemasonry developed into a distinctly interfaith movement. One need not be a Christian to be a Mason, for its members are drawn from a wide variety of faith traditions. At the lodge where Rudyard Kipling was initiated in Lehore, India, the sacred texts of no fewer than five different religions sat upon the altar. The only beliefs required of a Mason are faith in a Divine Builder, and the desire to fulfill one's own spiritual potential—a commitment to build yourself.

One great problem with this phenomenal history, however, is that traditionally only men are admitted to Masonry. Several years ago, I was invited by a friend to join a lodge that he was joining. I admit I was intrigued. I discussed the possibility with Kate, my spouse at the time, and you will probably not be surprised to hear she hit the roof. "How dare you join the Masons! They don't allow women!"

I pointed out that her monthly women's spirituality group excluded men, so why could I not join a men's spirituality group? She said, "It's not the same!" But I am still a bit unclear as to why. In any case, about a hundred years ago, co-masonic lodges began to spring up that initiated both men *and* women into the mysteries. Of course, my wife was not interested in joining one of those with me.

The Masons provide an excellent example of a mystical movement in which myth is more important than history. No one believes there was an historical Hiram Abiff, but it does not matter. It is the story of the archetypal builder that is operative in the lives of Masons today. All is symbol, all is drama, all is ritual, intended to point one to the Great Secret needed to complete the project that we are all—like it or not, know it or not, want it or not—working out: the completion of the Spiritual Temple that is our true Self and our divine calling.

Great Architect of Heaven,
you who built the earth and all that is within it,
help us to finish the project you have begun in us,
taking the raw materials of our lives
and fashioning of them a thing of beauty,
a Spiritual Temple worthy of being your dwelling place.
Help us to eschew dogma but cling to myth,
for it is through stories that our souls are instructed,
and the materials needed to complete the project
you have begun in us are to be found.
Give us the will to work,
that we may all discover the Great Secret for ourselves,
and bring to completion that which you have wrought in us.
For we ask this in the name of the chief cornerstone,
even Jesus Christ. Amen.

⊕ *Preached at Grace North Church on September 3, 2006.*

NOTE

1   I am indebted to the Summer 1997 edition *Gnosis* magazine for much of the information found in this sermon.

32 | krishnamurti

When I was a teenager, I struggled with how to please my father. I was terrible at sports, and to this day my mother still tells stories of how I embarrassed them when I tried. I still cringe when I remember my father ridiculing my vocabulary in front of his FBI agent friends. I was, apparently, using words in front of his co-workers that were so far beyond my grade level that once again, I embarrassed him.

I was fairly tortured by the degree to which, despite my best efforts, I was such a cause of shame to my folks. Then one morning I was sitting in church, and the pastor pointed at us—in that way that Baptist pastors always do—and said that he knew that God was calling some of us to preach.

I thought to myself, "Could he mean *me*? Is this what God wants me to do?" And then, suddenly, it all made sense. I had no talent whatsoever for the activities of "normal" little boys, but—I took a quick inventory of those talents which I did possess—I was a bookworm, had an almost fanatical fascination with theology, was an articulate speaker, and an irrepressible ham. "Good God!" I thought, "Maybe God *is* calling me to preach!"

About a month after having this epiphany I went forward at the altar call and surrendered to the ministry. I was sixteen years old, and was thereafter nicknamed "preacher-boy." This wasn't that unusual, as all of us who surrendered to preach were called "preacher-boys" until we were ordained, even the ones who were sixty years old. But I wore it as a badge of pride. I started attending our pastor's "school for prophets" and I began preaching. I still have a tape of my second sermon. It is one painful enterprise to sit through. Nevertheless, I was encouraged by my church family, and soon I found myself jumping to the tops of tables at the local roller rink, waving my big red bible over my head, proclaiming to the crowd that they were all going to Hell if they did not embrace our peculiar theology.

I even started preaching on my high school radio station—I may, in fact, have been the nation's youngest media evangelist at the time, a dubious honor at best.

I knew it was what God wanted me to do. I was actually good at it! And after one Sunday evening sermon, my father even told me he was proud of me. Even if I had been faking it, that would have made it all worth it. My dad was telling me he was proud of me for something I actually had native talent at! It was a shining moment.

But it was not to last. The church that nurtured this talent in me proclaimed that rock-n-roll was evil and commanded me to quit my radio show. When my father refused to let me do this, the pastor began a smear campaign against us, and all of our friends turned their backs on us. We eventually moved out to California to escape the orbit of that dangerous church, and I'm grateful we did, but the damage was done. I would not preach again for fifteen years.

Then, when God did call me back to the ministry, it was as a Catholic priest—once again beyond the pale of what my parents could support and which no doubt causes them great embarrassment to this day. Ah, well. I have become resigned to it as my lot.

But I still love preaching, and even though the messages that the Spirit gives me would no doubt continue to horrify my family, it seems I can do no other and be in my personal integrity.

I think today's mystic, Krishnamurti, would resonate with my journey—I certainly resonated with his. Like me, he desperately longed to please the adults in his young life, and as a man, he had to go his own way to discover his true calling.

He was born in 1895 to a middle-class Indian family near Madras, one of eleven children, six of whom survived childhood. He was of the Brahmin caste, and his father collected rents for the government. His mother died when he was ten, and he may have had some kind of innate psychic ability, because he admits to having seen her after her passing.

His father was also a member of the Theosophical Society, which will play a very large part in this story. The Theosophical Society was an organization that honored the religious heritages of both the East and the West, and was, in a way, an interfaith movement. It was keen on investigating the psychic powers latent in human beings, and sought to bring an era of enlightenment and peace beyond dogmas and the petty bickering of the religiously entrenched.

Unfortunately, as we have seen previously with the Sikhs, and to some extent the Bah'ias, the danger of interfaith movements is their tendency to want to set up dogmas of their own, and in so doing, they stop being interfaith movements and become religions in their own right, however eclectic they may be.

This is exactly what happened to the Theosophical Society. It's founder, Madame Blavatsky, claimed that there were "Ascended Masters" living in the Himilayas that were psychically guiding the spiritual evolution of humankind from their mountain lairs. Most Society members believed her, and when leadership of the Society passed to Annie Besant and her trusted sidekick, C.W. Leadbeater, messages from the Ascended Masters continued to

guide Theosophical Society affairs, mostly through the medi-
umship of Leadbeater.

Now Leadbeater is an interesting fellow to say the least. He
claimed to be a clairvoyant, and there are many people who
believe his talents in this area were beyond dispute. What was
also beyond dispute was that he was a pederast and a bit of a
charlatan. Like an early-twentieth century Michael Jackson, he
loved the company of children, especially boys, and relied on his
fame to exonerate him from any suspicion that might plague
"normal" people indulging in such activity.

Leadbeater proclaimed that the Masters had revealed to him
that the next world teacher was about to emerge, and was even
now among us, waiting to be recognized. This teacher would be
the second coming of Christ for the West, and the coming of the
Meitraya Buddha for the East, an enlightened sage that would
lead the world into the next stage of spiritual evolution.

He had already clairvoyantly identified a young boy from
America named Hubert as the World Teacher. But then one day
Leadbeater was enjoying the cool river near the Theosophical
headquarters in Adyar, India, when he saw a young boy bathing,
and the shining of his aura astounded him. He realized then that
he had been wrong about Hubert, and he identified Jiddu
Krishnamurti as the teacher the world had been waiting for.

Young Hubert and his family did not relinquish the throne of
the world quietly, but that is another story. Krishnamurti's family
were given better apartments, and Krishna and his brother Nitya,
who were inseperable, were given rooms that connected, not surprisingly, to Leadbeater's own.

Leadbeater almost immediately regretted his choice of messi-
ahs. He set out a strict educational regimen, intended to properly groom the boy for his role as spiritual teacher of the world, but
Krishna was not cooperative. It's not that he didn't want to
learn—he tried with everything that was in him to please his
mentor—but he was a slow learner. Leadbeater treated him cru-

276 | john r. mabry

elly at times, calling him "lazy" and "stupid," none of which helped Krishna's self-esteem one bit. My personal opinion is that Krishnamurti might even have been mildly autistic, which would actually explain a lot about his early difficulties, his later single-pointed brilliance, and his lifelong social awkwardness.

Eventually, in his late teens, Krishna and his brother were sent to England to continue their education, and Krishna's life became a series of pageants where he was trotted out like a performing animal to give his divine blessing to the Theosophical Society faithful at nearly every turn. This he deeply resented, but felt it was the price one pays to be the messiah.

He did indeed begin to accept his role, albeit reluctantly, as he was very shy. He had been told since he was ten that he was the savior of the world by the people he loved and trusted most—who was he to say differently? But he chafed at being "handled" at every turn, his complete lack of freedom, and his inability to be a normal teenager.

In his mid-twenties, however, everything changed. His brother Nitya died of tuberculosis, and he, even he, the messiah, despite his prayers and constant entreating of the Ascended Masters, was powerless to save him. That was when he realized it was all a sham, that he was being played. And he was determined that *he* would play no more.

At an international Theosophical Society meeting in 1929, Krishnamurti took the stage and horrified everyone in the crowd with a speech that has got to be near the top of the list of the top ten most unpopular public addresses in human history.

This is what he said: "…the devil and his friend were walking down the street when they saw ahead of them a man stoop down and pick up something from the ground, look at it, and put it away in his pocket. The friend said to the devil, 'What did that man pick up?' 'He picked up a piece of the truth,' said the devil. 'That is a very bad business for you, then,' said his friend. 'Oh, not at all,' the devil replied, 'I am going to help him organize it.'"

Krishnamurti then continued with words which would become immortal: "I maintain that truth is a pathless land, and you cannot approach it by any path whatsoever, by any religion, by any sect. That is my point of view, and I adhere to that absolutely and unconditionally. Truth, being limitless, unconditioned, unapproachable by any path whatsoever, cannot be organized; nor should any organization be formed to lead or coerce people along a particular path."

And with that he disavowed his affiliation with the Theosophical Society, denied his role as the World Teacher, dissolved the Order that was responsible for ushering him into his messianic role, returned all the funds that had been given to him by the Society, and for the first time in his life, walked out into the world his own man, a free man, and a very lonely man.

This was, of course, a very great blow to the Theosophical Society, which has never truly recovered. If you want to see sparks fly, just bring up Krishnamurti's name in Theosophical circles, even today. It is not a popular subject, but nevertheless one that they cannot stop talking about. Kind of like the Iraq war!

Krishnamurti was not totally abandoned. There were many who supported him, and indeed, he was taken care of for the rest of his life. From his home base in Ojai, California, he spent the rest of his life traveling the world and teaching. Even though he rejected the idea of being the messiah, he had been groomed to be a world teacher, and that was exactly what he was. I suppose you could say he was kind of a freelance religious philosopher, giving talks and engaging in Socratic-style dialogs wherever he went.

He denied the role of "guru" because he believed that, at some level, the guru-disciple relationship was always unequal and exploitative. But he nevertheless had followers, people who hung on his every word. To his credit, he never demanded obedience, money, or even belief from anyone. Instead, he insisted that, like Socrates, he knew nothing for sure, and that his philosophical

278 | john r. mabry

inquiries were like the mutual conversations and explorations between friends.

He denied all spiritual authority, including his own, and instead of being enslaved to any ideology or beliefs, entreated his listeners to pursue a radical freedom that would only be theirs by the hard process of letting go of preconceived ideas and dogmas. Freedom was his main message, and was no doubt to some degree neurotically driven by his own lack of freedom as a child and young man. It was nevertheless the catalyst for a profound teaching that continues to impact and liberate people from the cultural, psychological, and religious shackles that bind them.

He invited people into real relationship with one another, in which he said we can discern those things that cloud our true vision, and eventually understand our own consciousness, which is not ours alone, but is the common inheritance of all humanity. He taught that through this kind of real relationship and disciplined meditation, we can perceive the distinction between observer and the observed, and that it is this very distinction which is unreal and that leads to all human conflict, large and small.

But of course, like the Buddha, he never asked anyone to take his word for it, but to simply try it on for size. To the end of his life he proclaimed that there was no path to truth that could be taught, codified, or described in words, or—god forbid—rituals.

Krishnaji, as those who were fond of him called him, kept company with the greatest intellectual giants of his day. Aldous Huxley was a close friend, as was David Bohm. Krishnamurti was even awarded the United Nations Peace Medal in 1984, and he addressed the UN the next year.

He traveled and taught tirelessly until he finally succumbed to pancreatic cancer at the age of 90. He died surrounded by his friends and admirers. Though the world did not lose a messiah, it did most certainly lose its teacher.

There is so much in his story that moves me. I relate to the little boy, eager—but frustratingly unable—to please those responsible for him. And I certainly relate to his need to throw off the shackles of the dogmatic system he was reared in to find his authentic voice and a message that had integrity for him.

And even though most of us have not had this kind of childhood, there is much in his teaching to inspire all of us. He reminds us that we do not have to have the answers to teach the wisdom we have gleaned. We do not have to be believers to live a faithful life. We do not have to hand our souls over to any church or institution or guru or pastor or teacher or leader to pursue the truth. "Truth is a pathless land," and all of us must do the hard work to find our own way to discovery.

We cry out to you, source of life and truth,
which no words can describe, no image relate,
no rituals attain, no teachings contain,
no church can own, and to which no teacher can guide.
Give us the courage to take a road less traveled,
to seek you ourselves in our own way.
Grant us the discipline and the will to find you in unlikely places
and by means unique to us alone,
so that when we find you, we will know you as revealed to us
and not as described by another.
For we long to know you in spirit and in truth,
even as another great teacher described you,
who also demands no allegiance or alliance,
even Jesus Christ. Amen.

⊕ *Preached at Grace North Church on October 15, 2006.*

Printed in the United Kingdom
by Lightning Source UK Ltd.
118967UK00001B/284